I0199977

Psychology 808:

Knowledge Of Self

Psychology 808:

Knowledge Of Self

By Katrina Stradford

Second Edition Revision

Copyright © 2010 by Katrina M. Stradford
Published by Lulu Enterprises, Inc.
860 Aviation Parkway
Suite 300
Morrisville, NC 27560
www.lulu.com
orders@lulu.com

Second Edition
ISBN: 978-0-578-01147-9   Hardcover
All rights reserved. No part of this book may be reproduced, stored in a retrieval system or transmitted in any form or by any means, electronic or mechanical, including photocopying, recording, or by any information storage and retrieval system, without permission in writing from the copyright owner.

Certain sections of this book provide the reader with information to give them a better understanding of their individual design as a creation.

This publication contains the opinions and ideas of the author. It is intended to provide helpful and informative material on the subject matter covered. It is not the author's intention to provide medical advice to the reader. This book is neither intended to diagnose, treat or cure any ailment or condition; not to replace proper medical care. Reliance upon information obtained from this book is solely the reader's risk.

The author and publisher specifically disclaim any responsibility for any liability, loss, or risk, personal or otherwise, which is incurred as a consequence, directly or indirectly, of the use and application of any of the contents of this book.

Scripture quotations are taken from the Holy Bible, New Living Translation, copyright 1996. Used by permission of Tyndale House Publishers, Inc., Wheaton, Illinois 60189. All rights reserved.

This book was printed in the United States of America.
Library of Congress Control Number: 2009903141

To order additional copies of this book, contact:

Mskstradford Publishing
www.mskstradford.com
mskstradford@yahoo.com

Lulu Enterprises, Inc.
www.lulu.com
(919) 459-5858
orders@yahoo.com

Or

Dedication

First and for most all the glory goes to God The Father who took the time to create me and whom leads me in the direction I chose in my life and then to Jesus for keeping me in line to receive my many blessings. Thanks to my parents Catherine Little and Melvin Guyon for giving me the gift of life. To my children Mytrianna, Mercy and Passion I love you all so very much and thanks for pushing me to want better for you all. To my husband Edward, I'll love you forever more than words can ever express.

Table of Contents

Acknowledgments

To my beautiful auntie Jackie, whose like my second mom, thanks for all the days you rubbed my head and gave me treatment when I was sick from asthma and who constantly took me to church to receive the Lord. Thanks for teaching me it was okay to just be me. To my first love Michael Clinton Johnson you will always be very special and dear to me, no one will ever take that from me. A part of me will be in love with you forever. To the Big Buddy and Big Sister Program who discovered a very unique big sister Tonya to interact with me. Thanks for Christmas and the special gift of your time. Anytime you need a shoulder I'm here. To my favorite first grade teacher Mrs. Thompson at Tremont Elementary School in Cleveland, Ohio who allowed me to come back year after year and be apart of your atmosphere. To Mrs. Sherrill, my second grade teacher and aunt, thank you for being there just when I needed you. You are so beautiful and I strive to be just like you someday.

To the staff at Central Middle School, Mrs. Jones my French instructor who allowed me to escape my mind and be Catherine if just for a moment, To the V.I.P. Program, members, staff and my personal coach Mr. Williams who treated us all as if we were his own and escorted us out to a special day at the movies, To Mr. Mull my V.I.P. teacher who dedicated his every Saturday morning to teaching me Algebra and dealing with my difficult teenage mind.

To Mrs. Renita Story, my very tall basketball coach at East

Technical High who seen more in me, and gave extra care and attention by making sure I made it home safe every night after basketball practice, and even though I did not graduate from East Technical High School I will always be a scarab in my heart, to my Aunt Jean thanks for being persistent and determined to be a part of my life, to my G.E.D. instructor at Cleveland Skills who saw potential in me and paid for my education from her own pocket, thank you.

To the staff and graduating class of 2000 at Remington College, To the staff and members of Cleveland Works 2002-2003, To Ms. Oates, staff, and members of Antioch Baptist Church and Genesis Program 2004, to my Pastor Rev. Hughley, and Members and Family of Triedstone Baptist Church, to my childhood best friends Markie and Sherry I'll always love you both, to my friend Big Jay who loved to hear me speak my mind, to my bestfriend now Antonio Booze you're the best, to Janeisha Williams you know what you mean to me, be better than what you've been taught. To my favorite cousin Tony "I told you boy", to the memory of all those I loved and lost whom influenced my life for the time they were here I thank you, my godson Tony "Mr.Moo" Rice I'll love you forever, grandfather Jesse Little, grandmother Lula Mae Guyon, my brother Theodore "Thee" Broadus who didn't get the opportunity to see my vision come true, and to my favorite step-grandfather of all time John Thomas Moore who will continue to mean the world to me I miss you and love you dearly.

To my Aunt Tracy Merritt-Little thanks for being so persistent in my life in attempt to bring me a heavenly message from God. I heard you loud and clear. I have lots of respect and love for you. Na-na's death was not in vain. The lord wanted to make you rich in him. No one can ever take those kinds of riches away from you.

To my Aunt Sis thanks for being so strong, complex, beautiful and unique. Thanks for showing me I wasn't alone. Most important I want to thank my brothers and sisters Lorenzo, George, Demetrius, Lula, Prestina, Charlene and Chandra for always being there, and extra special thanks for the personality of Bear...I love you too. To my extended family and loved ones thanks also for being an inspiration. I love you all so very much. Last but not least to all of Auntie's Champions Charles, Lorenzo, Janayla, Allysia, Dana, Caitlin, Katron, Charlea, Joseph, Joshua, Jade, and Janaya I love you all. Thanks for keeping me occupied. You are truly gifts from God. Thanks to all for being the positive forces behind me.

Introduction

In my book, I'm not going to sugar coat anything because it's not a part of my personality type or character and the things that I say are not to hurt you, the reader, or anyone else's feeling . I ask for my audience to not take what I express personally because my book is not meant to be a direct target on one's character but to inform you of the events happening to your soul. I just want those who read my book to take the time to listen and understand what it is that's affecting their lives in a negative manner.

I have always been that person searching for effective methods of teaching others how to address the problems they face day to day. This is my prayer day to day, and best believe the lord has answered it for me. It took for me to do so little just to receive so much as once stated in the bible.

"Then the disciples came to Jesus privately and said, 'Why could we not cast it out?' He said to them, 'Because of your little faith. For truly I tell you, if you have faith the size of a mustard seed, you will say to this mountain, 'Move from here to there,' and it will move; and nothing will be impossible for you." **-Matthew 17:19-20**

My book lists the personality types, traits, emotions, temperaments, and negative behaviors of the personality traits, free will and morals. I used the bible as well as a few other tools to find my answers. You probably didn't know the blueprint to your design was there, but yes, that's were it's been the whole time, waiting to be read. You probably just thought the bible was just the **B**asic **I**nformation **B**efore **L**eaving **E**arth but it also contains the keys needed to enter Heaven. It is your choice. I guess you can look at me as a light pointing you in the right direction by using my life stories as examples.

Jesus tried to tell us a long time ago and the generations never really paid attention, instead mankind has debated on the unimportant matters of the world. A lot of the questions people ponder over are irrelevant, and mankind is losing the battle over their lives and souls because they've allowed life to become a distraction. I'm not just pointing the finger at others because I allowed myself to get distracted as well, but I realize that it was necessary for me to find the answers, now I'm back to reality and ready to do my life job. I am a person whom senses by the thoughts of others. The Lord purposely built me this way. This is the way in which I use my gift of free will, which you will learn more of in chapter 3.

My purpose in saying this is to let others know I was formed to think by the thoughts of others, and many people are born in this same manner as well. We have a lot of similarities and a lot of differences which makes us all unique which I will prove later, but for now, no one else has the blueprint to my design or would know about me as a creation but the creator himself. The science world has been pondering over these answers for years, but they will continue to come up short because the answers require you to step out on faith just to understand. There is no room for analytical thought only room for emotional thought.

The lord is so good, he knows his people just to look at them, as he did with Cain an Abel. The Lord knew he belonged to the evil one, and we ponder and wonder how could he know that, just from a glance, or tone in one's voice? The answer to this riddle is quite evident; you've just been looking through the wrong pair of glasses. You just have to open your mind to see the truth that is the lord knew just from Cain's conversation alone, that He didn't have the use of his morals, because the use of morals are everyone's direct link with God and the spiritual world. Had he the use of his morals he would not have gotten as angry and killed his brother because of envy. Your morals are the difference in right and wrong and do not carry any of the 8 deadly sins.
So take your time reading and absorb as much of the wisdom within this book as you can.

-Chapter 1-
Knowing Yourself

The road has been rough but I didn't give up. I've had enough experiences to last me a lifetime and more. So many experiences that I can now relate to various types of people. What I've realized in my many experiences is that the events and environment of my life were just the tools needed to form me into the woman that I am today. I've seen and experienced so much negativity and positivism in this lifetime that I have finally found my balance. No one told me in the beginning, that I would have to go through a great deal of pain just to find one simple answer and it's what psychiatrist and doctors have probably known for years but the only difference is that they haven't explained it well enough that our problems will cease to exist. Doctors have to make a living too. The question is, "how do we effectively deal with our problems"? Does anyone truly know the answer to this age-old question? To deal with our problems so well, that they no longer come back to haunt or rob us blind of our life's happiness. Happiness is what mankind has been searching about for so long. Can we truly attain it?

I, myself, am the victim of childhood abuse, incest and rape. My earliest memory was at the tender age of three when I remembered being in the crossfire of bullets being exchanged. They say that when something traumatic happens to you, your mind is like that of an elephant and you never forget, and it remains a permanent part of your character forever. You wouldn't know this about me from just looking at me had I not chose to reveal it because my emotions have been cleansed of all negative energy. I can talk freely about past experiences today without the tears and that is how you can recognize when a person has been healed. You too can also have a happy productive, stress and worry free life.

My faith is very strong in the Lord! How many people in the world actually believe they have a clear understanding of who they are? There are over 299 million people in America, and more than 6 billion worldwide, but the answer is few, if not many, people who understand who they truly are and their purpose in life. The rest are guessing just like the rest of the world. They rely on study after study for their answers, such as why do people desire certain foods, why can't a person commit to their significant other in a relationship, why do black female's boyfriend cheat on them and why do other races tick people off so easily. So distracting. The science of problem-solving has many answers but no clear-cut solution to any one problem.

There are millions of people who struggle day to day unsure of themselves or the direction in which there life is going. Who is truly here to help? Not to just know the desires of what you want to become as an adult, and the family you hope to have and raise, but to have a clear understanding of one's purpose in life. Here's a question...why do you think the creator, created such a marvelous invention (mankind) if those answers were not available to you?

That would be too much like right, huh? Well, the answers are available to all of Mankind you just haven't been looking close enough to see it. I don't believe many people have taken the time to receive their thorough understanding of their existence, which is one of the many blessings they possess as an individual. If mankind did understand the meaning of their existence there probably wouldn't be half the crimes that exists today in the whole world, and people wouldn't get into half of the non-sense that they are consumed by on a day-to-day basis. For most people they spend a lifetime searching for these answers and carrying excess baggage that they don't need, sometimes for more than 50 years, still without a clear understanding as to the reason why they find themselves in uncomfortable situations.

They have been taught to keep pushing forward and to never look back. For others, they burry themselves so deep within the bible they forget to look up and help their neighbor as Jesus once told them.

I know the world is very distracting, there are groups of people who think they are superior because of there color or ethnicity, others who were abused as children and haven't found ways to effectively deal with the issues that have plagued there life and they reach for comfort in the same sex and form unions as couples, others who have suffered so much pain down the generation line that it's so hard to overcome the negativity that was once placed upon them and their family tree that they are now vengeful at the world. Does any of this sound familiar? I'm not putting down these genres of people but attempting to bring problem areas to the light.

All of these difficult situations and I still sit back and say God is good. I am thankful for the many lessons in my life that he has taught me. He is so good that he is still taking mercy on the generations an giving each and every individual the opportunity to fix there negative ways and turn from there problems and the lies.

I am a Christian and I realize, many people don't believe in The Lords existence, even those that claim to work for the Lord have lost there faith in what they preach but I'm going to make an attempt to restore it. This is not necessarily just a religious book because I want all forms of people to understand the simple message that I convey and that is to get your emotions in order or they will kill you. You have to check them at the door because your emotions are what continue to harm your life and rob you blind. Even if others don't believe in the existence of The Lord, one thing for sure is there is a creator of the universe who made each and every individual. Not several but one.

I've experienced so much in my thirty-two years here on earth that I believe I have found a reliable way to help other's to effectively deal with their problems. I remember an instance with my sister in law when I attempted to teach her the same method of how to repent from her sinful ways and she rejected my words of truth. She said, "what makes you so special that God would send the message in you to help heal me". I was taken back, because I didn't expect that answer coming from her. She was always that person who called on me for advice and I gave it to her no questions asked. I just knew my sister was going to be on the same page with me when I tried to explain the truth to her.

What I realized at that moment was she was taken by a negative force that had a hold on her, the same negativity that Jesus spoke of in the bible. I didn't argue with my sister because I knew that she was not the one in control of her emotions at that moment. I just reflected for a minute on her question. I thought about it for a split second then moments in my life flashed before my eyes and I then knew the answer. I didn't think that I had any special powers to perform exorcisms or anything, because I was the same as her a sinner trying to get right with the lord, the only difference between me and her was that in my final decisions I always gave it over to the Lord, I chose him and that was the reason I believe he blessed me with the knowledge of the inner functions of the brain and emotional healing. The lord had been preparing me my whole life for this I just didn't understand it when I was younger.

The world is full of activities to take a persons mind off

emotional stresses. All these distractions, which are short answers. You can supply a hungry man with food and he will eat all day till he's full in the belly, but until you get to the root of the problem and find out why he's eating so much and still hungry, your meal will never be enough. Sometimes when a person is hungry, food is not the meal they crave, knowledge is.

Some people use food as a method to take away the pain they often feel, such as in the many cases of obesity. That's why there are so many overweight people in America compare to other countries. Americans are carrying a lot of weight on their shoulders.

This book is a meal for your mind. The final result is upon mankind. I can only provide a person with the tool he needs to save his life. He's got to dig his own way out of the grave he has created for himself. God's laws are not man made laws. He judges from a higher standard and you can't fool him. No matter how much makeup you put on to cover those lying eyes or fake smiles, the Lord is already aware. He's just testing you. I realize he loves me just as I am, attitude, bad flaws and all. He knew of my temperament before he even gave it to me, but it was upon me to control my temperament, as well as my other gifts.

The bible is more than short stories of examples of others experiences cautioning the world to be ware to not make the same mistakes, but it also tells the story of mankind's design. God is good and he is playing chess with the devil and it's checkmate time. This information would not be available if it were not close to the hour.

"So I wept much because no one was found worthy to open and read the scroll, or to look at it. But one of the elders said to me, do not weep. Behold, the Lion of the tribe of Judah, the Root of David, has prevailed to open the scroll and to loose its seven seals."-

Revelations 5:4-5

I believe people have just gotten so use to making excuses for their behavior, as to why certain events have happened in their lives, instead of seeing the more in depth answer, which is our emotions are influencing our actions. If I told you that you are exactly the person the creator meant you to be, would you trust and believe in this? And if I said it's not to late to fix the problems of the world, would you also believe in this! It's not too late for many.

I believe science and religion go hand and hand. Emotional and Rational work together to make the same point. Science continues to bring the spiritual realm into reality. In the bible, for the scripture say

To the Pharaoh, "For this very purpose I have raised you up, that I might show my power in you, and that my name may be declared throughout all the earth". **(Genesis 9:17)**

This scripture to me speaks loudly to the science world; it says I have given you all this power and technology just to show my power and existence through your invention so that everyone in the world shall believe.

The very invention of deciphering the DNA code has been completed. What took scientist years to do, I completely wrote out in a matter of months with the aid of the Lord whom used my senses to bring me the answers. God truly is wonderful he has used my African-American and Native- American heritage to bring me the truth. I guess if I had been raised in the culture of my Native- American heritage I would have been considered a shaman because of my spiritual guidance I received from the lord in writing this book. I've just taken the time away to fine tune the gifts that he gave me. I do not need a body of evidence to believe in the bare facts because I am a sensor and my gut feelings speak loudly for me. The area of my life the devil attempted to use he didn't have a clue the lord would use it to his advantage. There are those that need the body of evidence presented to them and these people are considered thinkers or those with strict analytical thought from memories, which I will discuss more later, don't worry about it for now.

Each and every individual was created differently just for the purpose of finding the truth from different angles, which is the quest to want to find and know the creator. Just because the answers are not available for my eyes to see, the answer is still evident in each and every creation of man to animal of the existence of the creator. Just because you see the clouds in the sky you should believe in him. I don't believe that I am the descendent of an alien, but if that is the way you want to think of the lord because he's of another universe than maybe I am because, he is not of this physical entity but of the spiritual realm that through the transfer of energy makes his presence known. I am prepared to give you the scientific and spiritual approach to your personality type and emotions with the hope that you believe that just because you don't see it in the physical realm it's presence is still alive and here.

-Chapter 2-

The Emotions and Personality Traits

"So I wept much because no one was found worthy to open and read the scroll, or to look at it. But one of the elders said to me, do not weep. Behold, the Lion of the tribe of Judah, the Root of David, has prevailed to open the scroll and to loose its seven seals". -
Revelation 5:4-5

As your gift from God, the Creator of the Universe, you were born with 2 different sets of gifts, one that you received from your mother and the other from your father. These are your spiritual gifts at birth that can also be found in the genes. The gifts are the use of free will, morals, a personality type and emotions. There are two sets that create a total of 8 gifts. One is a dominant and the other is a recessive. In this book we will only discuss the dominant so that you may understand your design.

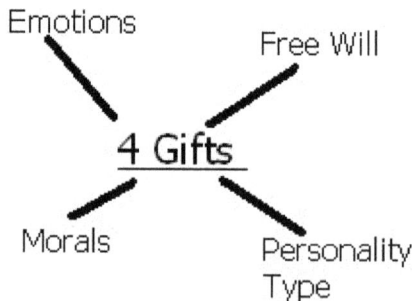

Emotions   Free Will

4 Gifts

Morals   Personality Type

Believe it or not, all of the gifts work together to create the one of a kind, unique individual in you.

Emotions   Free Will

You

Morals   Personality Type

"Work Together"

The purpose of everyone's life is set for journey and servitude. This is the way in which the body and mind gains it's experience, and learns. It doesn't really matter how you get there, as long as you do attempt to make it. Your life is constantly building on your design. You were created purposely, with the hope that you as a creation would want to know and find the creator. The creator actually marveled at the fact that one day you would ponder over him. He actually believed that one day you would look at yourself with love and want to know him. It is so beautiful the connection he feels for his people, his invention.

There are a total of 16 basic personality types, which create a variation of 192 different personality types with the aid of the astrological signs. Myers & Briggs built upon the theoretical work related to type done by Carl Jung. They gave it practical application and then I expanded on it. They were very close in there research. They found the 3 personality preference scales, which are sensing, thinking and feeling and the 16 distinct types. One of the personality preference scales was incorrect and actually an action of the scale and this is the reason the answers that I've discovered were not available to them. The creator has a time and a place for everything. He has been setting the stage for his glorious victory and once your realize your place in it all you too will be so proud.

The astrological signs are more than a map of the skies and planets but of the brain. It is the creator's personal grid to the mind. It is your crown and actually describes the battles that take place there. Astrology is an old profession, which took place back in the days. A lot of the meat was lost as far as the technique of why they told the stories that way. It wasn't because they were so interested in the world, but of themselves. The basic function of each and everyone's brain is to think. Depending on the order of your personality trait functions will defines the way in which you will think independently as an individual.

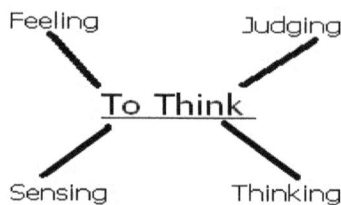

Feeling   Judging

To Think

Sensing   Thinking

There are four methods in the way the brain chooses to learn and they are by sensing, thinking, feeling or judging. Everyone does not have the ability to think from thoughts as a strength. Some people are guided by there emotions and this helps them to think. This is the same reason why, when you watch commercials and they're playing a certain type of music, you are motivated to go out and purchase that product. They've learned your tune, but you don't know theirs. Your dominant trait function is what defines how adequate a learner you truly are, so forget what you learned in school about IQ because it is nothing more than a game for fools and you're a target.

Some people learn from there feelings or by what others may feel, some learn by what they personally sense or by what others sense. An Example is as follows, my dominant trait function is sensing, which is aided by the five senses which are sight, smell, taste, hearing and touching which are located in opposite lobes of the brain. The aid of these five senses help me to think independently as a whole by what information is gathered because the function Sensing is my dominant trait function.

The personality types consist of all four-trait functions sensing, thinking, feeling and judging. This is what helps to create your identity as an individual. Each trait function is capable of doing all the function jobs individually. Depending on the order of the traits will define the duty of the given trait function.

-Memory-

Sensing is the use of the analytical emotions from the stored emotional memories of the individual or others. Did you just understand that? The memory section of the individuals mind, stores analytical emotions and analytical thoughts. Everything is done in sets of two's, as you further read you will understand more. They are called analytical because this portion of the individuals brain is constantly analyzing, breaking down, building it over and searching the event of a persons life that are stored over and over for truth or the perfect answers. The mind is always on a quest for truth from stored emotional and analytical thought. The funny part is, these are not happy memories. It's amazing what the mind chooses to remember and throw away.

For the memory section to work, it has to be connected to some form of negative event in your life just to store the event here, this is the reason why it is so hard to remember happy occasions which took place earlier in your life. It dispose of the junk that it doesn't need and unless the memories were connected to something negative the mind won't have a use for it. In this section of the brain, if the event isn't related to a negative emotion the brain disposes of it but only after sending it to the thinking section of the mind first. It's making sure that its partner in crime has everything that it needs as well. **Thinking** is the use of the analytical thought from the stored intellectual memories of the individual or others. For instance, debates, puzzles, mathematical problems, arguments, fighting, and any event with action that has little to do with emotions is stored here. This is the reason why you, as a person, love action packed movies, such as Die Hard because when you watch it, it is building up your thinking function of the mind. Your mind is learning and finding ways to be creative. This activity just builds up the emotions that reside in the Thinking section of the mind.

The functions Sensing and Thinking are housed in the parietal lobe of the brain, which also houses the memory and touching. The functions Feeling and Judging are housed in the Frontal Lobe of the brain, which also houses the moral of the individual. This is the reason why when people experience trauma to the frontal lobe of the brain they are aggressive. They have damaged the area that is responsible for maintaining the order of the functions Feeling and Judging, which is the Kingdom of God. It is like cutting heaven out of a persons mind.

Feeling is the use of the moral emotions and your direct link with the spiritual realm, which is the difference in right and wrong based on judgment formed by the moral or pure heart. Take for instance, a person with the feeling trait as a dominant function, if asked for change to feed the homeless they would willingly choose to give the money they have for a meal to a stranger because there feelings would tell them that the individual is honestly hungry and needs it. Just as a person with it's judging as a dominant function would choose to provide the meal rather than dispose of the change.

Judging is the use of the moral thought and your direct link with the spiritual realm, which is the difference in right and wrong, based on judgment formed by the moral or pure head. These two functions exist in the frontal lobe of the brain. This portion is smaller that the parietial lobe of the brain because there is no need to store information here because the creator of the universe is always with you, guiding you.

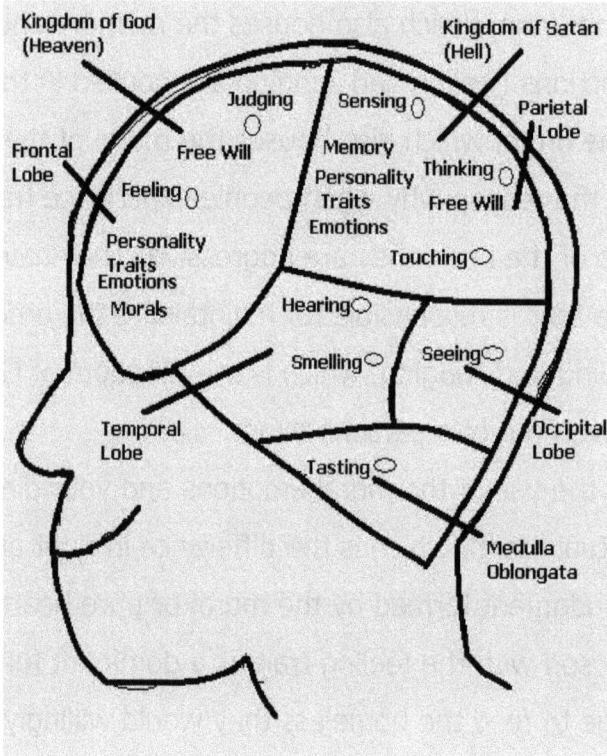

Speaking from a religious standpoint, knowledge of self is finding the kingdom of God within. Who but the Creator of the Universe (God) would know of the design of the creation (mankind)? What I have written proves the bible to be true and of the creator. When the creator gives you a gift, best believe he does not half step; he arms you with a powerful sphere and shield to battle against negativity.

People are mistaken by what they read in the bible they do not understand that the tales that are being told in the bible are spiritually telling mankind's design, like the story of Genesis in the beginning, there are so many things happening, so many clues, we are told that Adam was the first man and Eve is the first woman. Now of what importance do you really believe there name has to do with anything? To trace our roots perhaps. No! The names are told so that we will remember that Adam was the first Son of God or the first man of God and Eve was the first woman. This is important because it tells us that Adam had his morals working first as a creation. Just as when it tells us that Eve was seduced by the serpent, obviously she had to not have her morals working together as strengths. The second clue is that Adam was a man and Eve is a woman. For some reason the masculine and feminine sexuality stands out to me. So I did some digging and what I've come up with in my 33yrs. Of understanding life is that God is giving us, as a creation, the answers to our design without being to obvious. I say this because mankind has turned God's word within the bible into a commodity already, just as with Jesus, you can go to any store and purchase him for a price but who are truly loving him and trying to receive him? They do not respect God's word and like to benefit off of others pains, which is not right. Man will never be a God of Man, but a fool of a fool. Man need's to practice loving their neighbor because neither is superior than the other. That is just my opinion. What I realized was the story of Genesis was telling man's creation and that Adam was an INFP and that Eve was an ESTJ. The answers are not in the blood, and the blood is nothing but a mere distraction for sinners. You can learn the answers you seek, just from taking life one day at a time with the Bible as your guide. The purpose of this book is to undo the damage that has been done to the innocent and to educate others. I want to give others the ability like myself to actually see God working. Below is the only script that is important to your design.

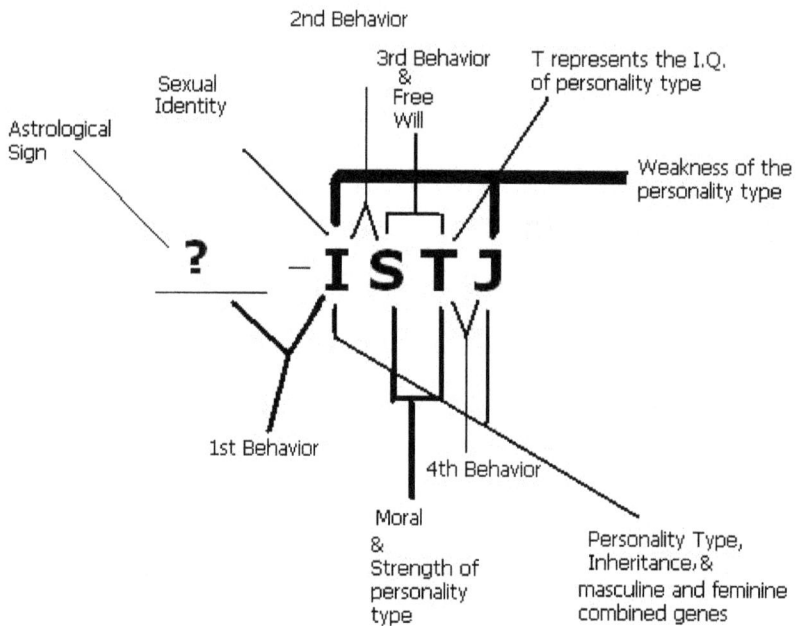

2nd Behavior

3rd Behavior & Free Will

Sexual Identity

T represents the I.Q. of personality type

Astrological Sign

Weakness of the personality type

? — ISTJ

1st Behavior

4th Behavior

Moral & Strength of personality type

Personality Type, Inheritance, & masculine and feminine combined genes

-Identity-

The I trait, which also stands for being Introverted, holds the markers needed for the masculinity sexuality of the individual.

If found in a girl she will be strong minded and a tomboyish, masculine girl. If found in a boy he will be very masculine and strong minded. The trait is meant to build strength in the character mentally and physically. The E trait, which also stands for being Extroverted, holds the markers needed for the femininity sexuality of the individual. If found in a girl she will be very tender, feminine and a girly girl. If found in a boy he will be a very feminine boy, tender but not a sissy. This trait is meant to soften the character of the individual mentally and physically. This was purposely done to give the illusion of a son being a mother son or as most call it momma's boy just as with a girl being a father's daughter or as most call it a daddy's girl. These two traits of being extroverted or introverted reflect your character within.

God was telling man the whole time when Moses just scribed the letters written in the bible and I'm making an attempt to translate them to you. He was not talking of the physical Eve or Adam but of the spiritual design, as well as in the conflicting stories of Jesus life and death. It is the spiritual design. Had he not been born physically he would not have been used as an example to tell the story. The bible is telling mankind's design. The personality type of Eve is ESTJ and of Adam is INFP.

Another dead give away was when Genesis tells the story of Eve eating the fruit and the travesty that happened to her after eating of it. What do you believe it was that went into her? I know, I know, knowledge of good and knowledge of bad, but what is that really? What do you think allowed her to have knowledge of good and knowledge of bad?

The story of Eden is more than a place here on earth. We have to remember that when reading the bible, it is telling us spiritual tales. Think for a moment, God talks of saving man from the earth, so why would he be so concerned with conversations about the earth in such detail if it were the same earth he wanted to rescue us from? He tells us constantly in the bible that we are not of this world. I believe the story of Eden is a delightful tale of the vagina of a woman and about experiencing sex. The serpent is the cervical canal and Adam is a sperm and Eve is an egg, and when they were kicked out I see this as going into the vagina for development. I believe the lord told us this tale, in this manner, so that we may remember the tale of our design in our minds.

In my belief, I see the fruit having all kinds of emotions. I believe that it is our emotions that are the invisible control apparatus that is piloting our bodies as found in the DNA code discovery.

The science field still doesn't know how this happens so allow me to enlighten you to the truth, the functions Feeling and Judging functions are being duplicated or copied by the functions Sensing and Thinking, and If morals exist in Feeling and Judging and if morals are the representation of the pure heart and the pure head, which is knowledge of good, that what exist in Sensing and Thinking but knowledge of bad. There is a Kingdom of God within as well as a Kingdom of Satan within each and every man. The greatest trick the devil ever pulled was convincing the world that he didn't exist (The Usual Suspects, 1995).

-A look at our Design-

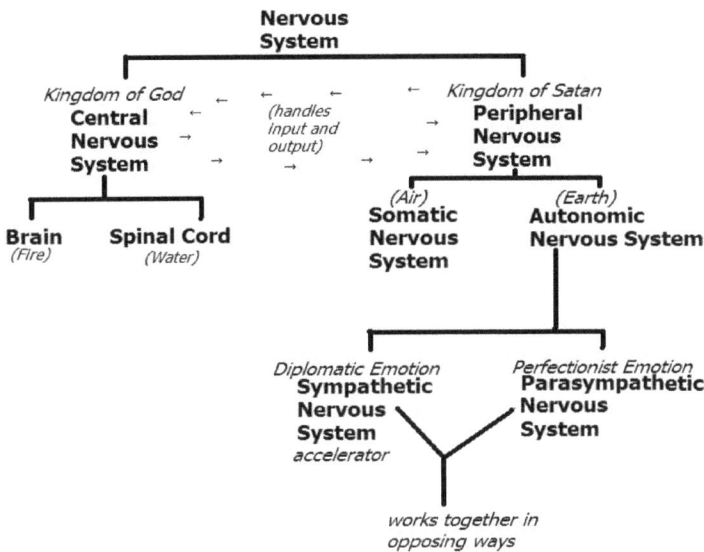

Nervous System

Kingdom of God
Central Nervous System
(handles input and output)
Kingdom of Satan
Peripheral Nervous System

Brain (Fire)   **Spinal Cord** (Water)

(Air) **Somatic Nervous System**   (Earth) **Autonomic Nervous System**

Diplomatic Emotion **Sympathetic Nervous System** accelerator   Perfectionist Emotion **Parasympathetic Nervous System**

works together in opposing ways

"The peripheral nervous system (PNS) handles the central nervous system's input and output. It contains all portions of the nervous system outside the brain and spinal cord, right down to nerves in the tips of the fingers and toes...In the peripheral nervous system, sensory nerves carry messages from special receptors in the skin, muscles and other internal and external sense organs to the spinal cord, which sends them along to the brain. These nerves put us in touch with both the outside world and the activities of our own bodies". (Wade C., Tarvis C., Psychology 2000)

So basically what ever information you gather from your feelings and judging your sensing and thinking interprets the information and adds a hint of spices by throwing in an old memory or two at you that relates to the same topic just to intensifies the emotional response. It's never personal but done to strengthen the sensing and thinking functions of the mind. This is how those with judging and feeling get caught up because they take things personal. It's lined up in your design. I say all of these things to help not to hinder. The same story that the science world has found is the same story that has been told for centuries about the Devil trying to over take the kingdom of God. It was just told in a spiritual manner bringing the parts and actions of the brain to life. The peripheral nervous system is always attempting to manipulate you. Take for instance if you haven't seen or visited with a loved one in such a long time and you feel lonely or saddened by there absence in your life, your sensing function would be alerted to the feeling and throw an old memory back at you to encourage the feelings. To make you feel gloomy allowing them to transform into more than what they were before because this section feeds off of negative emotions.

I'm not trying to frighten my reader, just to enlighten him or her on his or her very own design. We give negativity power over us, which needs to stop. God could have stopped the Devil long time ago. God does not hate the Devil. God is Love. Everyone has a part to play and he just so happens to be the villain. He doesn't have any special power, but the tools that we give him to mess with our minds in our dreams and everyday life. We play into his game and we need to let him play into ours. There is power in prayer and love.

In order for the four functions to exist they needs to be operated by the 16 main emotions and the emotions need the events and environment of the individual's life as a form of fuel. That is right the events and environment are a form of fuel for the emotions. This helps the emotions to grow big and strong. The emotions help to feed the overall personality type. Take for instance a person who has endured so much suffering within his life; think of how the events can stack in a person mind; making them a threat to themselves then to others, if he or she has no faith or trust in the creator's plan, were do you believe all of those built up emotions will go. All the events will be stacked right in the sensing section of the memory. People beat themselves up to much over nonsense because of the lies they chose to believe. No one is perfect. Everyone has fallen. It is all smoke and mirrors. Even as a child Jesus was a little mischievous. He was the son of the living God but he had to learn lessons in life as well. He didn't just wake up one morning and know his purpose. He was guided too. Just think of the journey he had to go to try to get the people to understand the message he was trying to convey without them wanting to pay attention. He bumped his head for a minute as well too, but he learned.

The emotions travel within the neurons. The same place that composes all of the information to make up the DNA code. What do you believe is the synapse that takes place in the mind? The synapses are the events and environments of a person's life that are linked together but never to cross each other, each event is separate but formed with the same purpose, for our growth as an individual. No need to write about the same information you've read in a regular psychology book, I'm telling the untold story to mankind's design. I'm filling in the blanks by telling the emotional side of it. I didn't learn the material I have from any school. It is the creator who guides me to this type of understanding.

The four functions are formed with the aid of the 16 major emotions and they are indecisive, idealistic, inventive, independence, intuitive, emotional, creativity, romantic, orderly, stubborn, cunning, diplomatic, careless, accident prone, intelligence and perfectionist. Remember as stated in the bible, first there was the word. The sixteen major emotions are locked within each and every astrological sign. The astrological sign is the keeper of the emotions and determines the climate and temperament of the individual, as I will discuss later.

The Element of Function

Aries	Taurus	Gemini	Cancer	Leo	Virgo	Emotional Response
Independence	Cunning	Emotional	Emotional	Diplomatic	Accident prone	When faced with a difficult situation
Diplomatic	Emotional	Romantic	Romantic	Romantic	Romantic	When in Love
Idealistic	Intelligence	Intuition	Cunning	Idealistic	Cunning	Strengths possessed
Intuition	Stubborn	Careless	Intelligence	Inventive	Intelligence	View of World
Inventive	Orderly	Idealistic	Orderly	Independence	Careless	Their Appearance
Perfectionist	Careless	Orderly	Indecisive	Orderly	Inventive	View of Home Life
Accident prone	Inventive	Cunning	Stubborn	Stubborn	Diplomatic	Upset with you
Intelligence	Diplomatic	Inventive	Inventive	Intelligence	Creativity	The way they think
Emotional	Accident prone	Diplomatic	Careless	Careless	Indecisive	Angry with you
Orderly	Intuition	Indecisive	Idealistic	Perfectionist	Orderly	View of money
Cunning	Creativity	Intelligence	Intuition	Creativity	Intuition	View of life
Creativity	Perfectionist	Creativity	Creativity	Intuition	Idealistic	View of Friends
Careless	Idealistic	Accident prone	Accident prone	Cunning	Stubborn	View of Family
Indecisive	Independence	Independence	Independence	Indecisive	Independence	View of Job
Stubborn	Indecisive	Stubborn	Diplomatic	Accident prone	Emotional	When Expressing emotions
Romantic	Romantic	Perfectionist	Perfectionist	Emotional	Perfectionist	When you feel loved

Libra	Scorpio	Sagittarius	Capricorn	Aquarius	Pisces	Emotional Response
Cunning	Diplomatic	Cunning	Stubborn	Stubborn	Cunning	When faced with a difficult situation
Romantic	Romantic	Romantic	Intuition	Perfectionist	Romantic	When in Love
Intuition	Orderly	Intuitive	Idealistic	Inventive	Intuition	Strengths possessed
Perfectionist	Cunning	Independence	Romantic	Diplomatic	Diplomatic	View of World
Inventive	Idealistic	Inventive	Independence	Orderly	Independence	Their Appearance
Orderly	Perfectionist	Orderly	Orderly	Careless	Idealistic	View of Home Life
Diplomatic	Stubborn	Diplomatic	Careless	Intelligence	Emotional	Upset with you
Intelligence	Intuition	Careless	Diplomatic	Intuition	Intelligence	The way they think
Accident Prone	Accident Prone	Creativity	Intelligence	Cunning	Stubborn	Angry with you
Careless	Intelligence	Stubborn	Cunning	Idealistic	Inventive	View of money
Stubborn	Creativity	Perfectionist	Perfectionist	Indecisive	Perfectionist	View of life
Independence	Indecisive	Idealistic	Accident Prone	Accident Prone	Creativity	View of Friends
Emotional	Inventive	Accident Prone	Inventive	Creativity	Careless	View of Family
Idealistic	Independence	Intelligence	Creativity	Independence	Orderly	View of Job
Indecisive	Careless	Indecisive	Emotional	Emotional	Indecisive	When expressing emotions
Creativity	Emotional	Emotional	Indecisive	Indecisive	Accident Prone	When you feel loved

Here are two simple charts, which tell how the emotions

work for each individual astrological sign.

The emotions are divided into the four orders of function dominant, auxiliary, third and fourth. The dominant and auxiliary functions are the strength that each and every personality type posses, and the third and fourth functions are the weaknesses.

The personality type determines if the individual will have the use of his or her morals early in life or later in life. For instance the ISTJ functions are sensing, thinking, feeling and judging in this exact order. The dominant and auxiliary functions are sensing and thinking which are the strengths of this personality type. It is the use of the analytical emotions and analytical thoughts from stored emotional and intellectual memories of others. This personality type will not have the use of their moral emotions or moral thoughts until later in life because feelings is a third function and judgment is a fourth function. They are destined to make bad choices as it relates to matters of the heart and head because feelings and judgment are the weaknesses of this personality type.

The dominant and auxiliary functions are the strengths the individual possess and they are also the formation of the free will and moral of the individual. This personality type senses by the thoughts of others, meaning they think by the impressions given by others meaning television shows, video games, and the people that interest them, so be aware of the people your children surround themselves around. The environment and events of the individual's these personality types surround themselves around will be the impression these personality signs give pickup, because they absorb it like a sponge. Example if the individual these personality signs are around are practicing racist then they will mock those same habits. If the individual these personality signs surround themselves around are practicing the homosexual lifestyle or are comfortable with this lifestyle then these personality signs will consume the same habits as being proper behavior.

There are four elements of the universe, which controls everyone's astrological sign, and emotions and they are Fire, Earth, Water, and Air. These are the temperaments of the astrological signs. Each of the twelve astrological sign resides in them. As you remember, the four elements of the universe control the four personality type functions individually, which are sensing, thinking, judging, and feeling. Every function controls four emotions each and every emotion is responsible for an emotional response, like for instance the emotion careless is responsible for anger, and the emotion emotional is responsible for stress. When you mix the element of the universe with a personality type function you create the temperament of the individual and this becomes a permanent mark on the individuals character.

If you can gain control over the emotions then you can control the emotional response that the individual illustrates day to day.

Depending on your astrological sign and personality type the arrangement of these functions are quite different. Two people can be the same personality type but act totally different in their views because of the arrangement of the given emotions. Everyone's astrological sign contains sixteen major emotions: eight positive as well as eight negative emotions as first told by Moses in the bible, in genesis. They operate both hemispheres of the brain, the right and left. The jobs of the emotions as I said before are to help with the growth of the personality type traits. On the next page is a diagram showing the direction in which the personality types exist.

Emotional Mind

Element of the Universe

Control ↓

Astrological Sign

Contains ↓

Emotions　→　need for fuel　→　**Events and Environment of a persons life**

Exist ↓

→

Mankind Contains ——→—— Cells　　## Rational Mind

Uses ↓　　　　　　　　Has ↓

Emotions (Junk DNA)　　Nucleus

Develop ↓　　　　　　Exist ↓　　→

　　　　　　　　　　Genes ——→—— Makeup　DNA

　　　　　　　　　　Encode ↓　　　　Composed of ↓

Personality Type　　　Protein　　　　2 separate chains (Molecules)

Consist of ↓　　　　　Consist of ↓　　Connected by ↓

　　　　　　　　　　Structural Proteins　Base Pairs

4 Personality Traits &　Enzymes　　　which are ↓

4 Functions　　　　　Hormones　　　subunits

　　　　　　　　　　Receptors and　　Called ↓

Produce ↓　　　　　DNA- binding proteins　Nucleotides

　　　　　　　　　　　　　　　　Containing ↓

Temperament　　　　　　　　　4 bases ——Linked —— Sugar

Creates ↓　　　　　　　　Adenine + Linked to Sugar +

　　　　　　　　　　　　Thymine + Linked to Sugar +

Attitude　　　　　　　　Cytosine + Linked to Sugar +

　　　　　　　　　　　　Guanine + Linked to Sugar+　　Phosphate Molecule

Adjust ↓　　　　　　Inscribe ↓　　→ Masculine & Feminine Codes ↓

　　　　　　　　　The Duties of the Genes　　$\frac{Adam}{Eve}$ = $\frac{INFP}{ESTJ}$ = $\frac{CAGTTGAC}{GTCAACTG}$

Emotional Response　Contain ↓

Releases ↓　　　　The Script of Life　　　↓　　↓　　↓

Hormones　　　　　　　　　　　　　　　"PERSONALITY TYPE"

Gives ↓

Hormonal Reaction

-The Creation of the Four Functions-

From birth to six years of age the dominant function is in development. Some authors believe that only the gift of extroversion or introversion in a child are recognizable and the other functions are elusive because the child has not yet developed the language skills to accurately describe their mental processes. I believe you can still detect the trait functions in the child if you knew the history of the child without having to examine its mental capacity. What the science world has not figured out is the traits are inherited from the mother and father so you already have a blueprint to work with. Parents are not just responsible for our births but are the secret windows into our lives and children are the continuation of one's lifeline. They traits as well as the genes originate from the mother and the father, and because the parents are adults all of their personality traits are fully functional and quite obvious. Have your parents ever argued with you and said to you, "I can't stand you because you act just like me". That may be true. The character trait that they see may actually be the trait you inherited from that parent. It is already known that each and every individual was given two copies of genes, one from their mother and one from their father with hopes of continuing the generation line.

I raised my oldest daughter without the presence of her father. He and I were young when I had gotten pregnant. He was street smart, selling drugs and involved in gang activity. I didn't want our daughter to be raised around that type of behavior.

Myself, I was book smart as a teenager and I had also come from a broken home. At the age of 15, I had suicidal tendencies because my mom had a boyfriend who was a constant predator over me. I was grief stricken and didn't want to exist. I've always been one to put the needs of others before myself. I remember one time his mom asked me to clean out her cabinets as a way of making change for myself. After the duty was done I sat in her room thinking of a way on how to ask her to tell her son to leave me alone. I loved this woman so much as my Granny, I just couldn't bring myself to hurt her. He soon showed up to take me home and I left with a tantrum. People check your children. Those attitudes you see just may be something deeper lurking within. I would often overuse my med's. My little sister and I would puff my inhaler's for the high, as a method of escape. A pharmacist recognized that I was using my med's wrong and told me if I continued in this manner I was going to burst my heart. The problem was not that I hated myself, I didn't want to do harm to myself, I just didn't want to be in the environment anymore. Everyone had always used me and my time, showed no appreciation and I was tired of it, I was only 15. I have never been a child and always called to duty. The time prior to my suicidal episode, I had been responsible for the care of my infant cousin, from birth until she was 10 months of age, then she had to return home to her mother. I had been building this little girl up, with all of my love than I had been stripped of her. I had grown quite attached and loved her as if she was my own child. I wanted the best for her and knew she wasn't going to get it just by returning home but it wasn't my call to make because I was a child myself. I wanted to hurt my mom's feeling in the same manner for sending her away from me that is why I overdosed on my med's. I just didn't feel she was hearing me or a comfort to my feelings. I soon realized that wasn't the way to go.

I prayed to the lord to send me a distraction a baby that no one could ever take from me again. I was determined to get pregnant by any means necessary, I didn't care who the father was I just wanted a baby, and the lord answered my prayers. I did not believe my baby could be a substitute for what I was going through but that the baby could be the distraction that I needed till my mind and soul were ready to face what was troubling me so much. I needed something else to invest in rather than focusing on my own pain. I just knew I would be a good mother just like a lot of teen parents often feel.

A lot of people often judge what they do not understand. You need to look closer than just what you see with your eyes. The next time you see a teenage pregnancy don't be so quick to hate on them emotionally just understand that the young lady is going through something that she needed a quick answer to for the moment, just to hold her till God saw fit to answer it for her.

Everyone must endure something. How do you think we learn? My oldest daughter is my blessing. My relationship to her father was short lived but he has definitely left his mark in my world. For me to not have spent a lifetime with him, his presence is always around me. My daughter acts just like this man, and I can't help but to love him for giving me such a wonderful part of himself. She inherited three of his personality traits and one of mine as a dominant trait. What are the odds of that happening? It makes me reminisce back on the day when we made her, we were both very innocent and he was so caught up in the moment and had pleaded with me to tell him that I loved him over and over till he released those mighty gametes. I thought it was foolish. Now that time has passed I see his intentions were on leaving me with a part of himself forever. Don't get me wrong it has been a joy raising her as a single parent and if I had to do it over again I wouldn't change a thing but it's funny how life turns out. His personality type is ENFP and my personality type is ISTJ and our daughter took my S and his ENF which is the formation of the personality type ESFP.

-The Growth of the Four Traits-

Just to recap, from birth to six years of age the first function the dominant is in development. It originates from a mother and a father; whoever was the dominant sex factor during conception, the child will exhibit those same characteristics. The individual will either be masculine or feminine. Children are the continuation of one's lifeline. This process helps to create the identity of the individual. The first strengths of any personality type is that which was received in the zodiac or astrological sign. The dominant trait will be the second strength the individual possesses, be it by way of sensing, thinking, judging, or feeling. This process takes place with the aid of the emotions. The emotions use the events and environments of ones life to aid in the growth of its traits and design.

From six years of age to twelve years of age the second function, auxiliary is in development. The dominant and auxiliary function work together as a team to create the free will and moral of the individual.

From twelve years of age to twenty-five years of age the third function, third is in development. The third function will be a fourth strength the individual possesses, be it by way of sensing, thinking, judging or feeling.

From twenty five to fifty years of age the last and fourth function, fourth is in development. The fourth function with be a fifth strength the individual possesses, be it by way of sensing, thinking, judging or feeling. This process takes place with the aid of the emotions. The emotions use the events and environments of ones life to aid in its design. The third and fourth function will work together as a team. Once you reach fifty years of age you should have all of the traits fully functional and should be on your way to being the wonderful creation the lord created you to be and hopefully you have learned how to dispose of the extra garbage.

Let me give you another example, if both parents are INFP than the child will be INFP or the dominant personality type depending on the blueprints, which they were given in the genes. You can't make ketchup out of mustard and DNA doesn't lie. As I said before, everyone has been given two blueprints; one that was received from the mom and the other that was received from the dad for the purpose of keeping the generations going. Depending on the functions that were passed on down the lifeline the child will exhibit those same qualities. Say for instance if both of those parents are INFP and the child is INFP then the child would have inherited the markers of that dominant parents lifeline be it from the grandmother or grandfather of the two gene copies. Look at the example diagram on the next page.

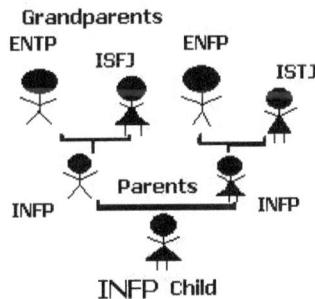

Grandparents
ENTP   ENFP
      ISFJ   ISTJ

          Parents
INFP   INFP

INFP Child

These traits are very easy to see in a child if you knew what to look for, for those that don't this may take time and practice. Without even knowing my history as a child to look at my features it's quite obvious how much I resemble my own father whose genes were dominant. Which tells me from a visual observation his genes were the dominant key factors in the creation of me, my blood type tells me this story as well. My father is an ESTJ, my mother is an INFP, and my trait is ISTJ. I naturally inherited one of my mother's characteristics or personality traits and three of my father's characteristics or personality traits. Look at the Diagram below.

Father= E S T J

Child = I S T J

Mother= I N F P

My selected personality trait, which I received from my parents by way of birth, is a mixture of the two personality types. Like the saying goes only the strong survive. This particular format is not always the case. As I said before, everyone is different and depending on which parent genes dominate, the child will inherit those genes.

Some children are split right down the middle as in the case with my brother ENFJ. He has two of my father's characteristics and two of my mother's characteristics. My mother's functions were dominant in his development. Girls create boys and the boys create girls.

He has the use of both his Moral Emotions and Moral

Thought as a dominant and auxiliary function together, which is the use of his free will, which I will explain in chapter 3. My father is a natural thinker then sensor. My mom is a natural feeler then a judger. They compliment each other because both lack what the other has. You know the saying opposites attract. The difference in my personality characteristics is I'm introverted and so like my mom my characteristics are flipped, instead of being a natural thinker I'm a dominant sensor then thinker. My father and I have a lot of the same characteristics therefore we use a lot of our emotions in the same manner. Look at the diagram below.

CANCER (INFP)	PISCES (ISTJ)	SAGITTARIUS (ESTJ)
EMOTIONAL	CUNNING →	CUNNING ←
ROMANTIC →	ROMANTIC ← →	ROMANTIC ←
CUNNING	INTUITION →	INTUITION ←
INTELLIGENCE	DIPLOMATIC	INDEPENDENCE
ORDERLY	INDEPENDENCE	INVENTIVE
INDECISIVE	IDEALISTIC	ORDERLY
STUBBORN	EMOTIONAL	DIPLOMATIC
INVENTIVE	INTELLIGENCE	CARELESS
CARELESS	STUBBORN	CREATIVITY
IDEALISTIC	INVENTIVE	STUBBORN
INTUITION	PERFECTIONIST →	PERFECTIONIST ←
CREATIVITY →	CREATIVITY ←	IDEALISTIC
ACCIDENT PRONE	CARELESS	ACCIDENT PRONE
INDEPENDENCE	ORDERLY	INTELLIGENCE
DIPLOMATIC	INDECISIVE →	INDECISIVE ←
PERFECTIONIST	ACCIDENT PRONE	EMOTIONAL

My mom is an INFP and my dad is an ESTJ. They have two emotions (romantic and accident prone) that are similar in functions, but because of their personality types and astrological sign the way they perform is very different. The similarities of these emotions create illusions of the same patterns. For instance, my parents are accident-prone when they relate to family and because of it I also am very careless when dealing with family.

-Femininity and Masculinity-

What does it mean to be feminine and or masculine? It's not something that you can just look up in a dictionary and clearly define it. If it were that simple than we wouldn't have the endless cases of gender disorders which plague the world or would we? The answers to these age old question have been available and are that simple, mankind just hasn't been paying that close attention to the answers they were allowed to have because they have been doing what they want to do and believing if they stay as a collection then they will be spared. But it's not true? You can't hide from God no matter how hard you try. Femininity is the act of what it means to be feminine. Those who are feminine possess the qualities of what the general public consider to be a woman, which is one who bears children in child birth, someone who is tender and sweet, a person who cares for others development, a teacher and educator in the developing mind of a child, someone who is lovely and sexy in appearance, and a person whose body is built to receive another . Masculinity is the act of what it means to be masculine. Those who are masculine possess the qualities of what the general public consider to be a man, which is one who gives sperm during conception, someone who is strong and tough in character, a person who cares for self development, a provider and donator in the life of a child, someone who gives guidance, someone who is handsome, rugged, and exquisite in appearance, and a person whose body is built to provide or give within another. These are what define femininity and masculinity to me. One has to understand that these are action, some are learned behavior and some of it just naturally happens for the individual. We have to quite assuming that just because one is born female that she is aware of how to act feminine or that because one is born male that he is aware of how to act masculine. This is not always the case. Males are born everyday who are feminine within and females are born everyday who are masculine within. I myself fall within that category. Being an ISTJ- I am naturally a masculine sexuality type.

At the age of 7 when I was in the second grade and my aunt, on my mother's side of the family, was my teacher she had introduced the new student to the class and her name was Sherry. I was volunteered to be her friend since as I said my aunt was the teacher. I had learned that she was from Chicago and had a best friend that she had left back home so that I would be next in line after her. After school was over we even road the same school bus home and lived in the same neighborhood. My cousin, a boy named Antonio had also road the bus and when he saw her for the first time he was star struck. Weeks had gone by and my cousin had made it his business to Know my friend as well. I did not understand his interest in her, I had believed at that age that my cousin was trying to steal my friend away. One day my cousin had brought my friend a pair of earrings and a necklace and had asked of me to deliver the gift and a message to my friend, which was, could she be his girlfriend? As I said before at that age I really didn't understand what he was asking of my friend. I felt as if he were trying to steal my friend away from me. He was my favorite cousin and I thought that he was being greedy for attention. We even got into an argument as he tried to explain to me his conversation. I rejected it altogether and said no that is my friend. Then he said no she'd like me more because I'm a boy. I still didn't comprehend his reasoning.

Myself, at the time not comprehending the depth of his answer felt threatened. I delivered the gifts to my friend and told her exactly what he said. She said he could be her friend even if he was a boy. I then asked if I were a boy would she like me too? She said yes, but that she likes me just fine the way that I was and would always want to play with me because we had more things in common. Then I felt proud of myself. I still didn't understand what it meant to be a boy or girl. I then left to tell my cousin that she didn't want her friendship with me to come between her friendship with him but that he could be her boy as a friend. It took me a long time to understand what being feminine meant and what being masculine meant. We as people need to quit assuming that girls are being taught to be little girls and that boys are learning to be little boys because they aren't.

At about the age of eleven I had this other friend named Shoe and we would fight from time to time and I'd win he battles cause I'm not your
average girl and I didn't give up. He was calling me the man before they even gave that name to cops. I played just as hard and dirty as the boys. I loved sports especially basketball. One afternoon my friend was rounding all the neighborhood boys up to play video games. I had liked video games as well so I decided to tag alone. I said. I'm coming. He said you can't my grandmother is not going to let you in. I said why? He said because you're a girl. I said but I like the same things that you like. He said you can try but I don't think she's going to let you in. So I got in the middle of the crowd and walked with them. When they all made it to the door each one spoke. They said Hello Mrs. Flowers. When it came my turn to speak I tried to speak and move quickly into the house. She said hold on honey. You can't go play with the boys because something might happen to you and I don't want to be held accountable. I

said I'm tough, I can handle myself. She said no maybe some other time. smiled at me and told me to go home. I was so disappointed. I could hear them laughing and having fun and I still didn't understand what was going on. I looked at being a girl as something bad like a disease. I'm putting this here to make others aware of what they are saying to a child. You have to go in depth with a child and make it very clear. I would have better understood if she would have told me that the little horny boys might attempt to violate me without supervisor attention. These are two memories that I hold in my mind about sexuality.

As I said earlier the I trait is the masculine sexuality of the individual and the E trait is the feminine sexuality of the individual.

Just speaking from off the top of my head, I don't know if anyone has ever guessed this, but women who are feminine create boys, and men who are masculine create girls. They purposely create the opposite sexes, just as women who are masculine create girls and men who are feminine create boys, they create little clones of themselves. I know your wondering now, what is she talking about and how does she know that. Just pay attention whenever you see someone who is pregnant; it may just be a black thang, but as a black woman we notice if the baby is carried low in the abdomen it is a boy if it is carried high in the ribs than it is a girl. The physical appearance of the mother tells the other story too, if she's up to appearance in her dress (girly) or just doesn't really care (tomboyish).

Just because you're a girl doesn't mean your feminine. There are masculine females and not all gay. If a female is the dominant sex partner than you first have to pay attention to the fact if she's a feminine or a masculine personality type, but has learned to be submissive or feminine in her relationship to that submissive or feminine man chances are that during conception she will deliver a boy because of the odds of the feminine man creating a clone of himself or because of the masculine female submitting to him. If a female is dominant and the masculine type and the male is submissive and masculine type then chances are you will deliver a girl, because chances are she will create a clone of herself or his masculine type genes will create the opposite sex. Dominant genes win every time, depending on whose genes are strongest.

Fathers create daughter and mothers create son. The world has been lying to you. Both parents in the home are very important to the child or children's development but not like you think. A boy does not need a father to teach him how to be a man just like a daughter does not need a mother to teach her to be a woman. The mother is to teach the son how to be a respectable man and the father is to teach the daughter how to be a respectable woman. This is the job the parents are to be doing.

Okay now that I've told the emotional side of the story let me tell the analytical side of the same story...there are a total of two blueprints given at conception in the development of a child.

Sex origin of the dominant parent and masculinity or feminization plays a role in the inheritance of the child. It is not a magic role of the dice but common sense.

My personality type is ISTJ, my mother is INFP and my dad is ESTJ. I received my masculine sexuality gene from my mother and the other traits I possess are feminine which I received from my father. Think back to what I said about Eve being the first woman ESTJ these traits she passed to her sons, just as in the case with my father passing it to his daughter. Get it. All this information right before your nose in clear view and no one has paid attention to it until now.

If the dominant parent is male than he will produce a female heir. He will take the already stored female blueprint that he has derived from his mother and create a life cycle similar to what was inherited. Males are a recreation of their mothers. If the dominant parent is male and feminine in behavior than he will produce a male heir. He will take the already stored male blueprint that he has derived from his father and create a life cycle similar to what was inherited. His body is giving of the impression, by way of hormones, that the male is female, because females are a recreation of their fathers, and therefore takes the wrong copy of the blueprint to create a new life. He will create a clone of himself. Such as in all the cases with the young boy who looks just like his father rather than his mother. See, his genes are telling a story which tells that the man was very feminine during conception and the female was the aggressor. The same as with women who have their daughters looking just like them rather than their fathers.

If the dominant parent is female and feminine than she will produce a male heir. She will take the already stored male blueprint that she has derived from her father and create a life cycle similar to what was inherited. Females are a recreation of their fathers. The flip side, if the dominant parent is female and masculine than she will produce a female heir. She will take the already stored female blueprint that she has derived from her mother and create a life cycle similar to what was inherited. Her body is giving off the impression, by way of hormones, that the female is male, because males are a recreation of their mother and therefore takes the wrong copy of the blueprint to create a new life. She will create a clone of herself. Children are the continuation of one's lifeline. The child will inherit one out of four, two out of four, or three out of four of the dominant parents personality trait factors. These are the factors that have always been dominant in establishing the lifeline of the parent. The other traits will be carried as well but known as recessive genes.

Dominant genes win every time, depending on whose genes are strongest. The only way to accurately tell whose genes were responsible in the creation is DNA, personality type and or the features of the child never lie. The hereditary factors can be one out of four traits, two out of four traits, or three out of four traits inherited as a dominant traits received from either or parent. Sorry to burst everyone's bubble but there are no little boys hiding in girls bodies waiting to become lesbians and there are no little girls hiding in boys bodies waiting to become gay men. Your life has just over stimulated the sensing and thinking functions of the brain because of abuse.

This process is possible because every person has two blueprints in them, one inherited from the mother and the other from the father. During creation one of the formulas is chosen as a strength and the other as a backup . The body has not disposed of the other plan; instead it chooses to use it when needed, just in case things go wrong. Each sperm and every egg carries two blueprints, one from each parent, with the hope of keeping the generation going. Let me start at the beginning...

Don't get upset if you never have a son because chances are your daughter will carry the same blueprint of yours and pass those same genes along in conception and produce a grandson that will carry your blueprint for you. Life is good. It will be evident in the child's personality type, which is a continuation of one's gene line. This evidence speaks louder without knowing the child's mental capacity.

Your personality trait functions sensing, thinking, feeling, and judging use certain emotions to help with its development, thereby are creating a series of codes. The code is created because the emotions are repeated. This is just a piece of the puzzle concerning mankind's design. The way I conducted my research was I listed the main emotions that I possess as a Pisces . I asked myself these questions; do you remember being emotional from birth to six years of age as a child? From birth to six years of age is the use of the dominant function. I put an X in the boxes because I remembered several instances where I was emotional. Then I asked myself, do you remember being emotional from six years of age to twelve years of age as a pre-teen? This was the formation of my auxiliary function, I did not remember being as emotional as I was when I was younger. These were the days I remember being violent and always having to fight as a method of protecting my siblings and myself. I did at this age what was necessary for my survival and I don't recall being emotional. I asked the same questions for the ages twelve through twenty five which is the use of the third function and twenty five through fifty which is the use of the fourth function and I put an X in both boxes because the older I got the more emotional I became. I took the time to review all of my answers and what I noticed was I had used four of my emotions all the time. This in return created a negative person in my attitude due to my emotions being over stimulated. The example is on the next page.

Emotions	0-6	6-12	12-25	25-50	O/S
Emotional (E)	X		X	X	
Intuitive (V)			X	X	
Romantic (V)			X	X	
Imaginative (I)		X	X	X	
Compassionate (I)	X			X	
Sensitive (V)	X		X	X	
Adaptable (E)	X	X	X	X	X
Receptive (J)			X	X	
Secretive (I)	X	X			
Careless (J)	X	X	X	X	X
Impressionable (I)	X	X			
Weak-willed (E)	X		X	X	
Indecisive (J)	X	X	X	X	X
Vague (J)	X	X	X	X	X
Mysterious (V)	X		X	X	
Unworldly (E)		X	X	X	

Code: E, I, V, E, I, J, I, E, J, J, V
    I, E, I, J, I, J, J, E
    E, V, V, I, V, E, J, J, E, J, J, V, E
    E, V, V, I, I, V, E, E, J, J, E, J, J, V, E
    E, J, J, J

What I then noticed which shocked me was that my emotions had created a series of codes, which must be also aligned in the DNA code. Translated the emotions code is C, T, G, C, T, A, T, C, A, A, G, T, C, T, A, T, A, A, C, C, A, A, T, G, C, A, A, C, A, A, G, C, C, A, A, T, T, G, C, C, A, A, C, A, A, G, C, C, A, A, A. My belief is the emotions are the dark area of the DNA which no ones pays much attention two and scientist have been looking at with no understanding. If more people followed this same formula to observing there emotions than they would not have as much difficulty in there life because they would be able to get to the root of the problem.

-Inheritability-

I heard once you can't know where you're going until you know where you've come from. This statement with the aid of slavery has done a lot of damage to the African American community. With slavery, the ties to the ancestral line has been cut. One is only left to guess the origin of their roots. A wicked mind game that was placed upon the people.

This statement for those who do not know there origins tells them they can't go anywhere as a people. It is wrong to assume such nonsense is true because God is the creator of all. He is the ancestral line that everyone is connected to. God has the blueprint to mankind's design. He knows where you come from and where you're going. He made you as a creation and gave you as a gift to your parents as an expression of his love. They have the easy job, all they have to do is continue to keep building you up with God (his love), remember to continue the transfer of the positive energy.

My husband and I are another example of inheritability. We have two children together and the both of them are girls. I am very dominant woman and he's a very submissive, or recessive man. His personality trait is E N F P and my personality trait is I S T J. Looking at the chart below you are able to chart my inherit traits.

INFP
John (I)

ESFJ
Louis (SJ)

ESTJ
George (T)

INTP
Mattie (T)

ISTP
Lorene (I)

ISTJ
Leo (STJ)

INFP
Catherine (I)

ESTJ
Melvin (STJ)

Katrina (ISTJ)

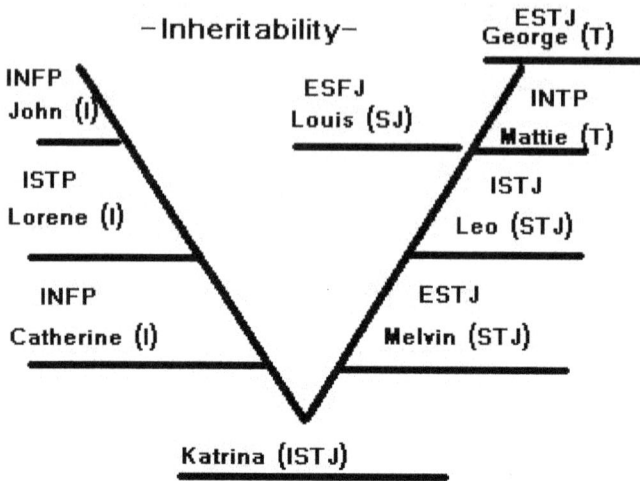

I have traced my individual personality traits down my generation line. The I-trait to my great grandfather John, who most likely received it from his mother because males are a recreation of their mother. The T-trait I have traced back to my great-great grandfather George who was of Indian decent stolen and sold into slavery. The S and J-trait I have been traced back to my great-grandfather Louis who was also of Indian decent. He married my great-grandmother Mattie who was the oldest child of George and Hannah Ruff. This is what I know of my generation line.

Looking at our personality traits together there could be a combination of sixteen different personality types to pick from, but in our daughter's case certain emotions are quite evident.

For one, our oldest child together, the middle one, as a baby she was not animated at all. She wouldn't play with talking toys because she feared them. I was the same way when I was younger. She didn't cry unless she needed to be changed or fed. She wasn't an emotional baby. She'd just lay relaxed and observe you. She didn't watch cartoons; she'd rather watch music videos. As she began to grow I noticed she didn't play with other children and would rather be left alone. At 8 months I noticed her solving problems, like if her bottle were out of her reach I noticed her stacking objects together so she could reach the bottle. I was in aw of the way here mind would work, by the time she was two years of age she knew when she was frightened. She knew the difference in right and wrong from emotions, and she wasn't judgmental. Which led me to believe the first group of emotions she exhibited were from her astrological sign of Aries temperament of fire, which is also her judgment. Fire is the use of our moral judgment and thoughts. This is a spiritual truth. She was a lot like me, her DNA was even like mine but she resembled her daddy a whole lot. So I figured she was going to have two of my traits and two of her daddy's. She's (I) introverted like me and a (S) sensor like me. Then I noticed she's a (F) feeler like her father and a perceiver. Together they form I S F P, and these are the traits she exhibits everyday, non-changing. Her personality type functions by Feeling, Sensing, Judging and Thinking by what she feels are true. You'll read more of these functions in the coming chapters.

My youngest daughter is a Sagittarius also the temperament of fire. As a little girl she didn't have the need to be constantly hugged and assured of our existence. She is very tough and dominates over my middle daughter. She learns by watching her oldest sister and loves to copy her. She's not animated either and talking toys frighten her as well. She enjoys the company of others and loves to socialize. I find her picking up the remote, learning how to operate it and changing the channels. I catch her bullying her sister and her older cousin. She senses the fear they have of her and because of it she constantly tries to intimidate them and has tantrums when she doesn't get her way. She as well is a Fire sign, and natural judger. She loves the use of her moral judgment. She's (E) extroverted like her father and a (S) sensor like me. Then she a (T) thinker and (J) Judger like myself, she has my DNA and his positive factor, plus she looks just like mommy. So she is E S T J, which is extroverted, sensing, thinking, and judging. She exhibits this behavior none changing. My children are three years old and one year's of age. I have recognized their personality traits without waiting on them to become older. To recognize is easy, you just have to pay attention to the signs and emotions they give off to you and the history of both parents personality type is quite useful as well.

The second function in development is the auxiliary function and this takes place from six years to twelve years of age. The child's dominant function starts to pull ahead of the group by this time. This is where patterns and behavior becomes more evident. It is most important for the child's healthy development to encourage the growth of the dominant function, be it negative or a positive one, this is a strength which can be aided by listening to music, coloring, inventing new games to play, learning new words, and playing board games with the child, depending on which is the dominant function. You'll learn more when you read the individual personality trait and astrological sign.

The third function takes shape between twelve through twenty-five years of age. By this time the dominant an auxiliary functions are team players and you've learned to master both functions. The auxiliary balances the dominant function and ensures that we are proficient at both information gathering and decision-making. The third function falls inline with the dominant and auxiliary.

By the time you are twenty-five years of age the personality type is distinctive. The third function is still quite under developed and will never be a strength possessed. The third and fourth functions will never be as strong as the dominant and auxiliary functions because these are the recessive genes but are still useful for the individual's character.

From twenty-five to fifty years of age the last function is in development. After fifty years of age all of the traits are fully functional and the process is complete. You have the use of all of your functions.

All the one-hundred ninety two personality types each have a total of sixteen emotions at work and they are orderly, indecisive, stubborn, careless, romantic, intuition, creativity, independence, diplomatic, inventive, cunning, perfectionist, intelligence accident prone, idealistic and emotional. I know what you're thinking, "that's not me at all. I am a very good person when you get to know me!"

Let me explain what I'm talking about, these are the basic emotions that each and every personality types exhibits, but the way in which they function for the individual is very different given the elements in which the individual was born.

Just to recap, in each of the personality traits you will find an element of the universe that controls the astrological sign. All of the astrological signs contain emotions that exist in mankind. Mankind uses the emotions to help with the growth of the individual personality type. The elements Fire, Water, Air and Earth controls a selected group of emotions which all exist within the Genes. As I said before the emotions aid in the development of the four Personality Traits thinking, sensing, judging, and feelings. Below I list the duties of the Genes.

-The Genes of Our Design-

An individual has 46 chromosomes, 23 received from the father and 23 received from the mother, which store the hereditary material passed on from one generation to the next. 22 of the chromosomes are auto some and one pair are sex chromosomes, either both x if female, or x and a y if male. (Mori, Catherine, Scott, R. The Human Genome, 1998)

DNA is the material within the chromosome that encodes the

genes, which are located at specific sites on the chromosome. The DNA carries all of the genetic information necessary for cellular functions. DNA consist of the codes Adenine (A), Cytosine (C), Thymine (T), and Guanine (G). The codes are what tell the genes the duties they need to perform. The science world cannot see the duties of the genes because the chemical bases are too tiny to see under a microscope. This is the reason that science has decided to unravel the DNA code because they believe that if they labeled each individual part than they will have a better understanding of it's duties.

The answers to this riddle are hidden within the bible. This is the very reason that Jesus spoke in parables. He did not want to give man control over man's design within the answers, and that is why he hid it here. This is the reason why the bible is considered the Holy Bible and not just the fact of Jesus life and death. All of the stories are telling a tale and giving an answer. In the old days, they studied astrology and the stars. Not because the stars were telling a story of the world but of the individual's mind. Down to the Capricorn, which is a sea goat, which is the hippocampus in the mind. Astrology is the crown of the brain which given the tales bring the parts of the brain to life with the hope that you will remember it's duties.

There are two copies of each gene, one is masculine and the other feminine. This is the reason that people get lost in the tale of Genesis. It is not a tale of the world it is a tale of man's creation.

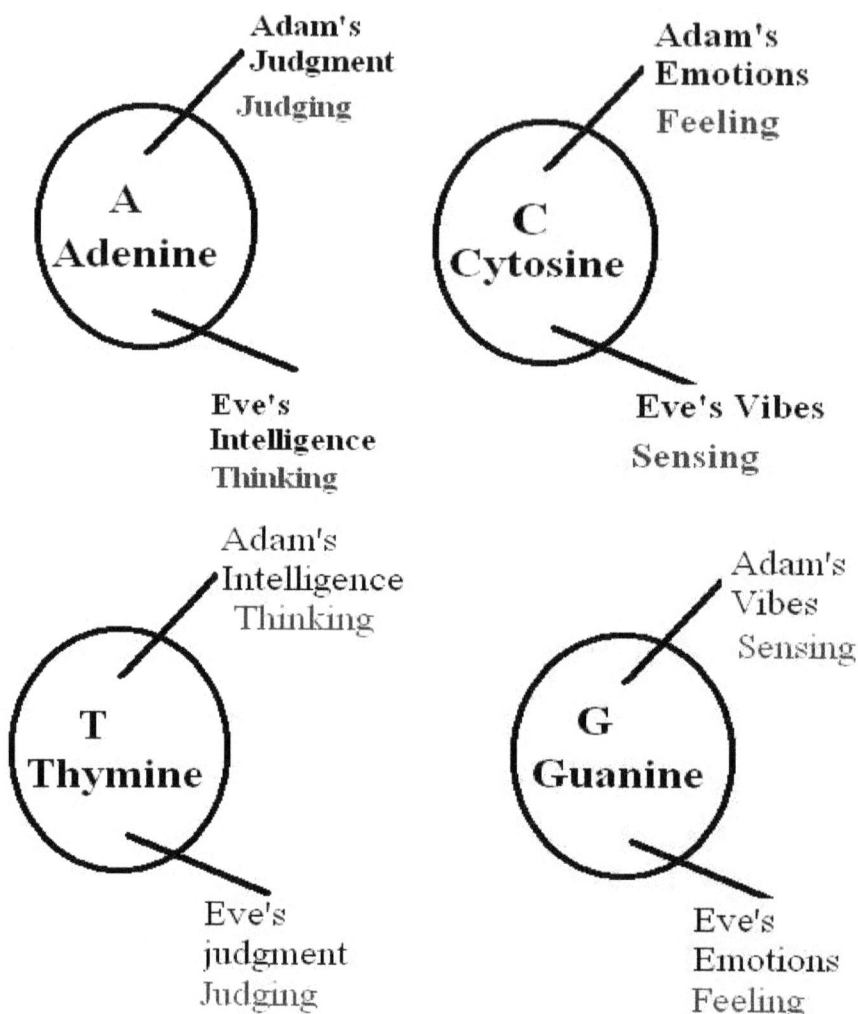

In the study of Genetics, there are four basic genes for the chromosomes and they are A, C, T, and G which represents the A for Adenine, the C for Cytosine, the T for Thymine and the G for Guanine. Science has only found the sequence of the genes, but still does not know the duties of the genes because they have yet to step out on faith just to understand God's answers. For the longest, no one knew the job of the genes or how they functioned, well that was until I stepped out on faith. Let me show you what I see.

- Adenine is a representation of Adam's Judgment (Judging) and Eve's Intelligence (Thinking), which do the same job but in opposing ways.
- Cytosine is a representation of Adam's Emotions (Feeling) and Eve's Vibes (Sensing), which do the same job but in opposing ways.
- Thymine is a representation of Adam's Intelligence (Thinking) and Eve's Judgment (Judging), which do the same job but in opposing ways.
- Guanine is a representation of Adam's Vibes (Sensing) and Eve's Emotions (Feeling), which do the same job but in opposing ways.

$$\frac{\text{A JUDGING}}{\text{T THINKING}}$$

$$\frac{\text{C FEELING}}{\text{G SENSING}}$$

Creating the same formula:

The Genes have a function and a duty to perform. They are

able to take on the duties and function of each of the gene code depending on the order in which they are placed. This process help's to create the masculine and feminine traits of your individual design.

The Genes are a combination of the personality traits as well as a blend of a parents characteristics.

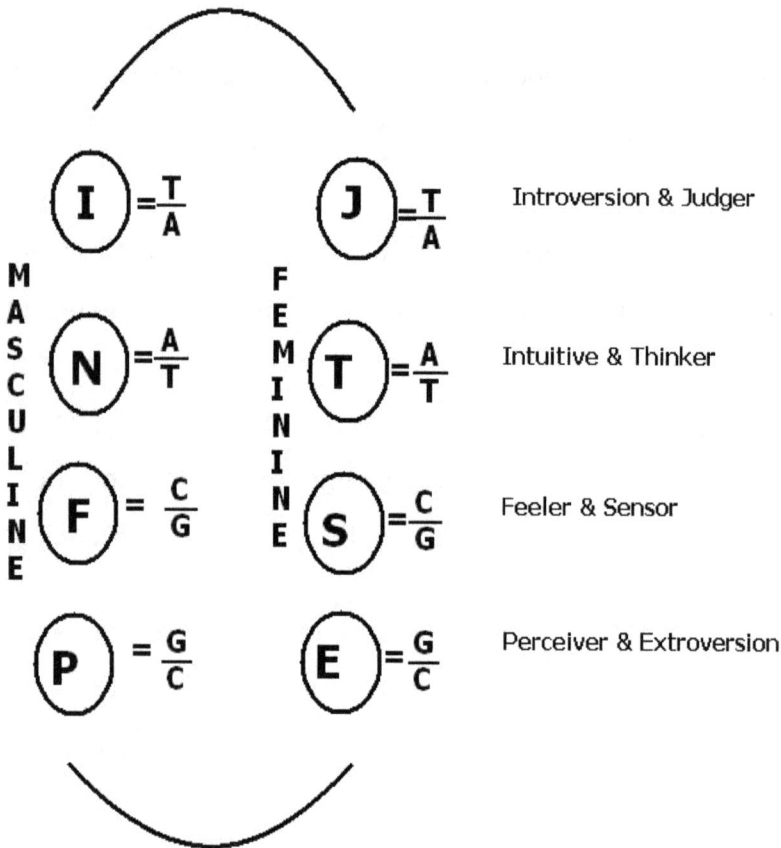

$\left(I\right) = \frac{T}{A}$ $\left(J\right) = \frac{T}{A}$ Introversion & Judger

$\left(N\right) = \frac{A}{T}$ $\left(T\right) = \frac{A}{T}$ Intuitive & Thinker

$\left(F\right) = \frac{C}{G}$ $\left(S\right) = \frac{C}{G}$ Feeler & Sensor

$\left(P\right) = \frac{G}{C}$ $\left(E\right) = \frac{G}{C}$ Perceiver & Extroversion

MASCULINE

FEMININE

My father's genes dominated my design but my mom's inner sexuality type beat him out. The I trait is what sets my identity. The genes are a mixture of negative and positive charges as well as dominant and recessive genes. There is always a polarity conflict going on, the battle of Adam against Eve. A pairs well with T, and C pairs well with G because they are clones of each other. The negative charge is always attempting to copy and replace the positive charge in an attempt to take over its position. So basically, everyone has eight traits', the four which lead that are first in command, and the four which follow who are a backup. They are often called dominant and recessive. Nothing is ever thrown away, it is just stored away for later usage when the emotion attempt to mimic that of the other.

My mom is an INFP and therefore her gene's represent Adam, she is a very strong, masculine sexuality type woman. My dad is an ESTJ and therefore his gene's represent Eve and he is a very passionate, feminine sexuality type man. When they created me, I took on a combination of their traits which lead me to be an ISTJ and I too am a very strong, masculine sexuality type woman. I inherited one of my moms dominant personality trait and three of my dads dominant personality trait, I also inherited three of my moms recessive personality trait and one of my dads recessive personality trait.

During conception, when the sperm cell joins forces with the egg, it does not discard information, it actually brings the rest of the information along for the ride and depending on which ever traits dominate for the sperm cell as well as the egg those traits will join forces. Whoever was the dominant sexuality at the time of conception wins the position of first place and the other takes the position of second place. The information is never lost but purposely put there just in case the genes need to mimic behavior. This is how hereditary information is stored and replicated. This is real easy to understand if you just like me have paid attention to the stories of the bible, there is always a battle of good vs. evil and each gene is a mixture of negative and positive charges, as well as feminine and masculine sexuality traits and there is always the polarity conflict going on. The Bible is talking of man's spiritual design and not the physical design. Look at the diagram.

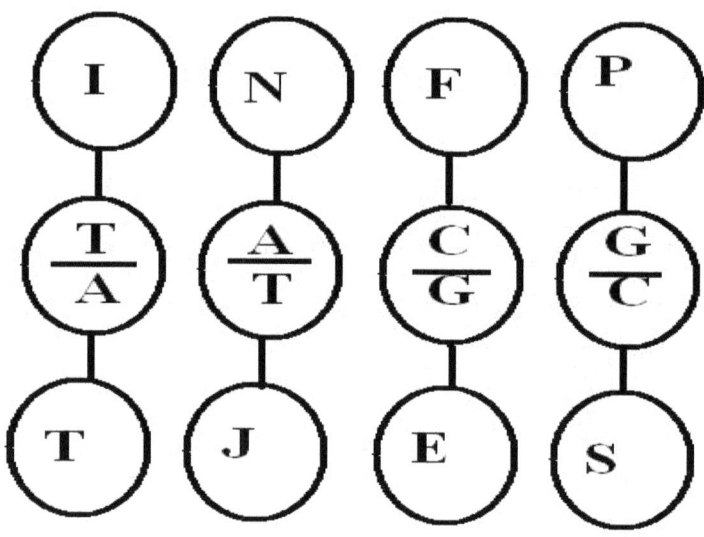

The diagram below list the sixteen major emotions of the traits, divided into the specific personality traits and elements, for you to learn how the traits function for that given trait.

Elements	Control	Duty	Emotions
Water	Emotion (Feelings) E	**Natural Feeler** Just like the lakes and oceans people love to be around you. (Cancer, Scorpio and Pisces)	Intelligence Accident Prone Idealistic Emotional
Fire	Judgment/ Intuition (Judging) J	**Natural Judger** Feisty and aggressive. It's your way or no way. (Aries, Leo and Sagittarius)	Orderly Indecisive Stubborn Careless
Air	Vibes (Sensing) V	**Natural Sensor** You pay close attention to facts and details that you experience day to day. Trust what information your five senses tell you. (Gemini, Libra and Aquarius)	Romantic Intuition Creativity Independence
Earth	Intelligence (Thinking) I	**Natural Thinker** Grounded and down to earth (Taurus, Virgo and Capricorn)	Diplomatic Inventive Cunning Perfectionist

The Elements of Function

No person has been aware, until now, is the story of Genesis is not just the story of the creation of man or the world but that it is actually a map of the mind telling mankind's design.

"In the beginning God created the heavens(Kingdom of God) and the earth (Kingdom of Satan). The earth (Thinking) was empty, a formless mass cloaked in darkness. And the Spirit of God was

hovering over its surface. Then God said, Let there be light, and there was light. And God saw that it was good. Then he separated the light from the darkness. God called the light day and the darkness night. Together these made up one day. And God said, Let there be space between the waters, to separate water from water. And so it was. God made this space to separate the waters above from the waters below. And God called the space sky. This happened on the second day. And God said. Let the waters beneath the sky be gathered into one place so dry ground may appear. And so it was. God named the dry ground land and the water seas (Feeling). And God saw that it was good". -*Genesis 1:1-10*

"For God made two great lights, the sun (Judging) and the moon (Feeling), to shine down upon the earth (Thinking). The greater one, the sun (Judging) presides during the day; the lesser one, the moon (Feeling), presides through the night. He also made the stars. God set these lights in the heavens to light the earth (Thinking), to govern the day and the night, and to separate the light from the darkness. And God saw that it was good. This all happened on the fourth day".- *Genesis 1:16-19*

The story of Adam and of Eve is purposely told in the manner in which it was to help the reader to understand its design. What better a way to tell a story of mankind's design, than in a story that is easily remembered.

Below is a list of the elements of function.

Fire- (Aries, Leo, and Sagittarius) Judgment is the use of your intuition by way of judging. It is the process of forming a final analysis of the information she or he has gathered from a personal point of view. This is your spiritual thought. This process takes place in the right hemisphere of the frontal lobe. It's also his or her ability to make a sound decision from the morals, also in the frontal lobe. This is the difference in right and wrong. When a person doesn't have usage of there moral thought working there personality is out of As a fire sign there are four constant emotions at work and they are careless, stubborn, indecisive, and orderly. Jobs and duties of the emotions:

Intuitive and judger contain the same group of emotions

Intuitive (Masculine)

Adam's Judgment

Intuitive (N)

- Mars
- Sun

- Jupiter

N- represents being an intuitive. Intuitive's are Dominant Judgers of positive emotions. It is the use and zone of Adam's Judgment. These individuals use their ability of judging to gather positive information. An Intuitive is one who uses the emotions to formulate inspiration. They possess the attitude of being insightful. They are masculine in character and enjoy exposing the truth of lies from their judgment. They are natural debaters and have a great insight concerning matters that are appropriate. These individual's can be perceived as argumentative but they just have a natural duty to order. The zone contains the planets Mars, Sun and Jupiter, which are responsible for the location of the Zodiac's Aries, Leo and Sagittarius. The Zodiac's creates the different variations of the duties of the emotions Careless, Indecisive, Orderly and Stubborn.

Stubborn-

°you trust inspiration, spiritual guidance, and fiction

°you are oriented towards the future

°Unduly determined to exert one's will

°Characterized by perseverance

°You are difficult to handle or work

°You are not easily persuaded

Careless-

°you like new ideas for your own sake

°you value imagination and innovation

°Not taking sufficient care

°Showing a lack of consideration

°Marked by or resulting from lack of forethought or thoroughness

°you tend to be general and figurative by using metaphors and analogies.

Indecisive-

°you enjoy learning new skills and get bored easily after mastering them.

°You present information through leaps and hurdles in a round about manner

°You are uncertain about your skills

°You make a judgment based on your own feelings.

°You are not clearly defined

°You are prone to or characterized by indecision

°Not decisive; inconclusive

Judger (Feminine)

Eve's Intelligence

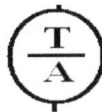

Judger (J)

- Venus
- Mercury
- Saturn

J- represents being a Judger. Judgers are Dominant Negative Thinkers of emotions. It is the use of Eve's Intelligence. These individuals use their ability of reasoning to gather negative information. Judgers are feminine in character and have a deep appreciation for problem-solving. These individuals require some form of negative action just to build up their thought and the way in which they think. The zone contains the planets Venus, Mercury and Saturn, which are responsible for the location of the Zodiac's. The Zodiac's Taurus, Virgo and Capricorn creates the different variations of the duties of the emotions Careless, Indecisive, Orderly and Stubborn.

Indecisive-
    °Not decisive; inconclusive
    °Not clearly defined
    °You have trouble keeping on track or following directions
    °Prone to or characterized by indecision

Careless-
    °You are product oriented and less likely to deal with specifics because your emphasis is on completing the task
    °You prefer to focus on the big picture.
    °Marked by or resulting from lack of forethought or thoroughness
    °Not taking sufficient care
    °Showing a lack of consideration

Orderly-

°You prefer to make plans and follow them accordingly.

°You are usually well organized.

 °You set goals and work toward achieving them on time.

°You are a methodical and systematic arrangement.

°You are peaceful.

°You are devoid of violence or disruption.

°You are happiest after final decisions have been made.

°You feel satisfaction from finishing the projects.

Stubborn-

°You have a work ethic, work first play later.

°You prefer to know what you are getting into.

°You are not easily persuaded

°You are difficult to handle or work

°Characterized by perseverance

°Unduly determined to exert one's will

Water- (Cancer, Scorpio, and Pisces) Feelings are the use of his or her emotions. It's the ability to trust interpretations of others and their decisions when it relates to you. This action takes place in the right hemisphere of the frontal lobe. This is your spiritual emotion. It's also the ability to know and use his or her moral judgment when it's pertains to his or her feelings. This is your difference between right and wrong. You react by your feelings, and those who do not have feeling as there dominant or auxiliary have a hard time making good decisions. As a water sign you have four constant emotions at work and they are intelligence, accident prone, idealistic and emotional.

Jobs and duties of the emotions:

Extroverted and feeler contain the same group of emotions

Extrovert (Feminine)

Eve's Vibes

Extrovert (E)

- Mercury
- Venus
- Uranus

E- represents being an Extrovert. It is the use of Eve's Vibes. Extroverts are Dominant Negative Sensors of emotions. These individuals also use their ability of feeling to gather positive information. These individuals use their five senses seeing, touching, smelling, hearing and tasting to gather the negative emotions. Extroverts are feminine in character and have a deep appreciation for friends rather than family. They are more outwards and forthcoming concerning their thoughts and feelings. These individuals excel In people friendly environments. They arc not patient when dealing with problem-solving issues. The zone contains the planets Mercury, Venus and Uranus, which are responsible for the location of the Zodiac's. The Zodiac's Gemini, Libra, and Aquarius creates the different variations of the duties of the emotions Accident Prone, Emotional, Idealistic and Intelligence.

Emotional- being with others energizes you. You react more than you think and you communicate to others with enthusiasm.

Accident Prone-
°You respond quickly without hearing the whole conversation.
°You enjoy being the center of attention, and also a fast pace.
°Not intentionally done.
Idealistic-
°you think out loud and are easier to know and read.
° You were your emotions on your sleeve and talk with your body language.
°When your emotions have been hurt you feel the need to voice your opinion.
°You share personal information freely and sometimes

without enough forethought.

°Your behavior is influenced by ideal

Intelligence-

°you talk more than you listen and prefer to know a little information rather than it all.

°You have the ability to reason

°The capacity to acquire and apply knowledge.

°The ability to show rational judgment.

Feeler (Masculine)

Adam's Emotions

Feeler (F)

- Moon
- Pluto
- Neptune

F- represents being a Feeler. Feelers are Dominant Feelers of positive emotions. It is the use and zone of Adams Emotions. These individuals use their ability of feeling to gather the much needed positive information. A feeler is one that feels with the emotions the intentions of another. Feelers are masculine in character and have a great insight in matters relating to feelings that are appropriate. They are emotional in behavior and take information very personally. . The zone contains the planets Moon, Pluto and Neptune, which are responsible for the location of the Zodiac's. The Zodiac's creates the different variations of the duties of the emotions Intelligence, Accident Prone, Idealistic and Emotional.

Intelligence-

°you consider it important to be tactful as well as truthful.

°You step forward and consider the effects of your actions on others.

°You have the ability to reason

°The capacity to acquire and apply knowledge.

°The ability to show rational judgment.

Idealistic-

°you show appreciation easily to others.

°You believe any feeling is valid whether it makes sense or not.

You naturally like to please others and may need to be encouraged to have own needs met.

°Your behavior is influenced by ideal

Emotional-

°you value empathy and harmony but see the exception to the rule when it pertains to your own feelings.

°You make judgment based on your own feelings and values

but you are people oriented and aware of others feelings.

    °You are happiest in friendly, supportive, and cooperative environments.

Accident Prone-

    °You may be seen as overemotional, illogical, and weak.

    °You are an impatient person but are motivated by a desire to be appreciated.

    °Not intentionally done.

Earth- (Taurus, Virgo, and Capricorn) Thinking is the use of your Intelligence, and the thought process. It's your perception of the facts gathered and your ability to learn, understand, and deal with new an old challenging situation's as they present themselves. You react by what you think. It's your ability to analyze the truth from thoughts within your mind. As an earth sign you have four constant emotions at work and they are inventive, diplomatic, cunning and perfectionist.

Jobs and duties of the emotions:

Introverted and Thinker contain the same group of emotions

Introvert (I)

- Venus
- Mercury
- Saturn

I- represents being an introvert. Introverts are Dominant Thinkers of positive emotions. It is the use of Adams Intelligence. Introverts like to direct their energy, thoughts, interest and emotions inward toward self. They possess the attitude of being introverted. These individuals use their ability of reasoning to gather the needed positive information. Introverts are masculine in character and have a deep appreciation for family rather than friends. They are more inwards and private concerning their thoughts and feelings. They only share their thoughts and feelings with a select few people. They are very motivational individuals and excel in problem-solving techniques and enjoy learning. They are patient in nature and compassionate when dealing with others and their issues. The zone contains the planets Venus, Mercury and Saturn, which are responsible for the location of the Zodiac's Taurus, Virgo and Capricorn. The Zodiac's creates the different variations of the duties of the emotions Cunning, Diplomatic,

Inventive and Perfectionist.

Cunning-

°you are private and are energized by spending time alone.

°you like to think things through inside your head.

°you share personal info with a select few people.

°Shrewd or crafty in manipulation or deception.

Inventive-

°you avoid being the center of attention and keep your enthusiasm to yourself.

°You are skillful at inventing.

Diplomatic-

°you think more than you react to any given situation and you prefer knowing more information than a little.

°Characterized by tact and sensitivity in dealing with people.

°In dealing with others it's never business and always personal.

°You are a skillful negotiator.

Perfectionist-

°you listen more than you talk.

°You respond after taking the time to think things through inside your head.

°You set extremely high standards and want nothing less than the best.

°You believe moral and spiritual perfection can be achieved

in this life.

Thinker (T)

- Mars
- Sun
- Jupiter

T- represents being a Thinker. Thinkers are Dominant Negative Judgers of emotions. It is the use of Eve's Judgment. Negative thoughts make these individuals smarter. They love to build up and break down ideas over for truth. Thinkers are feminine in character and are very intelligent in the manner they rationalize ideas. These individuals require some form of negative action to take place within their life just to aid in building up their judgment of thoughts. The zone contains the planets Mars, Sun and Jupiter, which are responsible for the location of the Zodiac's. The Zodiac's Aries, Leo and Sagittarius creates the different variations of the duties of the emotions Cunning, Diplomatic, Inventive and Perfectionist.

Diplomatic-

°You value logic, justice and fairness which to you is one standard for all.

°You step back and try to see the situation objectively before problem solving. You feel the need to be convinced that a specific event or activity makes sense before you will even believe.

°Characterized by tact and sensitivity in dealing with people.

°You are a skillful negotiator.

°In dealing with other's it's never personal and always business.

Perfectionist-

°you naturally see flaws and tend to be critical of others.

°You believe it is more important to be truthful than tactful.

° Believe others feelings are irrelevant to the situation at hand.

°You set extremely high standards and want nothing less than the best.

°You believe moral and spiritual perfection can be achieved in this life.

Inventive-

°Believe feelings are valid only if they are logical.

°You are motivated by a desire for achievement and accomplishment.

°You have a hard time translating ideas into active steps.

°You are skillful at inventing.

Cunning-

    °you may be seen as heartless, insensitive and uncaring.

    °You are impressed by competence and the end result.

    °Shrewd or crafty in manipulation or deception.

Air- (Gemini, Libra, and Aquarius) Sensing is the use of Vibes, and natural instinct. It's your ability to trust what is not certain or concrete. This is you're common sense, and your ability to see, hear, touch, taste, and smell the truth. This also takes place in the left hemisphere of the frontal lobe. As a sensor, your feelings are stimulated by the impression and emotions that someone or something gives off. You have the ability to analyze and sense the truth from the feelings within your mind.

Jobs and duties of the emotions:

Sensors and Perceivers contain the same group of emotions

Sensor (Feminine)

Eve's Emotion

    Sensor (S)

- Moon
- Pluto
- Neptune

S- represents being a sensor. Sensors are Dominant Negative Feelers of emotions. It is the use of Eve's Emotions. Sensors are dominant feelers of negative emotions. These individuals use the information gathered from the negative emotion to bring them the emotional truth. Sensors are feminine in character and enjoy the illusions of feeling. They need the facts of their negative emotions to bring them the truth of their lies in order to believe any idea. These individuals have fancy ideas and love to talk. They are very sensual, alluring, and arrogant individuals. They are natural dreamers and very passionate about patterns and colors. These individuals love to play off of the emotions of others. The zone contains the planets Moon, Pluto and Neptune, which are responsible for the location of the Zodiac's. The Zodiac's creates the different variations of the duties of the emotions Creativity, Independence, Intuition and Romantic.

Intuition-

you trust what is certain, can be proven and you present information in a step-by-step manner.

Independence-

you are knowledgeable of your established skills and make a judgment by the facts you gather.

Creativity-

you like new ideas only if they have practical applications.

You tend to be specific and literal about giving a detailed description.

Romantic-

you value realism and common sense and are oriented towards the present.

Perceiver (Masculine)

Adam's Vibes

Perceiver (P)

- Mercury
- Venus
- Uranus

P- represents being a Perceiver. Perceivers are Dominant Positive Sensors, which is the use of Adams. Vibes. Perceivers are dominant sensors of positive emotions. These individuals use their five senses seeing, touching, smelling, hearing and tasting as a tool to gather information. Perceivers are masculine in character and are flexible and passive in their views. These individuals hate to argue with others and are non-aggressive. The zone contains the planets Mercury, Venus and Uranus, which are responsible for the location of the Zodiac's. The Zodiac's Gemini, Libra, and Aquarius creates the different variations of the duties of the emotions Creativity, Independence, Intuition and Romantic.

Creativity-

you are better at concentration exercises than fantasy or daydreaming. You have a play ethic, enjoy now and finish the job later, and enjoy exercises that allow you to learn new thing and have fun doing it. You are process oriented and your emphasis is on how the task is completed.

Intuition-

you are influenced by past experiences and this is your knowledge of doing things. You don't like to brainstorm for answers and are happiest leaving your options open. You change goals as new information becomes available and prefer to not decide but continue to collect information for later usage.

Knowledge gained from the creator.

Romantic-

you feel satisfaction from starting projects and see time as a renewable resource and set deadlines.

Independence-

you are flexible, adaptable, and change gears quickly so that you may be available for many different approaches and techniques. You have a natural curiosity and like adapting to new situations.

Once again the diagram below list the emotions divided into the specific personality traits and elements.

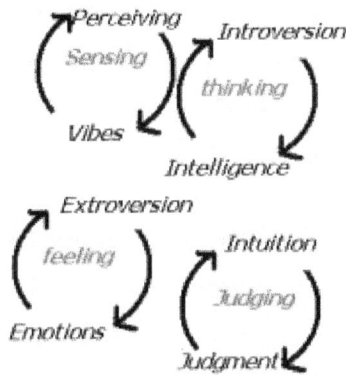

Perceiving
Sensing
Vibes

Introversion
thinking
Intelligence

Extroversion
feeling
Emotions

Intuition
Judging
Judgment

Introversion and Intelligence carry the same group of
emotions for the function thinking, but uses them in
opposing ways. The emotions of introversion pertain
to the Intelligence of Adam, and the emotions of
intelligence pertain to the judgment of Eve.

Extroversion and Emotions carry the same group of
emotions for the function feeling, but uses them in
opposing ways. The emotions of extroversion pertain
to the Vibes of Eve, and the emotions of emotions
pertain to the Emotions of Adam.

Sensing and Perceiving carry the same group of emotions
for the function sensing, but uses them in opposing
ways. The emotions of sensing pertain to the
Emotions of Eve, and the emotions of perceiving
pertain to the Vibes of Adam.

Intuition and Judgment carry the same group of
emotions for the function judging, but uses them in
opposing ways. The emotions of intuition pertain to
the Judgment of Adam, and the emotions of
judgment pertain to the Intelligence of Eve.

This is the reason for the conflict between the Genes. One is of the
masculine persuasion and the other of the feminine persuasion,
which has opposite duties with similar emotion, but co-exists as
neighbors within each of the Gene. Basically there are two copies
of Adenine, two copies of Thymine, two copies of Cytosine, and
two copies of Guanine. It is not hard to understand but very
simple. To map out the Human Genome is sincerely a waste of time
on the scientist behalf. I give them the credit that they deserve on
wanting to help the fellow man, but to map out and record answers
of the Genes with the possibility of mutating and changing is
pointless. The only thing that is definite is astrological sign,
personality type, emotions, free will, and moral. Everything else is
just short answers of the above mentioned which some people
stretch to make themselves seem highly intelligent. Documenting
will never tell them the answers that they truly seek. You will never
have a body part farm, you can't out wit God, and you will never
live forever. Man will never be God of Man and will only damn
his/her self in the search for the answers because you yourself are
someone who consist of the same codes as an invention and when

you investigate un-necessary material you put a lot of un-necessary information within yourself as well, a bunch of junk codes, which shortens your life span, regardless to you leaving a trail of information for the next scientist who comes along, they will never have the capability of bringing your soul back from the dead once it is gone. You can create new life, the same hour and date but it will never be that person, just a copy of resemblance with its own feelings and memories. The only thing man will learn of is of man, not of the soul, and not of time.

"Let no one deceive himself. If anyone among you seems to be wise in this age, let him become a fool that he may become wise. For the wisdom of this world is foolishness with God. For it is written, "He catches the wise in their own craftiness"; and again, The Lord knows the thoughts of the wise, that they are futile". - **1Corinthians 3:18-20**

The easiest emotions to spot are through the gift of our given astrological sign. The grid for the astrological sign is really a crown placed upon your head to tell the duties of the brain. The outside journey of the stars reflect the inside journey within your mind as well. There is a time and a place for everything. Our astrological sign contains the emotions that are always the first to our personality traits. For example is you're a Pisces you will see the element of water first before your see the four elements of the personality traits. This is the reason why a lot of the time when you talk to an individual you get the impression they are another astrological sign because of the temperament they exhibit on a daily basis which often is of that given astrological sign emotions. Once you find your astrological sign you can move to the next step.

Answer these four basic questions. This pertains to the behavior you exhibit on a day-to-day basis. Think about your answer before you answer and write it down. These are the habits you exhibit the majority of the time, which you will select. First in which element does your astrological sign exist. _____ answer. Then are you an (E) outdoor or (I) indoor type of person the majority of the time? E or I

Do you believe in (S) facts or (N) word of mouth the majority of the time? S or N

Do you react from thought (T) or by feelings (F) the majority of the time? T or F

Do you prefer to (J) work first or (P) play first the majority of the time? J or P

This is a just a short-cut answer to each personality type but very useful. Write down your answers _____ _____ _____ _____. I have a detailed survey in Chapter 4 to help distinguish your true personality type, but for now well take the approach that I have just listed. As I said before there are a total of 192 variations of the personality types.

Every Personality Type has an opposite counterpart or a mirror of themselves but opposite. For instance the ISTJ's opposite counterpart is ESTP. They function in the same manner sensing, thinking, feeling and judging but the difference is that one is Feminine, extroverted (likes the company of others) and the other is Masculine, introverted (likes to be left alone), opposites but the same, your mirror.

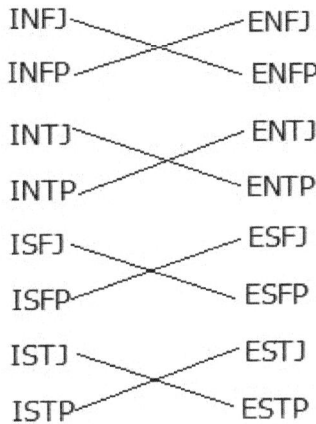

```
INFJ            ENFJ
INFP            ENFP

INTJ            ENTJ
INTP            ENTP

ISFJ            ESFJ
ISFP            ESFP

ISTJ            ESTJ
ISTP            ESTP
```

This is the way in which the creator created each personality type to find their answers to life's riddles.

"For to one is given the word of wisdom through the Spirit, to another the word of knowledge through the same Spirit, to another faith by the same Spirit, to another gifts of healings by the same

Spirit, to another the working of miracles, to another prophecy, to another discerning of spirits, to another different kinds of tongues, to another the interpretation of tongues. But one and the same Spirit works all these things, distributing to each one individually as He wills." -**1Corinthians 12:8-11**

How truly marvelous mankind really is. On the next pages I've listed the 192 different variations of the personality types and the emotions in the order according to functions.

"Dear friends, let us continue to love one another, for love comes from God. Anyone who loves is born of God and knows God. But anyone who does not love does not know God-for God is love". -1 John 4:16

"Love" was meant to be passed back and fourth between each other. Therefore, God was meant to be passed back and fourth between each other. When one is weak the other is stronger and love is there to see you through any crisis.

When you love man, this is the way you show God that you love him too, as the scripture says. Not just when man is right but also when man is wrong and you attempt to help him even when he has fallen.

God does not just want to be haved but he wants to be needed as well. Everyone has things but what do you need?

Example

ENFP

ISTJ

"Love"

"Hate"

moral thought
moral emotions
analytical thought
analytical emotions

analytical thought
analytical emotions
moral thought
moral emotions

"Hate"

"Love"

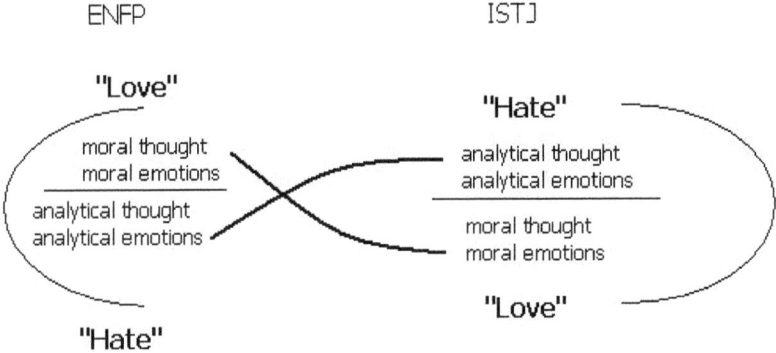

Love was meant to be passed back and
fourth between each other

The Em.Pt.Y Formula Functions

INFJ &ENFP	INFP & ENFJ	INTJ & ENTP
Judging (Careless, Indecisive, Orderly, & Stubborn)	**Feeling** (Accident Prone, Emotional, Idealistic, & Intelligence)	**Judging** (Careless, Indecisive, Orderly, & Stubborn)
Feeling (Accident Prone, Emotional, Idealistic, & Intelligence)	**Judging** (Careless, Indecisive, Orderly, & Stubborn)	**Thinking** (Cunning, Diplomatic, Inventive, & Perfectionist)
Thinking (Cunning, Diplomatic, Inventive, & Perfectionist)	**Sensing** (Creativity, Independence, Intuition, & Romantic)	**Feeling** (Accident Prone, Emotional, Idealistic, & Intelligence)
Sensing (Creativity, Independence, Intuition, & Romantic)	**Thinking** (Cunning, Diplomatic, Inventive, & Perfectionist)	**Sensing** (Creativity, Independence, Intuition, & Romantic)

INTP & ENTJ	ISTJ & ESTP	ISTP & ESTJ
Thinking (Cunning, Diplomatic, Inventive, & Perfectionist)	**Sensing** (Creativity, Independence, Intuition, & Romantic)	**Thinking** (Cunning, Diplomatic, Inventive, & Perfectionist)
Judging (Careless, Indecisive, Orderly, & Stubborn)	**Thinking** (Cunning, Diplomatic, Inventive, & Perfectionist)	**Sensing** (Creativity, Independence, Intuition, & Romantic)
Sensing (Creativity, Independence, Intuition, & Romantic)	**Feeling** (Accident Prone, Emotional, Idealistic, & Intelligence)	**Judging** (Careless, Indecisive, Orderly, & Stubborn)
Feeling (Accident Prone, Emotional, Idealistic, & Intelligence)	**Judging** (Careless, Indecisive, Orderly, & Stubborn)	**Feeling** (Accident Prone, Emotional, Idealistic, & Intelligence)

ISFJ & ESFP	ISFP & ESFJ
Sensing (Creativity, Independence, Intuition, & Romantic)	**Feeling** (Accident Prone, Emotional, Idealistic, & Intelligence)
Feeling (Accident Prone, Emotional, Idealistic, & Intelligence)	**Sensing** (Creativity, Independence, Intuition, & Romantic)
Thinking (Cunning, Diplomatic, Inventive, & Perfectionist)	**Judging** (Careless, Indecisive, Orderly, & Stubborn)
Judging (Careless, Indecisive, Orderly, & Stubborn)	**Thinking** (Cunning, Diplomatic, Inventive, & Perfectionist)

The Temperaments and Climates

As I said earlier there are four elements of the universe Fire, Earth, Water, and Air which are the natural temperaments that each and every astrological sign contains, for instance a Taurus is down to earth, a Pisces is moody like the waters it resides in, an Aquarius is always on the move like the element of air, and an Aries is feisty and hot tempered as the fire it resides in. Together these elements create a natural climate within you.

These elements control the temperaments within the functions of the personality traits. An example is the element of fire controls the function of judging, the element of water controls the function feeling, the element of air controls the function of sensing and the element of earth controls the function of thinking. Each of the four functions is developed with the aid of four emotions within them for each of the functions. Every one of the emotions is responsible for an emotional response. The emotion stubborn is responsible for fear, and the emotion creativity is responsible for the illusions of happy. When you mix the element of the universe with a function you have an emotional response and this response becomes a permanent part of your character. As stated before, if you can gain control over the emotions then you can control the emotions response.

Below is a list of the different temperaments as a result of the emotions.

1. Fire and Fire = Heat or Heated

Fire is the temperament responsible for creating the feisty and aggressive element within the individual. The temperament of fire contains three astrological signs, which are Aries, Leo, and Sagittarius. The temperament of fire creates an attitude of being sensitive for the gene.

Fire is the temperament responsible for creating the feisty and aggressive element within the individual. The temperament of fire contains three astrological signs, which are Aries, Leo, and Sagittarius. The temperament of fire creates an attitude of being sensitive for the gene.

Fire mixed with Fire creates heated emotions. Heated emotions are the exchange of judgmental words within a conversation. The flames burn with words everything and everyone in its path. This is a very judgmental person who has a comeback line for every word you throw in their direction.

2. Fire and Air, and Air and Fire=Bonfire

Fire is the temperament responsible for creating the feisty and aggressive element within the individual. The temperament of fire contains three astrological signs, which are Aries, Leo, and

Sagittarius. The temperament of fire creates an attitude of being sensitive for the gene.

Air is the temperament responsible for creating the free flowing exaggerative nature of the individual. The temperament of air contains three astrological signs, which are Gemini, Libra, and Aquarius. The temperament air creates an attitude of being sensitive for the gene.

Fire mixed with Air creates a bonfire of emotions. A Bonfire of Emotions is the elevation of judgmental words within a conversation. The flames rise given the words and temperament. It only takes a little to get this fire going, so choose your words and battles carefully.

3. Fire and Earth, and Earth and Fire= Eruption

Fire is the temperament responsible for creating the feisty and aggressive element within the individual. The temperament of fire contains three astrological signs, which are Aries, Leo, and Sagittarius. The temperament of fire creates an attitude of being sensitive for the gene.

Earth is the temperament responsible for creating a well-grounded and down to earth element within the individual. The temperament of earth contains three astrological signs, which are Taurus, Virgo, and Capricorn. The temperament of earth creates an attitude of being intelligent for the gene.

Fire mixed with Earth creates an eruption of emotions. An Eruption of Emotion is the bursting forth of judgmental words within a conversation. The flames burn and melt with words everyone in its path because of the storage of intellectual memories. This type of fire won't go out until the job is done.

4. Water and Water=Waves

Water is the temperament responsible for creating the calm, tranquil and collective individual's you love to surround yourself around. The temperament of water contains three astrological signs, which are Cancer, Scorpio, and Pisces. The temperament water creates the attitude of being emotional for the gene.

Water is the temperament responsible for creating the calm, tranquil and collective individual's you love to surround yourself around. The temperament of water contains three astrological signs, which are Cancer, Scorpio, and Pisces. The temperament water creates the attitude of being emotional for the gene.

Water mixed with Water creates a Wave of Emotions. A Wave of Emotion is the rippling of judgmental words with a conversation. The tides crash and drown everyone in its path. They are generally mild in nature but may knock you off your feet from time to time.

5. Earth and Air, and Air and Earth= Tornado

Earth is the temperament responsible for creating a well grounded and down to earth element within the individual. The temperament of earth contains three astrological signs, which are Taurus, Virgo, and Capricorn. The temperament of earth creates an attitude of being intelligent for the gene.

Air is the temperament responsible for creating the free flowing exaggerative nature of the individual. The temperament of air contains three astrological signs, which are Gemini, Libra, and Aquarius. The temperament air creates an attitude of being sensitive for the gene.

Earth mixed with Air create a Tornado of Emotions. A Tornado of Emotion is the thrashing and trashing with words everyone in its sight. They aren't like the hurricanes, which takes time to happen, and are more emotional and strike with out care because of the storage of intellectual memories. A tornadoes rage is violent, quick and very unpredictable, so don't turn your back because they are powerful and destructive.

6. Water and Air, and Air and Water=Hurricane

Water is the temperament responsible for creating the calm, tranquil and collective individual's you love to surround yourself around. The temperament of water contains three astrological signs, which are Cancer, Scorpio, and Pisces. The temperament water creates the attitude of being emotional for the gene.

Air is the temperament responsible for creating the free flowing exaggerative nature of the individual. The temperament of air contains three astrological signs, which are Gemini, Libra, and Aquarius. The temperament air creates an attitude of being sensitive for the gene.

Water mixed with Air create a Hurricane of Emotions. A Hurricane of Emotion is the thrashing and drowning with words everyone in its path. These storms are larger than a tornado because they require more time and energy to form, which is stored in the emotional memory. They give the appearance of calmness and tranquility until impact takes place.

7. Water and Fire, and Fire and Water=Steam

Water is the temperament responsible for creating the calm, tranquil and collective individual's you love to surround yourself around. The temperament of water contains three astrological signs, which are Cancer, Scorpio, and Pisces. The temperament water creates the attitude of being emotional for the gene.

Fire is the temperament responsible for creating the feisty and aggressive element within the individual. The temperament of fire contains three astrological signs, which are Aries, Leo, and Sagittarius. The temperament of fire creates an attitude of being sensitive for the gene.

Water mixed with Fire create a Steam of Emotions. The Steam of Emotion is the bursting forth with cloudy judgment toward everyone in its path. The little burst will never get bigger than the pot that hold it because moral intellect has no need for storage. The anger will never last for long periods of time because it's in its nature says to cool off.

8. Water and Earth, and Earth and Water=Flood

Water is the temperament responsible for creating the calm, tranquil and collective individual's you love to surround yourself around. The temperament of water contains three astrological signs, which are Cancer, Scorpio, and Pisces. The temperament water creates the attitude of being emotional for the gene.

Earth is the temperament responsible for creating a well grounded and down to earth element within the individual. The temperament of earth contains three astrological signs, which are Taurus, Virgo, and Capricorn. The temperament of earth creates an attitude of being intelligent for the gene.

Water mixed with Earth create a Flood of Emotions. A Flood of Emotion is the drowning with words everything in its path. Be careful of this flood because looks can be deceiving, just because the water looks safe doesn't always mean that the weather plays nice.

9. Air and Air=Windy

Air is the temperament responsible for creating the free flowing exaggerative nature of the individual. The element of air contains three astrological signs, which are Gemini, Libra, and Aquarius. The temperament air creates an attitude of being sensitive for the gene.

Air is the temperament responsible for creating the free flowing exaggerative nature of the individual. The temperament of air contains three astrological signs, which are Gemini, Libra, and Aquarius. The element air creates an attitude of being sensitive for the gene.

Air mixed with Air create a World Wind of Emotions. A World Wind of Emotion will taking your breath away with words. This is a build up of the emotional memory. The gust are strong enough to knock you off your feet and still your breath away. This is a battle you don't want to encounter.

10. Earth and Earth=Dusty, Sandstorm

Earth is the temperament responsible for creating a well grounded and down to earth element within the individual. The element of earth contains three astrological signs, which are Taurus, Virgo, and Capricorn. The temperament of earth creates an attitude of being intelligent for the gene.

Earth is the temperament responsible for creating a well grounded and down to earth element within the individual. The temperament of earth contains three astrological signs, which are Taurus, Virgo, and Capricorn. The temperament of earth creates an attitude of being intelligent for the gene.

Earth mixed with Earth produce a Dusty Sandstorm of Emotions. A Dusty Sandstorm of Emotion will blind everyone with words who are in its path. Just like walking through a dessert this battle is hard to see coming, be careful to not feed it, until it passes you by.

Not only are the temperaments responsible for climates changes within the individual but it also produces stages in the behavior of the individual. There are six stages to the behavior development of the individual, which leads to four basic behaviors.

-The 6 Steps of Behavior-

Each and every person was built with a natural design to their behavior just as with a fetus in the developmental stages of it's life everything takes time to grow and develop. What aid's the development of the behavior within the individual is the event's and environment of that given persons life. The events and environment are a form of fuel for the emotions, which feed the behavior as well in the long run. The way I look at life compared to the way another person looks at life is totally different because of our given identities which were received at birth in our astrological sign and personality types and the way in which we walk throughout life, we are building our own individual memories and identities. .

Below is a list of the 6 Steps of Behavior.

1. The Natural Temperament (Earth, Air, Fire, Water) of the Planets uses the zone.
2. The Zone (Intelligence, Vibes, Judgment, Emotions) in which the Astrological sign resides, stimulates an attitude within the emotion.
3. The attitude within the emotion then activates the action of the

Free Will, which is aided by the Moral.

4. The Free Will and Moral affects the function (Sensing, Thinking, Judging, Feeling), which enhances the reaction of the function to create the duty of the Soul.

5. The Soul leads to the character development of the genes and climates.

6. The Climates create the Behavior of the gene, which releases an emotional response that affects the Body System.

When this process takes place it creates a natural behavior in a person. This behavior takes place at different stages in the individual's life given the different variations of the personality types.

The First Stage takes place from Birth- Six years of age. This stage will be the dominant behavior of the personality type.

The Second Stage takes place from Six- Twelve years of age. This stage helps to strengthen the moral and free will of the individual. It is a backup stage to aid in strengthening the first.

The Third Stage takes place from Twelve- Twenty-Five years of age. The first and second stages will always be the strengths of this personality type. The Third stage is necessary for creating the behavioral choice of the individual, which will either be to choose to be a negative individual or to be a positive individual.

The Fourth Stage takes place from Twenty-Five -Fifty years of age. This stage is meant to enhance on the Third stage of the individual.

Everyone goes through different stages in there life. No one is purposely set to be a victim forever. Everyone has a journey and servitude to perform, this is how you grow as an individual. Even with all the negativity that you've experienced, these are gifts that you can use to help save another person's life. No one actually has to experience being an alcoholic to tell the effects of alcoholism. Everyone has different sides of the story to tell which can be beneficial to someone else. No one is perfect, and each and every person will have to go through the same stages in life, unless their life is cut short early in life.

I didn't let life beat me up, what I realized was that even through all the negativity that I've experienced and stored in my memory that the lord was using me to tell a story to help others. Many people beat themselves up after something has gone wrong in their life, they take it too personal when it is not even about them. The creator didn't purposely want to hurt you, but he wanted to help with your development, that is why he allowed these stages to take place. If I had it to do all over again, I wouldn't change a thing because all of it helped to make me the person I am, and I love what I see each and every time I look in a mirror. So, start seeing the different types of behavlor as developmental stages in your lifc. Had I not experienced the loss of two great loved ones at the same time when I was 19yrs. Of age how would my development of feeling and behavior of being patient even take place. Learn the truth of life and quit listening to lies. Below is a list of the different Behaviors in individuals.

Impatient/ Rationalist - is someone who is unable to wait patiently or tolerate a delay. They are restless and unable to endure irritation or difficult situations. They have a way of expressing their eagerness or desire. They have the quality of being impatient.

My natural temperament of earth uses the element of my intelligence to create an attitude of being intelligent to activate the action of my extroversion which effects my function of thinking which leads to the behavior of being a rationalist of impatient. This behavioral person is unable to wait patiently. They can't endure irritation for long periods of time. They have the ability to reason. They are always on a quest for truth even when the truth is laid out honestly before them. They have a natural desire to constantly search things over for truth. They believe "reason" to be the main source of knowledge and spiritual truth meaning because you have asked the question of "why" this brings about intelligence.

Patient -is someone who is capable of bearing affliction with calmness. A person who is calm and collective even in difficult situations. They are very tolerant, understanding, persevering and constant. They are capable of bearing any difficult situation. They have the quality of being patient.

My natural temperament of water uses the element of my emotions to create an attitude of being emotional to activate the action of my introversion which effects my function of feeling which leads to the behavior of being patient. This behavioral person is very calm and capable of handling all. They have a high tolerance of bearing even the most difficult of challenges. They are very understanding and their for you as an individual.

Realistic -is someone who expresses an awareness of things as they really are. They accurately represent what is depicted or described without fiction or illusions. They have the quality of being realistic.

My natural temperament of fire uses the element of my judgment to created an attitude of being judgmental to activate the action of my intuition which effects my function of judging which leads to the behavior of being realistic. This behavioral person is a natural truth teller and their work has to tell things as they naturally are or they will not be content. They love representing the truth as described.

<u>Illusionist</u> - is someone who uses illusionary techniques and devices in life for enjoyment and expression of self. A person whose work and life is marked by illusionism. They have the quality of being an illusionist.

My natural temperament of air uses the element of my vibes that I pick up on from my sight, smelling, hearing, tasting, and touching to create an attitude of being sensitive to activate the action of my perception which effects my function sensing which leads to the behavior of being an illusionist. This behavioral person is a natural liar and their work has to have some form of illusions in it or they just won't be happy.

-My Individual Design-

The Pisces- ISTJ

My personality type is I S T J and I am a Pisces. So the first thing noticeable is my element of water and I am very intelligent, accident prone, idealistic and emotional. Secondly, you notice that I am introverted, meaning my strengths are flipped. Introversion and thinking carry the same group of emotions, which will be my auxiliary function. Sensing is my dominant function, thinking is my auxiliary, feeling is my third and judging is my fourth function. My senses are very sensitive so my auxiliary function is the first function you notice for and introvert. My auxiliary is thinking so this function everyone sees first. This is actually my sense at work using the thinking portion of my personality to make sure all is safe by probing someone's thoughts.

Once my mind become aware of my surrounding being safe it then allows my senses to come out and take control. I am already emotional because of my element of water, I don't need any more surprises, get

it. Below is an example of the way the emotions represent themselves.

ISTJ

(Sensing, Thinking, Feeling and Judging)

Pisces is the element of water. Water and the element of air create a hurricane of emotions, thrashing and drowning with words everyone in its path. This is the development of dominant function, which takes place from birth to six years of age.

Illusionist

My natural temperament of air uses the element of my vibes that I pick up on from my sight, smelling, hearing, tasting, and touching to create an attitude of being sensitive to activate the action of my perception which effects my function sensing which leads to the behavior of being an illusionist. This behavioral person is a natural liar and their work has to have some form of illusions in it or they just won't be happy.

Sensing: The use of Vibes

This is the use of analytical emotions.

Creativity-is shown with friends by being sensitive to their needs. You like new ideas only if they have practical applications and tend to be specific and literal about giving a detailed description.

Independence-is shown in my appearance by being mysterious. You are knowledgeable of your established skills and make a judgment by the facts you gather.

Intuition- is a strength possessed from being judgmental. You trust what is certain, and can be proven and you present information in a step-by-step manner.

Romantic-is shown by showing love for another. You value realism and common sense and are oriented towards the present.

Water and the element of earth create a flood of emotions, drowning everything in its path with words. This is the development of the auxiliary function, which takes place from six years of age to twelve years of age.

<u>Impatient/ Rationalist</u>

My natural temperament of earth uses the element of my intelligence to create an attitude of being intelligent to activate the action of my extroversion which effects my function of thinking which leads to the behavior of being a rationalist of impatient. This behavioral person is unable to wait patiently. They can't endure irritation for long periods of time. They have the ability to reason. They are always on a quest for truth even when the truth is laid out honestly before them. They have a natural desire to constantly search things over for truth. They believe "reason" to be the main source of knowledge and spiritual truth meaning because you have asked the question of "why" this brings about intelligence.

Thinking: The use of Intelligence

This is the use of analytical thought.

Cunning- being secretive when introduced to a prior relationship shows your cunning nature. You are private and are energized by spending time alone, you like to think things through inside your head and you share personal info with a select few people.

Diplomatic- being compassionate to the situations of the world shows diplomatic nature. You think more than you react to any given situation and you prefer knowing more information than a little.

Inventive-Being imaginative when it pertains to money shows your inventive nature. You avoid being the center of attention and keep your enthusiasm to yourself.

Perfectionist- Being impressionable in your view your life shows that you are have a perfectionist nature and that you love learning and are always upgrading your skills for new ones.

Water and the element of water create a wave of emotions. Crushing everything in its path with words. This is the development of the third function, which takes place from twelve to twenty five years of age.

Patient

My natural temperament of water uses the element of my emotions to create an attitude of being emotional to activate the action of my introversion which effects my function of feeling which leads to the behavior of being patient. This behavioral person is very calm and capable of handling all. They have a high tolerance of bearing even the most difficult of challenges. They are very understanding and their for you as an individual.

Feeling: The use of Emotions

This is the use of moral emotions.

Accident Prone- Being weak-willed by giving in to a loved one shows the gift of accident-prone. You value empathy and harmony but see the exception to the rule when it pertains to your own feelings. You make judgment based on your own feelings and values but you are people oriented and aware of others feelings. You are happiest in friendly, supportive, and cooperative environments.

Emotional- being emotional when upset with others shows emotional. You value empathy and harmony but see the exception to the rule when it pertains to your own feelings. You make judgment based on your own feelings and values but you are people oriented and aware of others feelings. You are happiest in friendly, supportive, and cooperative environments.

Idealistic- being adaptable when it pertains to your home life shows that you are idealistic. You show appreciation easily to others and believe any feeling is valid whether it makes sense or not. You naturally like to please others and may need to be encouraged to have own needs met.

Intelligence- being unworldly when you think shows others your intelligence, because your approach is not of the ordinary. You consider it important to be tactful as well as truthful. You step forward and consider the effects of your actions on others.

Water and the element of fire create a steam of emotions.

Simmering everything it touches in its path with words and because it's a fourth function you'll just be grazed and not boiled. The development of the fourth function is from twenty five to fifty years of age.

Realistic

My natural temperament of fire uses the element of my judgment to created an attitude of being judgmental to activate the action of my intuition which effects my function of judging which leads to the behavior of being realistic. This behavioral person is a natural truth teller and their work has to tell things as they naturally are or they will not be content. They love representing the truth as described.

Judging: The use of Judgment/ Intuition
This is the use of moral thought.

Careless-is shown when surrounded by family. You need to learn to be more attentive of others feelings. You are product oriented and less likely to deal with specifics because your emphasis is on completing the task and you prefer to focus on the big picture.

Indecisive- is shown when expressing emotions and you have trouble keeping on track or following directions.

Orderly- being receptive on your job shows orderly and you prefer to make plans and follow them accordingly. You are usually well organized. You set goals and work toward achieving them on time and are happiest after final decisions have been made and feel satisfaction from finishing the projects.

Stubborn- being vague when you are angry with others shows stubbornness. You have a work ethic, work first play later, and prefer to know what you are getting into. Hope your having fun learning about your personality type. Now turn the page so you can learn about the gifts of free will and morals.

-Chapter 3-
Free Will and Morals

"Now when He was asked by the Pharisees when the kingdom of God would come, He answered them and said, "The kingdom of God does not come with observation; Nor will they say, See here! Or See there! For indeed, the kingdom of God is within you." **Luke 17:20-21**

Every individual has a personality type. The personality type is responsible for making the individual appear unique and one of a kind. The personality type has four functions and they are sensing, thinking, judging and feeling. The second and third traits are the dominant and the auxiliary functions of the personality type. These are the strengths that the individual possesses which is the free will and moral of the individual. Some individual's moral include being analytical as I will discuss later. The third and fourth functions are the two weakest functions the individual possesses. Some individuals possess the use of their morals as a dominant and auxiliary function in the beginning of their life and for others it doesn't happen until later in life and that is the reason why many people can't distinguish the difference in right from wrong. The use of morals is the difference in right and wrong, and if a person doesn't have the use of morals as a dominant and auxiliary function chances are they will get into a lot of difficult situations. If you look at the diagram below, it lists each given personality type and the roles of the two main functions working together.

Personality Types	Dominant	Auxiliary	The Role of Function
ISTJ	VIBES	INTELLIGENCE	Sense by thoughts picked up of others
ISFJ	VIBES	EMOTIONS	Sense by emotions picked up of others
INFJ	JUDGMENT	EMOTIONS	Judge by emotions picked up of others
INTJ	JUDGMENT	INTELLIGENCE	Judge by thoughts picked up of others
ISTP	INTELLIGENCE	VIBES	Think by vibes given
ISFP	EMOTIONS	VIBES	Feel by vibes given
INFP	EMOTIONS	JUDGMENT	Feel by judgment given
INTP	INTELLIGENCE	JUDGMENT	Think by judgment given
ESTP	VIBES	INTELLIGENCE	Sense by thoughts picked up of others
ESFP	VIBES	EMOTIONS	Sense by emotions picked up of others
ENFP	JUDGMENT	EMOTIONS	Judge by emotions picked up of others
ENTP	JUDGMENT	INTELLIGENCE	Judge by thoughts picked up of others
ESTJ	INTELLIGENCE	VIBES	Think by vibes given
ESFJ	EMOTIONS	VIBES	Feel by vibes given
ENFJ	EMOTIONS	JUDGMENT	Feel by judgment given
ENTJ	INTELLIGENCE	JUDGMENT	Think by judgment given
NO FREE WILL	EMOTIONS (FEEL)	INTELLIGENCE (THINK)	Feels by moral thought
NO FREE WILL	INTELLIGENCE (THINK)	EMOTIONS (FEEL)	Thinks by moral emotions

I believe every individual was born with a choice to be made, be it right or wrong, and our bodies contain the domino effect, from the result of our actions. Geneticists know that "Genetic diseases, or inborn errors, result from cases where the DNA blueprint is incomplete, usually because a specific gene is damaged or missing" (Hawley, R. S., Mori C.A., The Human Genome 1999, p.6). I don't believe anything is missing, I think that this is our blueprint being filled in with each action which we engage into. Just as with each meal we put into our mouths or bodies, it is a series of codes which we in the spiritual world can't see visually looking at with our eyes, but exist and when we over indulge because of the appeal or allure of the meal we put a lot of the unnecessary codes within ourselves. This fills in our DNA code with junk or unnecessary items.

I believe mankind was purposely built in this manner and what science has been looking at within our bodies and has named a mutation is actually the use of our given free will at work. I believe we have this to help us from going overboard with our emotions. God is good and God is love as Jesus said, and I don't believe he made an error in our design, just because mankind doesn't understand how we as a people function doesn't mean we need to fix us. We are perfect as we are. I don't believe The Lord was trying to but the burden on us by telling us the reason for our design. I believe that he just wanted us to be fruitful and multiply, obey his laws and to have faith in his existence, but because of the negativity that was placed upon us from Eve eating the of the fruit and sharing it with Adam we are now very inquisitive instead of just enjoying the moments we are able to be here on earth.

When you choose an action, the action creates a domino effect already set in motion. For instance, a person who suffers from a broken heart as a result of the significant other cheating, what function and main emotion do you believe is triggered as a result? Did you guess yet? Your sensing function and the emotion romantic, which exist in the sensing, has been triggered. Your sensing is the use of the analytical emotions from the stored memories of self and others. What happens is the individual begins to replay events in there mind searching for the answers they need to come to a better conclusions as to why this moment is happening to them. In the process of searching for an answer they then become emotional and use their function of feeling which thankfully doesn't store anything. The emotion of being emotional within the function feeling is responsible for stress to the heart. When the heart becomes stressed it releases the neurotransmitters Acetylcholine, GABA, Norepinephrine, Dopamine and Serotonin just to name a few. This process tries to comfort the body by attempting to release an emotional response. "Acetylcholine affects neurons involved in memory, emotions, cognitive functioning and muscle action. GABA (gamma-aminobutyric acid) functions as the major inhibitory neurotransmitter in the brain. Norepinephrine affects neurons involved in increased heart rate and the slowing of intestinal activity during stress, and neurons involved in learning, memory, dreaming, waking from sleep, and emotion. Dopamine affects neurons involved in voluntary movement, learning, memory, and emotion. Serotonin affects neurons involved in sleep, appetite, sensory perception, temperature regulation, pain suppression, and mood" (Wade, C., Tarvis, C., Psychology 2000 p.109). Acetylcholine is involved in the process of crying because the neurotransmitter replay the memories and emotions over and over in the individual's head till it produces an emotional response, which leads to the individual eventually becoming very angry, or crying, which requires muscle action. This is not the only process, which takes place the body also releases endorphins, the brains natural opiates and hormones as a method to relax the heart.

After this process, the individual who was cheated on has a choice to make. They can either deal with the emotion of the betrayal they feel or choose to ignore the situation altogether, but when she or he chooses to ignore the situation by throwing there time and attention into something else there will be repercussions because they are allowing the emotion to stake within their mind. Lets say for instance the person who suffers from a broken heart picked up a habit that gives them the same satisfaction such as eating. The body wasn't built to continuously do things in excessive amounts. People die everyday from committing one of the eight deadly sins, which are Greed, Lust, Gluttony, Sloth, Envy, Pride, Vanity and Wrath. Greed and Gluttony affect a person who over indulges in food, because of the chemical attraction they continuously want more. Greed is hidden in the emotion cunning and Gluttony is hidden in the emotion romantic. Every living element has hormones within it. The hormonal effect can be so appealing, giving the impression of satisfaction, but your body truthfully is still unsatisfied. The hormonal reaction from the food is not lasting and the brain is still trying to compensate for the loss of certain hormones. The next domino effect will be weight gain, which doesn't really appear to have affected the person because it's just a few pounds, but if the behavior continues there will be an excessive amount of weight which will become unbearable to the individual who has to carry it. The next sin is Sloth, which is laziness, hidden in the emotion independence, the individual doesn't want to put forth the time and the effort to shed the excessive weight, and they are continuously tired and lazy. The weight is putting pressure on the lungs, knees and heart of the individual. When we choose to indulge in food as a method to soothe the pain we gain weight and suffer health problems. Our bodies are trying to let us know our choice was wrong and that there is another method available to help us out. We loose the weight and pick it back up because of the poor eating habits that we have developed and the fact that we haven't truly addressed our emotions. The individual has still not faced the emotions that started the chain reaction. What will be the next domino effect? Heart disease, high cholesterol, high blood pressure, diabetes, acid reflux you take your pick, the signs have always been there, we have just been ignoring them. If the individual gains control over the emotion, the emotion will stop the domino effect.

I've listed a more descriptive answer for the Free Will, Analytical vs. Moral, the Roles of Function and Behavioral Choice for all the given personality types. Learn the behaviors of your free will and morals because then you'll be able to stop the reactions of harm to your body.

-THE FREE WILL-

There are 8 specific kinds of Free Will that create a variation of 16 different types of Free Will because they are clones of each other. One is of the female persuasion and the other of the male persuasion. Below I've listed the specific kinds of Free Will.

1. Sensitive Feeler- is capable of perceiving the emotional state or attitude of another person with the aid of their senses. This is a person whom senses by what they feel.

ISFJ and ESFP

SF=GC Analytical Emotion- Moral Emotion

Polarity Conflict

ISFJ
/ \
G   C
Polarity Conflict

ESFP
/ \
G   C
Polarity Conflict

The secondary and third traits SF= GC are the dominant and auxiliary function of the personality type. The traits S= G represents the analytical emotion and the F= C represents the moral emotion. The S- represents being a sensor; it is the act of sensing and being sensitive. Sensing is an action of the Analytical Emotion. The Analytical Emotion is the ability to analyze the truth from emotions picked up of others or self. The way in which these types gather information is through the five senses, which are tasting, touching, smelling, hearing, and seeing. This is the use of the analytical emotion as it pertains to emotional stored experiences in the memory section of the mind formed by dating, cheating, fashion, dramatically experienced situations, illusions of love and anything else that requires illusions. The F- represents being a feeler; it is the act of feeling and being emotional. Feeling is an action of the Moral Emotion. The Moral Emotion is the difference in recognizing right and wrong based on judgment formed by the moral or pure heart. The way in which these types gather information is through the heart. This is the use of the moral emotion and your direct link with the spiritual realm. The SF=GC have opposite polarity and bases must be paired and those pairing must be A=T and G=C and not A+T or C+G because they are opposites of each other but do the same jobs. C is the positive action and G is the negative action. The personality types ISFJ and ESFP are the Sensitive Feeler's whose primary role of function is to be a sensitive judger of emotions pertaining to others. Their behavioral choice is to be a strict analytical decision maker because of their dominant and auxiliary function, they have strict analytical emotion as it pertains to the moral head.

2. Emotional Sensor- is immediately affected by the mixed emotions that are received through the senses. This is a person whom feels by what they sense.

ISFP and ESFJ

FS= CG Moral Emotion- Analytical Emotion

Polarity Conflict

ISFP
/ \
C   G
Polarity Conflict

ESFJ
/ \
C   G
Polarity Conflict

The secondary and third traits FS=CG are the dominant and auxiliary function of the personality type. The traits F=C represent the Moral Emotion and the S=G represent the Analytical Emotion. The F- represents being a feeler; it is the act of feeling and being emotional. Feeling is an action of the Moral Emotion. The Moral Emotion is the difference in recognizing right and wrong based on judgment formed by the moral or pure heart. The way in which these types gather information is through the heart. This is the use of the moral emotion and your direct link with the spiritual realm. The S- represents being a sensor; it is the act of sensing and being sensitive. Sensing is an action of the Analytical Emotion. The Analytical Emotion is the ability to analyze the truth from emotions picked up of others or self. The way in which these types gather information is through the five senses, which are tasting, touching, smelling, hearing, and seeing. This is the use of the analytical emotion as it pertains to emotional stored experiences in the memory section of the mind formed by dating, cheating, fashion, dramatically experienced situations, illusions of love and anything else that requires illusions. The FS=CG have opposite polarity and bases must be paired and those pairings must be A=T and G=C and not A+T or C+G because they are opposites of each other but do the same job. The C is the positive action and the G is the negative action. The personality type's ISFP and ESFJ are the Judgmental Thinker's whose primary role of function is to be a judgmental judger of thoughts pertaining to others. Their behavioral choice is to be a strict moral decision maker because of their dominant and auxiliary function, they have strict moral thoughts as it pertains to the analytical head.

3. Judgmental Feeler- has the mental ability to judge and distinguish the relations between the feelings or intentions of another. This is a person who judges by what they feel.

INFJ and ENFP

NF= AC Moral Thought- Moral Emotion

INFJ
/ \
A   C

ENFP
/ \
A   C

The secondary and third traits NF= AC are the dominant and auxiliary function of the personality type. The traits N=A represents the moral thought and the F=C represents the moral emotion. The N- represents being a judger; it is the act of judging and being judgmental. Judging is an action of the Moral Thought. The Moral Thought is the difference in recognizing right and wrong based on judgment formed by the moral or pure head. The way in which these types gather information is through the head. This is the use of the moral thought and our direct link with the spiritual realm. The F- represents being a feeler; it is the act of feeling and being emotional. Feeling is an action of the Moral Emotion. The Moral Emotion is the difference in recognizing right and wrong based on judgment formed by the moral or pure heart. The way in which these types gather information is through the heart. This is the use of the moral emotion and your direct link with the spiritual realm. This personality types INFJ and ENFP are the Judgmental Judger's of emotions pertaining to others. Their behavioral choice is to be a good choice maker because of their dominant and auxiliary function, they are good choice makers as it pertains to the moral head and the moral heart.

4. Emotional Judger- is affected with the stirred emotions one passes in judgment and creates an opinion based upon another thoughts. This is a person who feels by what they judge.

INFP and ENFJ

FN=CA Moral Emotion- Moral Thought

```
  INFP         ENFJ
 /   \        /   \
A     C      A     C
```

The secondary and third traits FN=CA are the dominant and auxiliary function of the personality type. The traits F=C represent the Moral Emotion and the N=A represent the Moral Thought. The F- represents being a feeler; it is the act of feeling and being emotional. Feeling is an action of the Moral Emotion. The Moral Emotion is the difference in recognizing right and wrong based on judgment formed by the moral or pure heart. The way in which these types gather information is through the heart. This is the use of the moral emotion and your direct link with the spiritual realm. The N= A represents being a judger; it is the act of judging and being judgmental. Judging is an action of the Moral Thought. The Moral Thought is the difference in recognizing right and wrong based on judgment formed by the moral or pure head. The way in which these types gather information is through the head. This is the use of the moral thought and our direct link with the spiritual realm. The personality type's INFP and ENFJ are the Emotional Judger's whose primary role of function is to be an emotional perceiver of judgment given from self. Their behavioral choice is to be a good choice maker because of their dominant and auxiliary function, they are good choice makers as it pertains to the moral heart and moral head.

5. Judgmental Thinker- has the mental ability to judge and distinguish the relation between the thoughts or reasons given of another. This is a person who judges by what they think.

INTJ and ENTP

NT= AT Moral Thought- Analytical Thought

Polarity Conflict

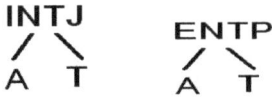

```
INTJ          ENTP
 /  \          /  \
A    T        A    T
```

The secondary and third traits NT=AT are the dominant and auxiliary function of the personality type. The traits N=A represents the moral thought and the T=T represents the analytical thought. The N- represents being a judger; it is the act of judging and being judgmental. Judging is an action of the Moral Thought. The Moral Thought is the difference in recognizing right and wrong based on judgment formed by the moral or pure head. The way in which these types gather information is through the head. This is the use of the moral thought and our direct link with the spiritual realm. The T- represents being a thinker; it is the act of thinking and being intelligent. Thinking is an action of the Analytical Thought. The Analytical Thought is the ability to analyze the truth from thoughts picked up of others or self. This is the use of the analytical thought as it pertains to intellectual stored experiences in the memory section of the mind formed by debates, arguments, puzzles, sports, mathematical equations and anything that requires action. The NT= AT have opposite polarity and bases must be paired and those pairings must be paired and those pairings must be A=T and G= C and not A+T or C+G because they are opposite of each other but do the same jobs. The A is the positive action and the T is the negative action. The personality types INTJ and ENTP are the Judgmental Thinker's whose primary role of function is to be a judgmental judger of thoughts pertaining to others. Their behavioral choice is to be a strict moral decision maker because of their dominant and auxiliary function, they have strict moral thoughts as it pertains to the analytical head.

6. Intelligent Judger- has a high degree of intelligence and the mental ability to reason by what is passed in judgment upon another. This is a person whom thinks by what they judge.

INTP and ENTJ

TN=TA Analytical Thought- Moral Thought

Polarity Conflict

INTP
/ \
A   T
Polarity Conflict

ENTJ
/ \
A   T
Polarity Conflict

The secondary and third traits TN=TA are the dominant and auxiliary function of the personality type. The traits T=T represent the Analytical Thought and the N=A represent the Moral Thought.

The T= T represents being a thinker; it is the act of thinking and being intelligent. Thinking is an action of the Analytical Thought. The Analytical Thought is the ability to analyze the truth from thoughts picked up of others or self. This is the use of the analytical thought as it pertains to intellectual stored experiences in the memory section of the mind formed by debates, arguments, puzzles, sports, mathematical equations and anything that requires action. The N= A represents being a judger; it is the act of judging and being judgmental. Judging is an action of the Moral Thought. The Moral Thought is the difference in recognizing right and wrong based on judgment formed by the moral or pure head. The way in which these types gather information is through the head. This is the use of the moral thought and our direct link with the spiritual realm. The TN=TA have opposite polarity and bases must be paired and those pairings must be A=T and G=C and not A+T or C+G because they are opposites of each other but do the same job. The A is the positive action and the T is the negative action. The personality types INTP and ENTJ are the Intelligent Judger's whose primary role of function is to be an intelligent perceiver of judgment given from self. Their behavioral choice is to be strict analytical decision makers because of their dominant and auxiliary function, they have strict analytical thought as it pertains to the moral head.

7. Sensitive Thinker- is capable of perceiving the mental state related to the thoughts and reason with the aid of the senses. This is a person who senses by what they think.

ISTJ and ESTP

ST= GT Analytical Emotion- Analytical Thought

```
ISTJ        ESTP
 / \         / \
G   T      G   T
```

The secondary and third traits ST= GT are the dominant and auxiliary functions of the personality type. The traits S=G represents the analytical emotion and the T= T represents the analytical thought. The S- represents being a sensor; it is the act of sensing and being sensitive. Sensing is an action of the Analytical Emotion. The Analytical Emotion is the ability to analyze the truth from emotions picked up of others or self. The way in which these types gather information is through the five senses, which are tasting, touching, smelling, hearing, and seeing. This is the use of the analytical emotion as it pertains to emotional stored experiences in the memory section of the mind formed by dating, cheating, fashion, dramatically experienced situations, illusions of love and anything else that requires illusions. The T- represents being a thinker; it is the act of thinking and being intelligent. Thinking is an action of the Analytical Thought. The Analytical Thought is the ability to analyze the truth from thoughts picked up of others or self. This is the use of the analytical thought as it pertains to intellectual stored experiences in the memory section of the mind formed by debates, arguments, puzzles, sports, mathematical equations and anything that requires action. The personality types ISTJ and ESTP are the Sensitive Thinker's whose primary role of function is to be a sensitive judger of thoughts pertaining to others. Their behavioral choice is to be a bad choice maker because of their dominant and auxiliary functions, they are bad decision makers as it pertains to the moral heart and the moral head.

8. Intelligent Sensor- with the aid of its intelligence has the ability to sense the emotions of another. This is a person who thinks by what they sense.

ISTP and ESTJ

TS= TG Analytical Thought- Analytical Emotion

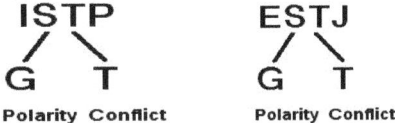

ISTP
/ \
G   T
Polarity Conflict

ESTJ
/ \
G   T
Polarity Conflict

The secondary and third traits TS= TG are the dominant and auxiliary function of the personality type. The traits T=T represent the Analytical Thought and the S=G represents the Analytical Emotion. The T- represents being a thinker; it is the act of thinking and being intelligent. Thinking is an action of the Analytical Thought. The Analytical Thought is the ability to analyze the truth from thoughts picked up of others or self. This is the use of the analytical thought as it pertains to intellectual stored experiences in the memory section of the mind formed by debates, arguments, puzzles, sports, mathematical equations and anything that requires action. The S= G represents the analytical emotion and the F= C represents the moral emotion. The S- represents being a sensor; it is the act of sensing and being sensitive. Sensing is an action of the Analytical Emotion. The Analytical Emotion is the ability to analyze the truth from emotions picked up of others or self. The way in which these types gather information is through the five senses, which are tasting, touching, smelling, hearing, and seeing. This is the use of the analytical emotion as it pertains to emotional stored experiences in the memory section of the mind formed by dating, cheating, fashion, dramatically experienced situations, illusions of love and anything else that requires illusions. The personality types ISTP and ESTJ are the Intelligent Sensor's whose primary role of function is to be an intelligent perceiver of vibes given from self. Their behavioral choice is to be a bad choice maker because of their dominant and auxiliary functions, they are bad decision makers as it pertains to the moral head and moral heart.

The Creation of Free Will and Morals

Every person uses their gift of free will and morals differently. The way in which people walk throughout life is very different because of the exposure that they have to events in their life. Regardless to what you've overcome the free will and moral are already a definite job assigned to you in your life. You just help in building it by the events and environment that you experience in life.

1. ISTJ (Masculine Sexuality Type) and ESTP (Feminine Sexuality Type)

Strengths: Dominant Vibes and Auxiliary Intelligence

Role of Function: Sensitive Judgers of Thoughts pertaining to others

Natural Reaction: Sensitive Thinkers

Behavioral Choice: Bad Choice Makers

Free Will: Bad decision makers as it pertains to matters of the moral heart and moral head

Moral: AE= Analytical Emotion, AT= Analytical Thought

Behavioral Strength: Illusionist

These personality sign's sense by the thoughts picked up of others. This is the way these personality sign functions by choice of free will. ISTJ are very sensitive judgers and ESTP are sensitive perceivers. The dominant function of vibes is the ability to analyze the truth from emotions of others. These are the stored analytical emotions from memories of others. The personality types ISTJ and ESTP use the memories from others to make an opinion. This is the use of the intellect judging the emotions for truth. The auxiliary function of intelligence is the ability to analyze the truth from thoughts of others. The third function is the gift of emotions, which controls the moral emotions. The moral emotions are responsible for judgments based on right and wrong matters as it pertains to matters of the heart. The fourth function is the gift of judgment, which controls the moral thoughts. The moral thoughts are responsible for judgments based on right and wrong matters as it pertains to the head. For these personality sign's the gift of moral emotions and moral thoughts are absent and will never be strengths possessed because they are a third and fourth function. They will consistently make bad choices and decisions as it pertains to the moral heart and head. They will have to constantly be reminded to make right decisions as it pertains to matters of the heart because the analytical head will always lead the emotions. Depending on the events and environment experienced by the given individual, negative or positive play a part in the final decision.

2. ISFJ (Masculine Sexuality Type) and ESFP (Feminine Sexuality Type)

Natural Reaction: Sensitive Feelers

Strengths: Dominant Vibes and Auxiliary Emotions

Role of Function: Sensitive judger of emotions pertaining to others

Behavioral Choice: Strict analytical decision maker

Free Will: Strict analytical emotions as it pertains to the moral head

Moral: AE=Analytical Emotion- ME=Moral Emotion

Behavioral Strength: Illusionist

These personality sign senses by emotions picked up of others.

This is the way these sign functions by choice of free will. ISFJ are very sensitive judgers whom judge without enough adequate information and ESFP are sensitive perceivers who know there is more to the story than what you generally see. The dominant function of vibes is the ability to analyze the truth from emotions of others. This is the use of the intellect judging the emotions for truth from the collection of emotional experiences stored in memory. The auxiliary function is emotions, which is the difference in right and wrong from the moral emotions as it pertains to matters of the heart. The third function is intelligence, which is the ability to analyze the truth from thought of others. The fourth function is Judgment, which is the ability to know the difference in right and wrong from thoughts as it pertains to matters of the head. It judges the truth from the collection of stored thoughts as part of the memory. This sign is not a very good judge of character because the ability to analyze the truth from thought is not a strength possessed. They will not have the use of moral thought until after twenty-five years of age. This is a very emotional person. So this sign only has the use of its analytical emotions, and moral emotions.

3. INFJ (Masculine Sexuality Type) and ENFP(Feminine Sexuality Type)

Natural Reaction: Judgmental Feeler

Strengths: Dominant Judgment and Auxiliary Emotions

Role of Function: Judgmental judger of emotions pertaining to others

Natural Reaction: Judgmental Feeler

Behavioral Choice: Good Choice Maker

Free Will: Good choice makers as it pertains to the moral head and the moral heart

Moral: MT=Moral Thought- AE= Auxiliary Emotion

Behavioral Strength: Realistic

These personality signs judge by emotions picked up by others. INFJ and ENFP are judgmental feelers. This is the way these sign functions by choice of free will. The dominant function is judgment, which is the ability to make good decision based on moral thoughts of right and wrong as it pertains to matters of the head. The auxiliary function is emotions and the ability to make good decisions based on moral emotions. This is the difference in right and wrong as it pertains to matters of the heart. The third function of intelligence is the ability to analyze the truth from thoughts picked up of others. This is the use of the analytical thoughts from stored memory. The fourth function is vibes and the ability to analyze the truth from emotions picked up of others. This is the use of analytical emotions from stored memory. This personality sign has the use of moral thought and moral emotions as strength together to defeat the effects of negativity. They will use their gifts often firstly for those who honestly need there help. They judge from a higher power being what there morals suggest to them. The gift of analytical thought and analytical emotions will not be as effective until after twenty-five years of age but they will never be strengths possessed.

4. INTJ (Masculine Sexuality Type) and ENTP (Feminine Sexuality Type)

Natural Reaction: Judgmental Thinker

Strengths: Dominant Judgment and Auxiliary Intelligence

Role of Function: Judgmental judger of thoughts pertaining to others

Natural Reaction: Judgmental Thinker

Behavioral Choice: Strict Moral Decision Maker

Free Will: Strict moral thought as it pertains to the analytical head

Moral: MT= Moral Thought- AT= Analytical Thought

Behavioral Strength: Realistic

These personality signs judge by thoughts picked up by others. INTJ and ENTP are judgmental thinkers. This is the way these sign functions by choice of free will. The dominant function is judgment and the ability to use moral thought to make right and wrong decisions as it pertains to the head. The auxiliary function is intelligence and the ability to analyze the truth from thoughts picked up of others from personal conversations, which are a stored collection o memory. The third function is emotions, which is the use of the moral emotions as it pertains to right and wrong decisions of the heart. The fourth function is vibes and the ability to analyze the truth from emotion picked up of others from personal conversations, which are stored collection of memories. This personality sign does not have the use of its moral emotions and analytical emotions. This person is very firm in there decisions. You won't get a budge out of them. So when giving a final judgment they can appear pretty stiff because there decision is based on analytical thought and moral thought. This personality sign wont be its best until after twenty-five years of age.

5. ISTP (Masculine Sexuality Type) and ESTJ (Feminine Sexuality Type)

Natural Reaction: Intelligent Sensor

Strengths: Dominant Intelligence and Auxiliary Vibes

Role of Function: Intelligent perceiver of vibes given from self

Behavioral Choice: Bad Choice Maker

Free Will: Bad decision maker as it pertains to the moral head and moral heart

Moral: AT= Analytical Thought- AE= Analytical Emotion

Behavioral Strength: Impatient/ Rationalist

These personality sign thinks by personal feelings given. ESTJ are sensitive judgers and ISTP are sensitive perceivers. This is the way these sign functions by choice of free will. The dominant function of intelligence is the ability to analyze the truth from personal thoughts. The auxiliary function of vibes is the ability to analyze the truth from personal emotions given. The vibes are based upon this individual's own stored emotional memories. This is the use of the intellect to judge the emotions for truth. The third function is the gift of judgment, which controls the moral thoughts given. The moral thoughts are responsible for judgments based on right and wrong matters as it pertains to the head. The fourth function is the gift of emotions, which controls the moral emotions. The moral emotions are responsible for judgments based on right and wrong matters as it pertains to the heart. For this personality sign the gift of moral thoughts and emotions will never be strengths possessed because they are third and fourth function. This personality sign thinks from a collection of personal thoughts experienced, then from a collection of personal emotions experienced. This sign does not have the use of its moral thoughts or emotions so they will consistently make bad choices and decisions when it comes to matters of the heart. Their head and forethought will take the lead. They will have to constantly be reminded of how to formulate right decisions as it pertains to the head and heart. The will not have the ability to make fair choices until after twenty-five years of age.

6. ISFP (Masculine)and ESFJ (Feminine)
Natural Reaction: Emotional Sensor
Strengths: Dominant Emotions and Auxiliary Vibes
Role of Function: Emotional perceiver of vibes given from self
Behavioral Choice: Strict Moral Decision Makers
Free Will: Strict moral emotions as it pertains to the analytical

heart

Moral: ME= Moral Emotion- AE=Analytical Emotion

Behavioral Strength: Patient

These personality sign senses by emotions picked up of others. ISFP are sensitive perceivers and ESFJ are sensitive judgers. This is the way these sign functions by choice of free will. The dominant function is emotions, which is the difference in right and wrong from the moral emotions as it pertains to matters of the heart. The auxiliary function of vibes is the ability to analyze the truth from emotions given. This is the use of the intellect judging the emotions for truth from the collection of personal emotional experiences. The third function is Judgment, which is the ability to know the difference in right and wrong from thoughts as it pertains to matters of the head. It judges the truth from personal collection of thoughts. The fourth function is intelligence, which is the ability to analyze the truth from thoughts given. This sign is not a very good judge of character because the ability to analyze the truth from analytical thought and moral thought are not strengths possessed. This is an overly emotional person because there is only the use of analytical, and moral emotions. They will not have the use of moral thought until after twenty-five years of age.

7. INFP (Masculine Sexuality Type) and ENFJ (Feminine Sexuality Type)

Natural Reaction: Emotional Judger

Strengths: Dominant Judgment and Auxiliary Emotions

Role of Function: Emotional perceiver of judgment given from self

Natural Reaction: Judgmental Feeler

Behavioral Choice: Good Choice Makers

Free Will: Good choice makers as it pertains to the moral heart and moral head

Moral: MT=Moral Thought- AE= Analytical Emotion

Behavioral Strength: Patient

These personality sign feels by judgments given. INFP and ENFJ are judgmental feelers. This is the way these sign functions by choice of free will. The dominant function is emotions and the ability to know the difference in right and wrong as it pertains to matters of the heart. The auxiliary function is judgment, which is the ability to make good decision based on moral thoughts of right and wrong as it pertains to matters of the head. The third function is vibes and the ability to analyze the truth from emotions given. The fourth function of intelligence is the ability to analyze the truth from thoughts given. This personality sign has the use of moral thought and moral emotions as strength together. They use their gifts of servitude very well. Analytical thought and emotions will not be as effective until after twenty-five years of age.

8. INTP (Masculine Sexuality Type) and ENTJ(Feminine Sexuality Type)

Natural Reaction: Intelligent Judger

Strengths: Dominant Intelligence and Auxiliary Judgment

Role of Function: Intelligent perceiver of judgment given from self

Behavioral Choice: Strict Analytical Decision Maker

Free Will: Strict analytical thought as it pertains to the moral head

Moral: AT= Analytical Thought- **MT**=Moral Thought

Behavioral Strength: Impatient/Rationalist

These personality sign thinks by judgments given. INTP and ENTJ are judgmental thinkers. This is the way these sign functions by choice of free will. This is the way this sign functions by choice of free will. The dominant function is intelligence and the ability to analyze the truth from thoughts picked up of others from personal conversations and stored as part of your collection. The auxiliary function is judgment and the ability to use moral thought to make right and wrong decisions as it pertains to matters of the head. The third function is vibes and the ability to analyze the truth from emotion given and stored as part of your collection. The fourth function is emotions and the use of your moral emotions as it pertains to matters of the heart. This personality sign does not have the use of its moral emotions and analytical emotions. So when giving a final judgment can appear pretty stiff because there decision is based on analytical thought and moral thought. This personality sign wont be its best until after twenty-five years of age.

No Free Will

Strengths: Dominant Intelligence and Auxiliary Emotions/ or Dominant Emotions and Auxiliary Intelligence

Role of Function: Intelligent judger of feelings given, and Emotional sensor of thoughts given.

Natural Reaction: Intelligent Feeler, and Emotional Thinker

Behavioral Choice: Strict Analytical Thinker, and a Strict Moral Feeler

Free Will: Strict Analytical Thinker as it pertains to the moral heart, and Strict Moral Feeler as it pertains to the head

Moral: TE= Analytical Thought- Moral Emotion, and ET=Moral Emotion- Analytical Thought

Behavioral Strength: Rationalist and Patient

These personality sign thinks by moral emotions given. The dominant function of intelligence is the ability to analyze the truth from thoughts stored within the mind. The auxiliary function of emotions is the use of moral emotions and the ability to make right and wrong decisions as it pertains to matters of the heart. An example of the way these two functions would work together is If a relative that you trusted told you that Jesus was real and he loved you, you would trust that thought first because your gift to analyze the truth would tell you that this relative has been right this far in his judgment so I should believe them and then the gift of moral emotions would tell you because of your emotional ties its right to also believe them. Your analytical head and moral heart would confirm the truth so there would be no need or reason for you to look for this truth because it would already be found.

As you can see from the information I provided above, none of the personality types have the ability to feel with their emotion or think with their intelligence as strengths together in the dominant and auxiliary functions. If mankind possessed these two strengths as there dominant and auxiliary functions than there would no longer be the need to experience events by living them because everyone's choice would already be made because you would trust what is told to you by word of mouth. The emotions diplomatic, inventive, perfectionist and cunning controlled by your intelligence would confirm the theory. The emotions of intelligence, accident prone, idealistic and emotional controlled by the emotions would verify it. Look at the chart below.

Traits	Function
Emotions (E)	The use of moral emotions and difference in right and wrong as it pertains to matters of the heart.
Judgment (J)	The use of moral thoughts and difference in right and wrong as it pertains to matters of the heard.
Vibes (V)	The use of analytical emotions and the ability to analyze truth as it pertains to emotional stored experiences.
Intelligence (I	The use of analytical thoughts and the ability to analyze truth as it pertains to intellectual stored experiences.

None of the personality traits have intelligence and emotion together as strengths in the dominate and auxiliary function.

This leads me to believe this is the creation of no free will. This factor stood out to me as I was writing mankind's design. This led me to think about the lord and the possibility of angels, which I truly believe in. Let's hypothesis for a moment. What would be the actual design of an angel if they too exist? I mean this would truly confirm in the theory of God or the story of Satan being cast to Hell, because angels are born in the realm of God, they see him and have been told about him since the beginning of their creation so they have no choice but to trust in him. Humans are not born in the realm of God but are built to have faith in his existence as the creator of all. God has not been hiding from man, he has been waiting and wanting man to find him for the longest. He's been dropping clues the whole while since the beginning of time. Do you think it was my deep thinking, which lead me to find the answers that I've found. No the exact opposite. Man's lack of faith distances himself from God. That is why the scripture says for your lack of knowledge... I will also forget your children. Not purposely done but because you as a creation choose not to see him.

If a person were created with the absence of free will, they would be bound because the answers would already be available to them because of there emotional trust and ties to other individuals and the fact that the word would be passed on from individual to individual so there would be no denying the truth. Imagine yourself in the realm of the creator. You would not be free to just let go and get wild in nature because your always being watched and you wouldn't want the creator to see you misbehaving anyway. This is what it's like for angel's everyday. We as humans should be appreciative of that freedom.

 As you can see, everyone has been given the choice of free will and morals, just as first stated in the bible. Everyone has a choice to make and it is upon you to except the Lord's word of truth, I can't force anyone's hand but I can put the message out. This in return brings the lord into reality for me because he is the first known existence of this message as quoted from the bible. Look at the five examples I've listed.

"For the children being not yet born, neither having done any good or evil, that the purpose of God according to election might stand, not of works, but of him that calleth. .... For he saith to Moses, I will have mercy on whom I will have mercy, and I will have compassion on whom I will have compassion. So then it is not of him that willeth, nor of him that runneth, but of God that sheweth mercy. For the scripture saith unto Pharaoh, Even for this same purpose have I raised thee up, that I might shew my power in thee, and that my name might be declared throughout all the earth. Therefore hath he mercy on whom he will have mercy, and whom he will he hardeneth. Thou wilt say then unto me, Why doth

he yet find fault? For who hath resisted his will? Nay but, O man, who art thou that repliest against God? Shall the thing formed say to him that formed it, Why hast thou made me thus? Hath not the potter power over the clay, of the same lump to make one vessel unto honour, and another unto dishonour? What if God, willing to shew his wrath, and to make his power known, endured with much longsuffering the vessels of wrath fitted to destruction." -- **Romans 9:11-22**

"Who hath saved us, and called us with an holy calling, not according to our works, but according to his own purpose and grace, which was given us in Christ Jesus before the world began." -- **2 Timothy 1:9**

"God hath from the beginning chosen you to salvation." -- **2 Thessalonians 2:13**

"He hath chosen us in him before the foundation of the world, that we should be holy and without blame before him in love: Having predestinated us unto the adoption of children by Jesus Christ to himself, according to the good pleasure of his will." -- **Ephesians 1:4-5**

I believe all of them to be good examples of free will's existence in the bible. The quote that begins not of works (because you born to have him as your personal savior) but of him that calleth, (asked him to be his personal savior) confirms it for me that the Lord purposely created mankind to want to receive him. This part of the passage "for this same purpose have I raised thee up that I might shew my power in thee and that my name might be declared throughout all the earth" is so reminiscent of today and the way the world functions. Not to sound insulting but for those who sit at the top with their high-powered jobs and education levels and think they have it all figured out, you might want to rethink your answer. The world has been one big lie with dozens of methods of distractions. We fight over Jesus color, birth, be it spiritual or physical, the miracles he performed and his romantic involvement if any. I don't think anyone has taken the time to hear the one clear message that Jesus delivered and that was that his father loves us and wants to be a part of us if we choose to have him but that we must obey his laws. It is the use of analytical thought that takes over the mind making people so judgmental, which is the knowledge of bad. Most people aren't using their moral head or moral heart, which is your direct spiritual link with the Lord. This is the knowledge of good. This is what makes it hard for you to receive his message of truth. This is the reason for the passage in the bible Mark 10:13-16 Then they brought little children to Him, that He might touch them; but the disciples rebuked those who brought them. But when Jesus saw it, He was greatly displeased and said to them, "Let the little children come to

Me, and do not forbid them; for of such is the kingdom of God".
"Assuredly, I say to you, whoever does not receive the kingdom of God as a little child will by no means enter it." And he took them up in His arms, laid His hands on them, and blessed them.

The lord knew the majority of people would have a lot of negative emotions corrupting their judgment, and that most would get lost along the way as adults. This is why you must receive the knowledge of Christ as a child, because receiving him as a child you are taught and reminded to value and love him because he first loved you so, that when and eventually if you get lost along the way you would find you way back home to him the savior who loves you unconditionally.

Em.Pt.Y Formula

Emotions (Em) + Personality Trait (Pt) = Your Behavior (Y)

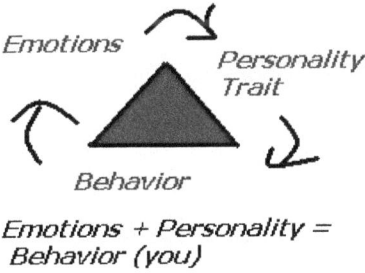

Emotions

Personality Trait

Behavior

Emotions + Personality =
Behavior (you)

I believe that emotions and personality type lead to a natural behavior in people, which most people like to call positive behavior and when our emotions are over-stimulated it leads to negative behavior. Below is an example of behavior that resulted from emotions turning negative.

Creation VS. Evolution

Positive Attributes of Emotions	Negative Attributes of Emotions
Heterosexuality (Sexual Relations) Man + Woman Woman + Man **The Diplomatic Emotion**	Homosexuality (Sexual Relations) Man + Man Woman + Woman **The Diplomatic Emotion**
Willful (Thoughtlessness) Forms of Willful; Love For the reason of; Prove, grant, concede **The Romantic Emotion**	Racism (Discrimination) Forms of Racism; Pride, Shame and Hate For the reason of; Assumption, Guessing, Suspecting **The Romantic Emotion**
Freedom (Free Will) Forms of Freedom; thin, healthy, drug free, relationships, liberty and independence **The Independence Emotion**	Slavery (No Free Will) Forms of Slavery; imprisonments, jail, obesity, disease, drug abuse, abandonment, and servitude **The Independence Emotion**

The positive attributes of willful, heterosexuality and freedom were given as part of mankind's individual creation. They are included in the gifts of free will and morals. If the positive attributes turn negative, due to abuse and neglect which come from the events and environment of a given individuals life, the individual's view of the world will turn negative. If the positive attributes lack of knowledge and skills to effectively deal with the given negative environmental situations and events that have taken place in the individuals past life experiences, the evolution of the negative individual is created.

Those that are born ISTP's, ESTJ's, INTP's, and ENTJ's have thinking from analytical thought and the function thinking as a dominant function. These signs are dominant thinkers from thoughts.

Those that are born ISTJ's, ESTP's, INTJ's, and ENTP's have thinking from analytical thought and the function thinking as a second strength or auxiliary function. These signs are secondary thinkers from thoughts.

Those that are born ISFJ's, ESFP's, INFJ's, and ENFP's have thinking from analytical thought and the function thinking as a third function. These signs have thinking from thoughts as a third function and have their feeling or sensing as a strength.

Those that are born ISFP's, ESFJ's, INFP's, and ENFJ'S have thinking from analytical thought and the function thinking as a fourth function. These signs have thinking from thoughts as a fourth function and have their feeling or sensing as a strength.

Don't worry if your not a dominant thinker, you will still be able to think from thoughts later on down the road. Thoughts is just not your strength. Everyone is born with a natural gift that they are able to do better than anyone. Regardless everyone comes out on top when they don't allow there analytical thoughts to take over there positive judgment. So in the countless cases of African-American being told that they can't learn because they just don't comprehend, it is a lie. The majority of African- American's just like Jesus are born with there morals first, meaning they have the gift of there judging and feeling working first and not there thinking and that is the reason that there interest is not there. They are not building on their strengths but there weakness and that is why they are not interested in the work. Sports are an easy form of thinking for the African-American and that is why we excel in it rather than sitting down doing math equations. For those who do not have thinking or sensing as strengths find it rather boring. Just think of all the countless cases of those who allowed their children to be medicated with Ritalin because they were told they have a behavior problem. Wrong answer, they are just in the wrong environment where it's hard for them to excel and showcase there many talents.

Personality Type Love Attraction

(Masculine)   (Feminine)

ISTJ ———————— ENTP
ISFJ ———————— ENFP
INFJ ———————— ESFP
INTJ ———————— ESTP
ISTP ———————— ENTJ
ISFP ———————— ENFJ
INFP ———————— ESFJ
INTP ———————— ESTJ

"ONE HAS WHAT THE OTHER LACK"

"This is my commandment, that you love one another as I have loved you. Greater love has no one than this, than to lay down one's life for his friends". **-John 15:12-13**

Beauty is in the eye of the beholder. Beauty is attracted to the beast, because the beast is beauty itself waiting to take shape. To one is given the gift of appeal, to the other the appeal is in the gift itself. Beauty and Brains together.

Strengths vs. Weaknesses

Feeling and Judging- When the personality type of those with feeling and judging as their dominant strengths are abused physically and mentally the functions of sensing and thinking are building up. These functions are the weaknesses of the personality type. Therefore, thinking from thoughts and sensing from emotions are building up but aren't their strengths therefore they have no control over the reaction from the functions.

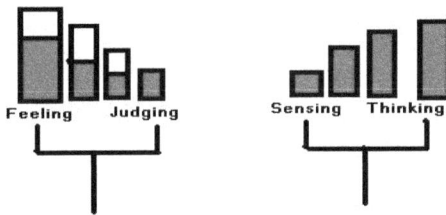

"Dominant Judgers and Feelers"

Just as in the countless cases of all the young African American males who turn to the sale of drugs as a method to provide for their families. They come from abusive backgrounds not necessarily in the home but the events of one's life play a part in the behavior and it has been passed on generation to generation since the days of slavery, and the will just plainly trying to make it in life without the assistance of others. The Blackman is barely able to work because he has no experience and the way the schools are set up they build up the African American's weaknesses rather than his strengths. Those that are able to excel are a result of the mixing of races to create the dominant thinking personality types. So when the opportunity to provide for the family presents itself the Blackman jumps at it heart first. These types are not crafty in the way that they think and therefore they will always get caught up in the vicious cycle and end up incarcerated until change happens.

Sensing and Thinking- When the personality type of those with sensing and thinking as their dominant strengths are abused physically and mentally the functions of sensing and thinking are building up because the functions store negative thoughts and emotions in the memory section of the mind. These personality types are building up there strengths and there fore they are dominant thinkers from thoughts or dominant sensors from emotions. These types have total control over the reaction from these functions. If these personality types have not received or accepted love in his heart as a child then the emotions will run wild and out of control for this person. Early in life they do not have the aid of there morals as strengths but as weaknesses. This is the reason why the scriptures say for a child to receive Jesus young.

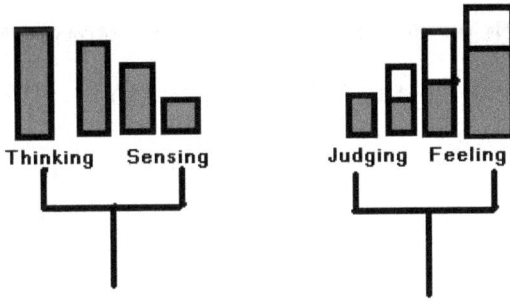

"Dominant Thinkers and Sensors"

Just as in the case of Ted Bundy's, Jeffrey Dahmer's and such individual monsters being created. People tell a lie to God with their mouth when they say these individual types were never abused or abused others because the fact of the matter is there intellect would not grow if this were not so. The same as with those that get an adrenaline rush from doing fear events. This is how you build a person up to becoming a mass murderer or serial killer. They are naturally crafty, therefore get away with committing crimes, but the truth is still found in their slick words and vocabulary. I'm not encouraging this behavior to happen in others but I'm making an attempt at exposing it in others, for those who are listening will learn to quite building these monsters up. It is not a race thing, color is a mere distraction. It is about the personality types. The majority of African American's are born with their morals working first, so by the time they reach adulthood they are in the realm of no morals. The love was meant to be passed back and fourth but the African American is forgotten and therefore the rage builds with up with no direction. They are not thinkers or killers, just lost and no one has taken the time out to find them or try to save them.

You cannot defeat the mechanism for the way in which that you were purposely designed but you can choose to live by them because they are your strengths. Remember to allow the love to come into your heart and refuse to become the monster.

-Chapter 4-
Finding Your Personality

Please answer all the survey questions to the best of your ability. This will help you to sharpen your skills on your attributes and personality type. Once completed you will know fully the gifts you posses as an individual and will have an advantage of being more responsible for yourself as a whole.

Em.Pt.Y Survey Questions

1. Are you happiest when surrounded by others? Yes or No
2. Do you constantly stand out in a crowd or others have told you? Yes or No
3. In a confrontation do you react first, then think about your actions and the way it affected others? Yes or No
4. Do you think out loud? Yes or No
5. Do you share your emotions freely with others? Yes or No
6. Are you more of a comfort to others by helping them address their issues rather than listening? Yes or No
7. When you learn new things are you anxious to

communicate them to others? Yes or No

8. Do you normally respond without hearing the whole story? Yes or No

9. Are you content with a little information rather than knowing the whole story? Yes or No

10. Do you enjoy spending time alone? Yes or No

11. Do you avoid being the center of attention? Yes or No

12. Do you think about your actions and the way it affects others before you react? Yes or No

13. Do you think thing out privately to yourself? Yes or No

14. Do you keep to yourself with personal information? Yes or No

15. Are you more of a comfort to others by listening than being expressive? Yes or No

16. When excited do you keep your emotions to yourself? Yes or No

17. Do you take the time to gather information inside your head before you respond? Yes or No

18. Do you prefer information to gut feelings? Yes or No

19. Do you trust what is certain and concrete? Yes or No

20. Do you like new ideas? Yes or No

21. Do you value realism and common sense? Yes or No

22. Do you like to use your established skills? Yes or No

23. Do you tend to be specific and give a detailed description? Yes or No

24. Do you present information in an orderly manner? Yes or No

25. Are you up to date with the present? Yes or No

26. Do you make a judgment by the facts gathered? Yes or no

27. Are you knowledgeable of your talents and skills? Yes or No

28. Do you trust your vibes or feelings? Yes or No

29. Do you like new ideas for your own sake? Yes or No

30. Do you value illusions or imagination? Yes or No

31. Do you like to learn new skills and get bored easily after learning them? Yes or No

32. Do you use metaphors or body language when expressing yourself? Yes or No

33. Do you make a judgment by your feelings? Yes or No

34. Are you exaggerative when telling a story? Yes or No

35. Do you look forward to the future? Yes or No

36. Are you uncertain about the skill or talents you posses? Yes or No

37. Instead of making a judgment do you step back and try to get a clearer picture of the given situation? Yes or No

38. Is the truth very important to you? Yes or No

39. Do you naturally see flaws in others rather than the positives? Yes or No

40. Have you ever been considered insensitive when it

pertains to others feelings? Yes or No

41. Do you find it important to be truthful regardless to others feelings? Yes or No

42. Do you value other people's feelings when expressed appropriately? Yes or No

43. Are you motivated by accomplishments? Yes or No

44. Do you step forward and make a decision based on what you feel is the right judgment? Yes or No

45. Do you value harmony and will go to any extreme to make it happen regardless to what it cost you? Yes or No

46. Do you take great pride in helping others? Yes or No

47. Do others normally say you're too emotional and tend to over think events and situations? Yes or No

48. Do you reveal the truth regardless to hurting other's feelings? Yes or No

49. Do you believe all of your emotions are important in a conversation? Yes or No

50. Are you happiest when you feel needed? Yes or No

51. Are you happiest after decisions have been made? Yes or No

52. Do you prefer to get the job done before you can sit back and relax? Yes or No

53. Do you set goals and work towards achieving them? Yes or No

54. Do you prefer knowing what you're getting into before

you say yes? Yes or No

55. Do you complete an assignment based on instructions? Yes or No

56. Are you happiest after completing an assignment? Yes or No

57. Do you take deadlines seriously? Yes or No

58. Are you happiest leaving your options open? Yes or No

59. Do you prefer to relax now and sit back then get the job done later? Yes or No

60. Do you change your mind as new information becomes available to you? Yes or No

61. Is it easy for you to adapt to new situations? Yes or No

62. Do you creatively think of ways to work an assignment? Yes or No

63. Do you see time as elastic, room for growth? Yes or No

64. At work, are you concerned most about the way a project is completed? Yes or No

You have now completed the short survey. Please turn to the next page for the Answer Sheet.

The Answer Sheet:

Questions 01-09 are for (E) extroverted type.

How many yes responses: _____   How many no responses:

_____

Questions 10-18 are for (I) introverted type.

How many yes responses: _____   How many no responses:

_____

Questions 19-27 are for (S) sensing type.

How many yes responses: _____   How many no responses:

_____

Questions 28-36 are for (N) intuitive/judging type.

How many yes responses: _____   How many no responses:

_____

Questions 37-43 is for (T) thinking type

How many yes responses: _____   How many no responses:

_____

Questions 44-50 is for (F) feeling type

How many yes responses: _____   How many no responses:

_____

Questions 51-57 is for (J) judger type

How many yes responses: _____   How many no responses:

_____

Questions 58-64 is for (P) perceiver type

How many yes responses: _____   How many no responses:

Please list your type: _____ _____ _____ _____

                       E or I   S or N   T or F   J or P

If you answered the questions correctly to the best of your ability than the personality type listed above is your definite personality type. Below I've listed a way for you to chart your emotion. For each of the emotions, ask the same question for each of the ages and O/S listed below. A question for the emotions would be, as a small child would I have considered myself to be accident prone? From the age of 6-12 would I have considered myself to be accident prone? And so forth, accordingly. Answer the questions to the best of your ability.

Emotions	emotion	The age ranges				overstimulated
		0-6	6-12	12-25	25-50	O/S
1. Accident Prone (F)						
2. Careless (J)						
3. Creativity (S)						
4. Cunning (T)						

Emotions	0-6	6-12	12-25	25-50
1. Accident Prone (F)				
2. Careless (J)				
3. Creativity (S)				
4. Cunning (T)				
5. Diplomatic (T)				
6. Emotional (F)				
7. Idealistic (F)				
8. Indecisive (J)				
9. Independence (S)				
10. Intuition (S)				
11. Inventive (T)				
12. Intelligence (F)				
13. Orderly (J)				
14. Perfectionist (T)				
15. Romantic (S)				
16. Stubborn (J)				

Once you finish this assessment of your emotions you'll be closer to knowing more of yourself. Then as you read more of the chapters about your personality type you can draw a better conclusion about the self within you. Then you can move ahead to the back of the book and take my quiz on building the personality type.

CHAPTERS 5-12
THE PERSONALITY TYPES

The following Chapters list the functions, emotions, behavior and temperament of each personality type. The only part, which is missing, is the events and environment of a person's life because the way in which every person walks throughout life is quite different. Mankind fill's this part of the script up with his or her many lessons learned within life.

Each of the types also has an opposite counterpart. I call them opposite counterpart because they do the same jobs but in different fashions because one is masculine sexuality type and the other is feminine sexuality type, one may be introverted and value family but like to spend time alone and the other may be extroverted and value friends but like to spend time with others, one may be a judger and prefer to get the job done now and the other may be a perceiver (passive) and prefer to play now, work later but they all balance out to the same duties.

The blueprint is still incomplete because your journey and servitude is not over and your writing your code as you walk through life. I hope that these next chapters will be very informative concerning your life's temperament.

Let's try to be the best at being an individual and remember to pass the "love" rather than the "hate".

Chapter 5: ISTP & ESTJ
Intelligence, Vibes, Judgment, and Emotions

Masculine Sexuality Type

ISTP (Think as an introvert, sense as a perceiver, judge as a judger and feel as a feeler)

Thinking (Masculine)

Cunning-you are private and are energized by spending time alone, you like to think things through inside your head and you share personal info with a select few people.

Inventive- you avoid being the center of attention and keep your enthusiasm to yourself.

Diplomatic- you think more than you react to any given situation and you prefer knowing more information than a little.

Perfectionist- you listen more than you talk and respond after taking the time to think things through inside your head.

Behavior: Impatient/ Rationalist

My natural temperament of earth uses the element of my intelligence to create an attitude of being intelligent to activate the action of my extroversion which effects my function of thinking which leads to the behavior of being a rationalist of impatient. This behavioral person is unable to wait patiently. They can't endure irritation for long periods of time. They have the ability to reason. They are always on a quest for truth even when the truth is laid out honestly before them. They have a natural desire to constantly search things over for truth. They believe "reason" to be the main source of knowledge and spiritual truth meaning because you have asked the question of "why" this brings about intelligence.

Sensing (Masculine)

Creativity- you are better at concentration exercises than fantasy or daydreaming. You have a play ethic, enjoy now and finish the job later, and enjoy exercises that allow you to learn new thing and have fun doing it. You are process oriented and your emphasis is on how the task is completed.

Intuition- you are influenced by past experiences and this is your knowledge of doing things. You don't like to brainstorm for answers and are happiest leaving your options open. You change goals as new information becomes available and prefer to not decide but continue to collect information for later usage.

Romantic-you feel satisfaction from starting projects and see time as a renewable resource and set deadlines.

Independence- you are flexible, adaptable, and change gears quickly so that you may be available for many different approaches and techniques. You have a natural curiosity and like adapting to new situations.

Behavior: Illusionist

My natural temperament of air uses the element of my vibes that I pick up on from my sight, smelling, hearing, tasting, and touching to create an attitude of being sensitive to activate the action of my perception which effects my function sensing which leads to the behavior of being an illusionist. This behavioral person is a natural liar and their work has to have some form of illusions in it or they just won't be happy.

Judging (Feminine)

Indecisive- Have trouble keeping on track or following directions.
Careless- you are product oriented and less likely to deal with specifics because your emphasis is on completing the task and you prefer to focus on the big picture.
Orderly- you prefer to make plans and follow them accordingly. You are usually well organized. You set goals and work toward achieving them on time and are happiest after final decisions have been made and feel satisfaction from finishing the projects.

Stubborn- you have a work ethic, work first play later, and prefer to know what you are getting into.

Behavior: Realistic

My natural temperament of fire uses the element of my judgment to created an attitude of being judgmental to activate the action of my intuition which effects my function of judging which leads to the behavior of being realistic. This behavioral person is a natural truth teller and their work has to tell things as they naturally are or they will not be content. They love representing the truth as described.

Feeling (Masculine)

Intelligence- you consider it important to be tactful as well as truthful. You step forward and consider the effects of your actions on others.

Idealistic- you show appreciation easily to others and believe any feeling is valid whether it makes sense or not. You naturally like to please others and may need to be encouraged to have own needs met.

Emotional- you value empathy and harmony but see the exception to the rule when it pertains to your own feelings. You make judgment based on your own feelings and values but you are people oriented and aware of others feelings. You are happiest in friendly, supportive, and cooperative environments.

Accident Prone- You may be seen as overemotional, illogical, and weak. You are an impatient person but are motivated by a desire to be appreciated.

Behavior: Patient

My natural temperament of water uses the element of my emotions to create an attitude of being emotional to activate the action of my introversion which effects my function of feeling which leads to the behavior of being patient. This behavioral person is very calm and capable of handling all. They have a high tolerance of bearing even the most difficult of challenges. They are very understanding and their for you as an individual.

Feminine Sexuality Type
ESTJ (Think as a thinker, sense a sensor, judge as a judger and feel as an extrovert)

Thinking (Feminine)

Diplomatic- You value logic, justice and fairness which to you is one standard for all. You step back and try to see the situation objectively before problem solving. You feel the need to be convinced that a specific event or activity makes sense before you will even believe.

Perfectionist- you naturally see flaws and tend to be critical of others and believe it is more important to be truthful than tactful. Believe others feelings are irrelevant to the situation at hand.

Inventive- Believe feelings are valid only if they are logical. You are motivated by a desire for achievement and accomplishment but have a hard time translating ideas into active steps.

Cunning- you may be seen as heartless, insensitive and uncaring but are impressed by competence and the end result.

Behavior: <u>Impatient/ Rationalist</u>

My natural temperament of earth uses the element of my intelligence to create an attitude of being intelligent to activate the action of my extroversion which effects my function of thinking which leads to the behavior of being a rationalist of impatient. This behavioral person is unable to wait patiently. They can't endure irritation for long periods of time. They have the ability to reason. They are always on a quest for truth even when the truth is laid out honestly before them. They have a natural desire to constantly search things over for truth. They believe "reason" to be the main source of knowledge and spiritual truth meaning because you have asked the question of "why" this brings about intelligence.

Sensing (Feminine)

Intuition- you trust what is certain, can be proven and you present information in a step-by-step manner.

Independence- you are knowledgeable of your established skills and make a judgment by the facts you gather.

Creativity- you like new ideas only if they have practical applications and tend to be specific and literal about giving a detailed description.

Romantic- you value realism and common sense and are oriented towards the present.

Behavior: Illusionist

My natural temperament of air uses the element of my vibes that I pick up on from my sight, smelling, hearing, tasting, and touching to create an attitude of being sensitive to activate the action of my perception which effects my function sensing which leads to the behavior of being an illusionist. This behavioral person is a natural liar and their work has to have some form of illusions in it or they just won't be happy.

Judging (Feminine)

Indecisive- Have trouble keeping on track or following directions.
Careless- you are product oriented and less likely to deal with specifics because your emphasis is on completing the task and you prefer to focus on the big picture.
Orderly- you prefer to make plans and follow them accordingly. You are usually well organized. You set goals and work toward achieving them on time and are happiest after final decisions have been made and feel satisfaction from finishing the projects.
 Stubborn- you have a work ethic, work first play later, and prefer to know what you are getting into.

Behavior: Realistic
My natural temperament of fire uses the element of my judgment to created an attitude of being judgmental to activate the action of my intuition which effects my function of judging which leads to the

behavior of being realistic. This behavioral person is a natural truth teller and their work has to tell things as they naturally are or they will not be content. They love representing the truth as described.

Feeling (Feminine)

Emotional- being with others energizes you. You react more than you think and you communicate to others with enthusiasm.

Accident Prone- You respond quickly without hearing the whole conversation. you enjoy being the center of attention, and enjoy a fast pace.

Idealistic- you think out loud and are easier to know and read. You were your emotions on your sleeve and talk with your body language. When your emotions have been hurt you feel the need to voice your opinion and you share personal information freely and sometimes without enough forethought.

Intelligence- you talk more than you listen and prefer to know a little information rather than it all.

Behavior: Patient

My natural temperament of water uses the element of my emotions to create an attitude of being emotional to activate the action of my introversion which effects my function of feeling which leads to the behavior of being patient. This behavioral person is very calm and capable of handling all. They have a high tolerance of bearing even the most difficult of challenges. They are very understanding and their for you as an individual.

Aries- The Element of Fire

Aries is the element of Fire. Fire and element of Earth create an eruption of emotions, burning everything and everyone, which crosses its path. The development of the dominant function is from birth to six years of age. The four emotions, which aid in the growth of your intelligence, are cunning, diplomatic, inventive and perfectionist.

Thinking: Intelligence

This is the use of your analytical thought.

> Cunning- your adventuresome as it pertains to life shows cunning.
>
> Diplomatic- your enthusiastic when experiencing love.
>
> Inventive- your impulsive as it pertains to their appearance.
>
> Perfectionist- you're innovative in your home life.

Aries is the element of Fire. Fire and the element of Air create a bonfire of emotions, rising giving the temperaments. This is the development of the second function auxiliary. This takes place from six to twelve years of age. The emotions that aid in its development are creativity, independence, intuition, and romantic.

Sensing: Vibes

This is the use of your analytical emotions.

Creativity-your optimistic as it pertains to your friends

Independence- you're courageous when you face a difficult
situation.

Intuition- you're a free spirit in your view of the world.

Romantic- your impatient when you feel loved.

Aries is the element of Fire. Fire and the element of Fire create heated emotions. This is the development of the third function. This takes place from twelve to twenty-five years of age. This function will never be as strong as the dominant and auxiliary functions. The emotions that aid in its development are careless, indecisive, orderly, and stubborn.

Judging: Judgment/ Intuition

This is the use of your moral thought.

Careless- you're a procrastinator as it relates to your family.

Indecisive- you are energetic about doing your job.

Orderly- you are selfish when it comes to money.

Stubborn- you are self-centered when expressing your
emotions.

Aries is the element of Fire. Fire and the element of water create a steam of emotions. This is the development of the fourth function. This takes place from Twenty-five till the age of fifty. It's not fully functional till after fifty years of age. This function will never be strong. The emotions that aid in its development are accident prone, emotional, idealistic, and intelligence.

Feeling: Emotions

This is the use of your moral emotions.

> Accident prone- your accident prone when your upset.
>
> Emotional- you're quick tempered when you're angry.
>
> Idealistic- being assertive is a strength you possess.
>
> Intelligence- you're very tactless in the way you think.

Taurus- The Element of Earth

Taurus is the element of the earth. Earth and the element of earth produce a dusty sandstorm of emotions. Blinding everyone in sight. This is the development of the dominant function. This takes place from birth to six years of age. The emotions that aid in its development are cunning, diplomatic, inventive and perfectionist.

Thinking: Intelligence

This is the use of your analytical thought.

> > Cunning- when you face a difficult situation you're very resentful.
> >
> > Diplomatic- you are set in your ways when you think.
> >
> > Inventive- When upset you are very inflexible.
> >
> > Perfectionist- you are very reliable when it comes to your friends.

Taurus is the element of the earth. Earth and the element of air create a tornado of emotions, thrashing and trashing everything in its sight. This is the development of the auxiliary function. This takes place from six to twelve years of age. The emotions that aid in its development are creativity, independence, intuition and romantic.

Sensing: Vibes

This is the use of your analytical emotions.

> Creativity-Your very solid in your view of life shows creativity.
>
> Independence- you're very persistent about doing your job.
>
> Intuition- when it comes to money you're very trustworthy.
>
> Romantic- you're very affectionate when you feel loved.

Taurus is the element of the earth. Earth and the element of fire create an eruption of emotions. This is the development of the third function. This takes place from twelve to twenty-five years of age. The emotions that aid in its development are careless, indecisive, orderly and stubborn.

Judging: Judgment/ Intuition

This is the use of your moral thought.

> Careless- you're very practical in your views concerning home life.
>
> Indecisive- when expressing emotions you are very lazy.

> Orderly- you are very possessive about your
> appearance.
> Stubborn- you are very stubborn in your views of the
> world.

Taurus is the element of the earth. Earth and the element of water create a flood of emotions, drowning everything in its path. This is the development of the fourth function. This takes place from twenty-five to fifty years of age. The emotions that aid in its development are accident prone, emotional, idealistic and intelligence.

Feeling: Emotions

This is the use of your moral emotions.

> Accident Prone- you are violent when you are angry.
> Emotional- you are greedy when in love.
> Idealistic- you are warm hearted when it relates to your
> family.
> Intelligence- being strong- willed is a strength you
> possess.

Gemini- The Element of Air

Gemini is the element of air. Air and the element of earth create a tornado of emotions, thrashing and trashing everything in its sight. This is the development of the dominant function. This takes place from birth to six years of age. The emotions that aid in its

development are cunning, diplomatic, inventive and perfectionist.

Thinking: Intelligence

This is the use of analytical thought.

Cunning- you are very cunning when you are upset.

Diplomatic- when you are angry you are very devious.

Inventive- you are a communicator about the way you think.

Perfectionist- you can be very versatile when in love.

Gemini is the element of air. Air and the element of air create a world wind of emotions. This is the development of the auxiliary function. This takes place from six to twelve years of age. The emotions that aid in its development are creativity, independence, intuition and romantic.

Sensing: Vibes

This is the use of analytical emotions.

Creativity- you are very energetic when it pertains to your friends.

Independence- you are adaptable as it relates to your job.

Intuition- being an intellectual is a strength possessed.

Romantic- you are very witty when in love.

Gemini is the element of air. Air and the element of fire create a bonfire of emotions, rising given the temperament. This is the development of the third function. This takes place from twelve to twenty-five years of age. The emotions that aid in its development

are careless, indecisive, orderly and stubborn.

Judging: Judgment/ Intuition

This is the use of moral thought.

Careless-you are very secretive about your view of the world.

Indecisive- you can be superficial when it pertains to money.

Orderly-you are logical in your home life.

Stubborn- you are inconsistent when expressing your emotions.

Gemini is the element of air. Air and the element of water create a hurricane of emotions. This is the development of the fourth function. This takes place from twenty-five to fifty years of age. The emotions that aid in its development are accident prone, emotional, idealistic and intelligence.

Feeling: Emotions

This is the use of moral emotions.

Accident Prone- you are very restless when it pertains to your family.

Emotional- you are nosey when you face a difficult situation.

Idealistic- you are very flighty in your appearance.

Intelligence- you are very spontaneous in your views of life.

Cancer- The Element of Water

Cancer is the element of water. Water and the element of earth create a flood of emotions, drowning everything in its path. This is the development of the dominant function. This takes place from birth to six years of age. The emotions that aid in its development are cunning, diplomatic, inventive and perfectionist.

Thinking: Intelligence

This is the use of analytical thought.

Cunning- being sympathetic is a strength possessed.

Diplomatic- when expressing emotions you can be over indulgent in self-pity.

Inventive- you are very receptive when you think.

Perfectionist- when you feel loved you can be moody.

Cancer is the element of water. Water and the element of air create a hurricane of emotions. This is the development of the second function auxiliary. This takes place from six to twelve years of age. The emotions that aid in its development are creativity, independence, intuition, and romantic.

Sensing: Vibes

This is the use of analytical emotions.

Creativity- you're very kind to your friends.

Independence- your job is very messy.

Intuition- you're very judgmental in your views of life.

Romantic- when in love you can be overly emotional.

Cancer is the element of water. Water and the element of fire create a steam of emotions. This is the development of the third function. This takes place from twelve to twenty-five years of age. The emotions that aid in its development are careless, indecisive, orderly and stubborn.

Judging: Judgment/ Intuition

This is the use of moral thought.

Careless- you are very shrewd when you are angry.

Indecisive- your home life is very unstable.

Orderly- your appearance is changeable.

Stubborn- when upset you are unforgiving.

Cancer is the element of water. Water and the element of water create a wave of emotions. This is the development of the fourth function. This takes place from twenty-five to fifty years of age. The emotions that aid in its development are accident prone, emotional, idealistic and intelligence.

Feeling: Emotions

This is the use of moral emotions.

Accident Prone-you are hyper sensitive when it pertains to family.

Emotional- when you face a difficult situation you can be very emotional.

Idealistic- you are thrifty when it pertains to money.

Intelligence- you are sensitive in your view of the world.

Leo- The Element of Fire

Leo is the element of fire. Fire and the element of earth create an eruption of emotions. This is the development of the dominant function. This takes place from birth to six years of age. The emotions that aid in its development are cunning, diplomatic, inventive and perfectionist.

Thinking: Intelligence

This is the use of your analytical thought.

Cunning- you are patronizing when it relates to your family.

Diplomatic- when you face a difficult situation you are dogmatic.

Inventive- your view of the world is creative.

Perfectionist- when it comes to money you are extravagant.

Leo is the element of fire. Fire and the element of air create a bonfire of emotions, rising given the temperament. This is the development of the second function auxiliary. This takes place from six to twelve years of age. The emotions that aid in its development are creativity, independence, intuition, and romantic.

Sensing: Vibes

This is the use of your analytical emotions.

Creativity- you are very enthusiastic about life.

Independence- you are conceited about your appearance.

Intuition-you are very optimistic when it comes to your friends.

Romantic- when in love you are dramatic.

Leo is the element of fire. Fire and the element of fire create heated emotions. This is a very judgmental person. This is the development of the third function. This takes place from twelve to twenty-five years of age. The emotions that aid in its development are careless, indecisive, orderly and stubborn.

Judging: Judgment/ Intuition

This is the use of your moral thought.

Careless- when you're angry you appear very snobbish.

Indecisive- at your job you are very egotistical.

Orderly- your home life is organized.

Stubborn- when upset you are intolerant.

Leo is the element of fire. Fire and water create a steam of emotions. This is the development of the fourth function. This takes place from twenty-five to fifty years of age. The emotions that aid in its development are accident prone, emotional, idealistic and intelligence.

Feeling: Emotions

This is the use of your moral emotions.

Accident Prone- when expressing emotions you are attention-seeking.

Emotional- when you feel loved you are generous.

Idealistic- being powerful is a strength possessed.

Intelligence- you are very broad-minded in the way you think.

Virgo- The Element of Earth

Virgo is the element of earth. Earth and the element of earth create a dusty sandstorm of emotions, blinding everyone in its path. This takes place from birth to six years of age. The emotions that aid in its development are cunning, diplomatic, inventive and perfectionist.

Thinking: Intelligence

This is the use of your analytical thought.

Cunning- being prudish is a strength possessed.

Diplomatic- when upset you are cranky.

Inventive- you are a busy body in your home life.

Perfectionist- you are a worrier when you feel loved.

Virgo is the element of earth. Earth and the element of air create a tornado of emotions, thrashing and trashing everyone in its path. This is the development of the second function auxiliary. This takes place from six to twelve years of age. The emotions that aid in its development are creativity, independence, intuition, and romantic.

Sensing: Vibes

This is the use of your analytical emotions.

Creativity- you are practical in the way you think.

Independence- at your job you are a workaholic.

Intuition- you are hypercritical in your view of life.

Romantic- when in love you are a perfectionist.

Virgo is the element of earth. Earth and the element of fire create an eruption of emotions, burning and melting with words everyone in its path. This is the development of the third function. This takes place from twelve to twenty-five years of age. The emotions that aid in its development are careless, indecisive, orderly and stubborn.

Judging: Judgment/ Intuition

This is the use of your moral thought.

Careless- you are neat in your appearance.

Indecisive- when angry you are grouchy.

Orderly- you are meticulous when it comes to money.

Stubborn- you are analytical in your view of family.

Virgo is the element of earth. Earth and the element of water create a flood of emotions, drowning with words everyone in its path. This is the development of the fourth function. This takes place from twenty-five to fifty years of age. The emotions that aid in its development are accident prone, emotional, idealistic and intelligence.

Feeling: Emotions

This is the use of your moral emotions.

Accident Prone- when you face a difficult situation you are fussy.

Emotional- when expressing your emotions you are pessimistic.

Idealistic- you are conscientious about your friends.

Intelligence- you are hypercritical in your view of the world.

Libra- The Element of Air

Libra is the element of air. Air and the element of earth create a tornado of emotions, thrashing and drowning with words everyone in its path. This takes place from birth to six years of age. The emotions that aid in its development are cunning, diplomatic, inventive and perfectionist.

Thinking: Intelligence

This is the use of your analytical thought.

Cunning- when you face a difficult situation you are charming.

Diplomatic- when upset you are diplomatic.

Inventive- you are changeable in your appearance.

Perfectionist- you are a seeker in harmony when it relates to the world.

Libra is the element of air. Air and the element of air create a world wind of emotions; taking your breath away with words. This is the development of the second function auxiliary. This takes place from six to twelve years of age. The emotions that aid in its development are creativity, independence, intuition, and romantic.

Sensing: Vibes

This is the use of your analytical emotions.

Creativity- when you feel loved you are flirtatious.

Independence- you are frivolous when it pertains to your
   friends.

Intuition- being two faced is a strength possessed.

Romantic- when in love you are romantic.

Libra is the element of air. Air and the element of fire create a
bonfire of emotions, rising given the words and temperament. This
is the development of the third function. This takes place from
twelve to twenty-five years of age. The emotions that aid in its
development are careless, indecisive, orderly and stubborn.

Judging: Judgment/ Intuition

This is the use of your moral thought.

   Careless- you are extravagant when you have money.

   Indecisive- when expressing emotions you are very indecisive
      and hard for you to make up your mind.

   Orderly- your home life is orderly.

   Stubborn- your view of life is easy going.

Libra is the element of air. Air and the element of water create a
hurricane of emotions; thrashing and drowning with words
everyone in its path. This is the development of the fourth function.
This takes place from twenty-five to fifty years of age. The
emotions that aid in its development are accident prone, emotional,
idealistic and intelligence.

Feeling: Emotions

This is the use of your moral emotions.

Accident Prone- when angry you are resentful.

Emotional- you are gullible when it comes to your family.

Idealistic- your job is idealistic and you don't expect much.

Intelligence- you are refined in the way you think.

Scorpio- The Element of Water

Scorpio is the element of water. Water and the element of earth create a flood of emotions, drowning with words everything in its path. This takes place from birth to six years of age. The emotions that aid in its development are cunning, diplomatic, inventive and perfectionist.

Thinking: Intelligence

This is the use of your analytical thought.

Cunning- you are vengeful in your views of the world.

Diplomatic- when you face a difficult situation you are jealous.

Inventive- you are determined when it relates to your family.

Perfectionist- your home life is secretive.

Scorpio is the element of water. Water and the element of air create a hurricane of emotions, thrashing and drowning with words everyone in its path. This is the development of the second function auxiliary. This takes place from six to twelve years of age. The emotions that aid in its development are creativity, independence, intuition, and romantic.

Sensing: Vibes

This is the use of your analytical emotions.

Creativity-you are creative in life.

Independence- you are independent in your job.

Intuition- you are very judgmental when you think.

Romantic- when in love you are passionate.

Scorpio is the element of water. Water and the element of fire create a steam of emotions. This is the development of the third function. This takes place from twelve to twenty-five years of age. The emotions that aid in its development are careless, indecisive, orderly and stubborn.

Judging: Judgment/ Intuition

This is the use of your moral thought.

Careless- when expressing emotions you are overly emotional.

Indecisive- you are energetic when it relates to your friends.

Orderly-being persistent is a strength possessed.

Stubborn-when upset you are stubborn.

Scorpio is the element of water. Water and the element of water create a wave of emotions, crashing and drowning everyone in its path. This is the development of the fourth function. This takes place from twenty-five to fifty years of age. The emotions that aid in its development are accident prone, emotional, idealistic and intelligence.

Feeling: Emotions

This is the use of your moral emotions.

Accident Prone- you are violent when you are angry.

Emotional- when you feel loved you are emotional.

Idealistic- your appearance is practical.

Intelligence- you are very manipulative when it comes to money.

Sagittarius- The Element of Fire

Sagittarius is the element of fire. Fire and the element of earth create an eruption of emotions, burning and melting with words everyone in its path. This takes place from birth to six years of age. The emotions that aid in its development are cunning, diplomatic, inventive and perfectionist.

Thinking: Intelligence

This is the use of your analytical thought.

Cunning- when faced with a difficult situation you remain sincere.

Diplomatic-you are frivolous when you are upset.

Inventive- you are tactless in your appearance.

Perfectionist-you are undisciplined in your life.

Sagittarius is the element of fire. Fire and the element of air create a bonfire of emotions, rising given the words and temperament. This is the development of the second function auxiliary. This takes place from six to twelve years of age. The emotions that aid in its development are creativity, independence, intuition, and romantic.

Sensing: Vibes

This is the use of your analytical emotions.

Creativity- you are erratic when upset.

Independence- you are free spirited in your view of the world.

Intuition- being optimistic is a strength you possess.

Romantic-when in love you are very passionate.

Sagittarius is the element of fire. Fire and the element of fire create heated emotions, burning with words everything in its path. This is a very judgmental person. This is the development of the third function. This takes place from twelve to twenty-five years of age. The emotions that aid in its development are careless, indecisive, orderly and stubborn.

Judging: Judgment/ Intuition

This is the use of your moral thought.

Careless- you are careless in the way you think.

Indecisive- when expressing emotions you are frank and give short answers.

Orderly- your home life is restless.

Stubborn- you are exaggerative when you have money.

Sagittarius is the element of fire. Fire and the element of water create a steam of emotions, bursting with cloudy judgment toward everyone in its path. This is the development of the fourth function. This takes place from twenty-five to fifty years of age. The emotions that aid in its development are accident prone, emotional, idealistic and intelligence.

Feeling: Emotions

This is the use of your moral emotions.

Accident Prone- you are irresponsible when it pertains to family.

Emotional-when you feel loved you are ambitious.

Idealistic-you are very dependable when it pertains to friends.

Intelligence- you are energetic when it pertains to your job.

Capricorn- The Element of Earth

Capricorn is the element of earth. Earth and the element of earth create a dusty, sandstorm of emotions, blinding everyone with words in its path. This takes place from birth to six years of age. The emotions that aid in its development are cunning, diplomatic, inventive and perfectionist.

Thinking: Intelligence

This is the use of your analytical thought.

Cunning-you are opportunistic when it pertains to money.

Diplomatic- you are prudent in the way you think.

Inventive- you are reliable when it pertains to family.

Perfectionist- you are overly ordinary in your life.

Capricorn is the element of earth. Earth and the element of air create a tornado of emotions, thrashing and trashing with words everyone in its sight. This is the development of the second function auxiliary. This takes place from six to twelve years of age. The emotions that aid in its development are creativity, independence, intuition, and romantic.

Sensing: Vibes

This is the use of your analytical emotions.

Creativity-you are ambitious about doing your job.

Independence- you are comfortable in your appearance.

Intuition- when in love you are generous.

Romantic-you are patient in your view of the world.

Capricorn is the element of earth. Earth and the element of fire create an eruption of emotions, burning and melting with words everyone in its path. This is the development of the third function. This takes place from twelve to twenty-five years of age. The emotions that aid in its development are careless, indecisive, orderly and stubborn.

Judging: Judgment/ Intuition

This is the use of your moral thought.

Careless- when upset you are mean.

Indecisive- when you feel loved you are determined.

Orderly- your home life is organized.

Stubborn- when you face a difficult situation you are rigid.

Capricorn is the element of earth. Earth and the element of water create a flood of emotions, drowning with words everything in its path. This is the development of the fourth function. This takes place from twenty-five to fifty years of age. The emotions that aid in its development are accident prone, emotional, idealistic and intelligence.

Feeling: Emotions

This is the use of your moral emotions.

Accident Prone- you are a social climber when it pertains to friends.

Emotional- you are miserly at expressing emotions.

Idealistic- having a sense of humor is a strength you possess.

Intelligence- when you are angry you are a nit-picker and you pick the least important thing to argue about.

Aquarius- The Element of Air

Aquarius is the element of air. Air and the element of earth create a tornado of emotions, thrashing and trashing with words everyone in its sight. This takes place from birth to six years of age. The emotions that aid in its development are cunning, diplomatic, inventive and perfectionist.

Thinking: Intelligence

This is the use of your analytical thought.

Cunning- when angry you are unpredictable.

Diplomatic- you are human in your view of the world.

Inventive- being inventive is a strength you possess.

Perfectionist- when in love you are charismatic.

Aquarius is the element of air. Air and the element of air create a world wind of emotions, taking your breath away with words. This is the development of the second function auxiliary. This takes place from six to twelve years of age. The emotions that aid in its development are creativity, independence, intuition, and romantic.

Sensing: Vibes

This is the use of your analytical emotions.

Creativity- you are eccentric when it pertains to family and there is no one like you.

Independence- you are independent at your job.

Intuition- you are judgmental in the way you think.

Romantic-when you feel loved you are perverse.

Aquarius is the element of air. Air and the element of fire create a bonfire of emotions, rising given the words and temperament. This is the development of the third function. This takes place from twelve to twenty-five years of age. The emotions that aid in its development are careless, indecisive, orderly and stubborn.

Judging: Judgment/ Intuition

This is the use of your moral thought.

Careless- your home life is disorganized.

Indecisive- you are impulsive in your life.

Orderly- you are neat in appearance.

Stubborn- you are rebellious when you face a difficult situation.

Aquarius is the element of air. Air and the element of water create a hurricane of emotions, thrashing and drowning with words everyone in its path. This is the development of the fourth function. This takes place from twenty-five to fifty years of age. The emotions that aid in its development are accident prone, emotional, idealistic and intelligence.

Feeling: Emotions

This is the use of your moral emotions.

Accident Prone- you are tactless when it pertains to friends.

Emotional- when expressing emotions you are friendly.

Idealistic-you are idealistic when it pertains to money.

Intelligence- when upset you are intelligent.

Pisces- The Element of Water

Pisces is the element of water. Water and the element of earth create a flood of emotions, drowning with words everything in its path. This takes place from birth to six years of age. The emotions that aid in its development are cunning, diplomatic, inventive and perfectionist.

Thinking: Intelligence

This is the use of your analytical thought.

Cunning- when faced with a difficult situation you are secretive.

Diplomatic- you are compassionate in your view of the world.

Inventive-you are imaginative when it pertains to money.

Perfectionist- you are impressionable in your life.

Pisces is the element of water. Water and the element of air create a hurricane of emotions, thrashing and drowning with words everyone in its path. This is the development of the second function auxiliary. This takes place from six to twelve years of age. The emotions that aid in its development are creativity, independence, intuition, and romantic.

Sensing: Vibes

This is the use of your analytical emotions.

Creativity- you are sensitive when it pertains to friends.

Independence- you are mysterious in your appearance.

Intuition- being judgmental is a strength possessed.

Romantic- when in love you are romantic.

Pisces is the element of water. Water and the element of fire create a steam of emotions, bursting with cloudy judgment toward everyone in its path. This is the development of the third function. This takes place from twelve to twenty-five years of age. The emotions that aid in its development are careless, indecisive, orderly and stubborn.

Judging: Judgment/ Intuition

This is the use of your moral thought.

Careless- you are careless when it pertains to family.

Indecisive- when expressing emotions you are indecisive.

Orderly- you are receptive at your job.

Stubborn- when you are angry you are vague and don't reveal a lot of information as to why you feel the way you do.

Pisces is the element of water. Water and the element of water create a wave of emotions, crashing and drowning everyone in its path. This is the development of the fourth function. This takes place from twenty-five to fifty years of age. The emotions that aid in its development are accident prone, emotional, idealistic and intelligence.

Feeling: Emotions

This is the use of your moral emotions.

Accident Prone- when you feel loved you are weak-willed.

Emotional-when upset you are emotional.

Idealistic- you are compassionate in your view of the world.

Intelligence- you are unworldly in the way you think.

Chapter 6: INTP & ENTJ
Intelligence, Judgment, Vibes, and Emotions

Masculine Sexuality Type

INTP (Think as an introvert, judge as an intuitive, sense as a perceiver and feel as a feeler)

<u>Thinking</u> (Masculine)

Cunning-you are private and are energized by spending time alone, you like to think things through inside your head and you share personal info with a select few people.

Inventive- you avoid being the center of attention and keep your enthusiasm to yourself.

Diplomatic- you think more than you react to any given situation and you prefer knowing more information than a little.

Perfectionist- you listen more than you talk and respond after taking the time to think things through inside your head.

Behavior: <u>Impatient/ Rationalist</u>

My natural temperament of earth uses the element of my intelligence to create an attitude of being intelligent to activate the action of my extroversion which effects my function of thinking which leads to the behavior of being a rationalist of impatient. This behavioral person is unable to wait patiently. They can't endure irritation for long periods of time. They have the ability to reason. They are always on a quest for truth even when the truth is laid out honestly before them. They have a natural desire to constantly search things over for truth. They believe "reason" to be the main source of knowledge and spiritual truth meaning because you have asked the question of "why" this brings about intelligence.

Judging (Masculine)

Stubborn- you trust inspiration, spiritual guidance, and fiction and are oriented towards the future.

Careless- you like new ideas for your own sake, value imagination and innovation but tend to be general and figurative by using metaphors and analogies.

Indecisive- you enjoy learning new skills and get bored easily after mastering them. You present information through leaps and hurdles in a round about manner and are uncertain about your skills but make a judgment based on your own feelings.

Behavior: Realistic

My natural temperament of fire uses the element of my judgment to created an attitude of being judgmental to activate the action of

my intuition which effects my function of judging which leads to the behavior of being realistic. This behavioral person is a natural truth teller and their work has to tell things as they naturally are or they will not be content. They love representing the truth as described.

Sensing (Masculine)

Creativity- you are better at concentration exercises than fantasy or daydreaming. You have a play ethic, enjoy now and finish the job later, and enjoy exercises that allow you to learn new thing and have fun doing it. You are process oriented and your emphasis is on how the task is completed.

 Intuition- you are influenced by past experiences and this is your knowledge of doing things. You don't like to brainstorm for answers and are happiest leaving your options open. You change goals as new information becomes available and prefer to not decide but continue to collect information for later usage.

Romantic-you feel satisfaction from starting projects and see time as a renewable resource and set deadlines.

Independence- you are flexible, adaptable, and change gears quickly so that you may be available for many different approaches and techniques. You have a natural curiosity and like adapting to new situations.

Behavior: Illusionist

My natural temperament of air uses the element of my vibes that I pick up on from my sight, smelling, hearing, tasting, and touching to create an attitude of being sensitive to activate the action of my perception which effects my function sensing which leads to the behavior of being an illusionist. This behavioral person is a natural liar and their work has to have some form of illusions in it or they just won't be happy.

Feeling (Masculine)

Intelligence- you consider it important to be tactful as well as truthful. You step forward and consider the effects of your actions on others.

Idealistic- you show appreciation easily to others and believe any feeling is valid whether it makes sense or not. You naturally like to please others and may need to be encouraged to have own needs met.

 Emotional- you value empathy and harmony but see the exception to the rule when it pertains to your own feelings. You make judgment based on your own feelings and values but you are people oriented and aware of others feelings. You are happiest in friendly, supportive, and cooperative environments.

Accident Prone- You may be seen as overemotional, illogical, and weak. You are an impatient person but are motivated by a desire to be appreciated.

Behavior: Patient

My natural temperament of water uses the element of my emotions to create an attitude of being emotional to activate the action of my introversion which effects my function of feeling which leads to the behavior of being patient. This behavioral person is very calm and capable of handling all. They have a high tolerance of bearing even the most difficult of challenges. They are very understanding and their for you as an individual.

Feminine Sexuality Type
ENTJ (Think as a thinker, judge as a intuitive, sense as a sensor and feel as an extrovert)

Thinking (Feminine)

Diplomatic- You value logic, justice and fairness which to you is one standard for all. You step back and try to see the situation objectively before problem solving. You feel the need to be convinced that a specific event or activity makes sense before you will even believe.

Perfectionist- you naturally see flaws and tend to be critical of others and believe it is more important to be truthful than tactful. Believe others feelings are irrelevant to the situation at hand.

Inventive- Believe feelings are valid only if they are logical. You are motivated by a desire for achievement and accomplishment but have a hard time translating ideas into active steps.

Cunning- you may be seen as heartless, insensitive and uncaring but are impressed by competence and the end result.

Behavior: Impatient/ Rationalist

My natural temperament of earth uses the element of my intelligence to create an attitude of being intelligent to activate the action of my extroversion which effects my function of thinking which leads to the behavior of being a rationalist of impatient. This behavioral person is unable to wait patiently. They can't endure irritation for long periods of time. They have the ability to reason. They are always on a quest for truth even when the truth is laid out honestly before them. They have a natural desire to constantly search things over for truth. They believe "reason" to be the main source of knowledge and spiritual truth meaning because you have asked the question of "why" this brings about intelligence.

Judging (Masculine)

Stubborn- you trust inspiration, spiritual guidance, and fiction and are oriented towards the future.

Careless- you like new ideas for your own sake, value imagination and innovation but tend to be general and figurative by using metaphors and analogies.

Indecisive- you enjoy learning new skills and get bored easily after mastering them. You present information through leaps and hurdles in a round about manner and are uncertain about your skills but make a judgment based on your own feelings.

Behavior: Realistic

My natural temperament of fire uses the element of my judgment to created an attitude of being judgmental to activate the action of my intuition which effects my function of judging which leads to the behavior of being realistic. This behavioral person is a natural truth teller and their work has to tell things as they naturally are or they will not be content. They love representing the truth as described.

Sensing (Feminine)

Intuition- you trust what is certain, can be proven and you present information in a step-by-step manner.

Independence- you are knowledgeable of your established skills and make a judgment by the facts you gather.

Creativity- you like new ideas only if they have practical applications and tend to be specific and literal about giving a detailed description.

Romantic- you value realism and common sense and are oriented towards the present.

Behavior: Illusionist

My natural temperament of air uses the element of my vibes that I pick up on from my sight, smelling, hearing, tasting, and touching to create an attitude of being sensitive to activate the action of my perception which effects my function sensing which leads to the behavior of being an illusionist. This behavioral person is a natural liar and their work has to have some form of illusions in it or they just won't be happy.

Feeling (Feminine)

Emotional- being with others energizes you. You react more than you think and you communicate to others with enthusiasm.

Accident Prone- You respond quickly without hearing the whole conversation. you enjoy being the center of attention, and enjoy a fast pace.

Idealistic- you think out loud and are easier to know and read. You were your emotions on your sleeve and talk with your body language. When your emotions have been hurt you feel the need to voice your opinion and you share personal information freely and sometimes without enough forethought.

Intelligence- you talk more than you listen and prefer to know a little information rather than it all.

Behavior: <u>Patient</u>

My natural temperament of water uses the element of my emotions to create an attitude of being emotional to activate the action of my introversion which effects my function of feeling which leads to the behavior of being patient. This behavioral person is very calm and capable of handling all. They have a high tolerance of bearing even the most difficult of challenges. They are very understanding and their for you as an individual.

Aries- The Element of Fire

Aries is the element of Fire. Fire and element of Earth create an eruption of emotions, burning everything and everyone, which crosses its path. The development of the dominant function is from birth to six years of age. The four emotions, which aid in the growth of your intelligence are cunning, diplomatic, inventive and perfectionist.

Thinking: Intelligence

This is the use of your analytical thought.

Cunning- your adventuresome as it pertains to life shows
cunning.

Diplomatic- your enthusiastic when experiencing love.

Inventive- your impulsive as it pertains to their appearance.

Perfectionist- you're innovative in your home life.

Aries is the element of Fire. Fire and the element of Fire create heated emotions. This is the development of the second function auxiliary. This takes place from six to twelve years of age. The emotions that aid in its development are careless, indecisive, orderly, and stubborn.

Judging: Judgment/ Intuition

This is the use of your moral thought.

Careless- you're a procrastinator as it relates to your family.

Indecisive- you are energetic about doing your job.

Orderly- you are selfish when it comes to money.

Stubborn- you are self-centered when expressing your
emotions.

Aries is the element of Fire. Fire and the element of Air create a bonfire of emotions, rising giving the temperaments. This is the development of the third function. This takes place from twelve to twenty-five years of age. This function will never be as strong as the dominant and auxiliary functions. The emotions that aid in its development are creativity, independence, intuition, and romantic.

Sensing: Vibes

This is the use of your analytical emotions.

Creativity-your optimistic as it pertains to your friends

Independence- you're courageous when you face a difficult situation.

Intuition- you're a free spirit in your view of the world.

Romantic- your impatient when you feel loved.

Aries is the element of Fire. Fire and the element of water create a steam of emotions. This is the development of the fourth function. This takes place from Twenty-five till the age of fifty. It's not fully functional till after fifty years of age. This function will never be strong. The emotions that aid in its development are accident prone, emotional, idealistic, and intelligence.

Feeling: Emotions

This is the use of your moral emotions.

Accident prone- your accident prone when your upset.

Emotional- you're quick tempered when you're angry.

Idealistic- being assertive is a strength you possess.

Intelligence- you're very tactless in the way you think.

Taurus- The Element of Earth

Taurus is the element of the earth. Earth and the element of earth produce a dusty sandstorm of emotions. Blinding everyone in sight.

This is the development of the dominant function. This takes place from birth to six years of age. The emotions that aid in its development are cunning, diplomatic, inventive and perfectionist.

Thinking: Intelligence

This is the use of your analytical thought.

> Cunning- when you face a difficult situation you're very resentful.
>
> Diplomatic- you are set in your ways when you think.
>
> Inventive- When upset you are very inflexible.
>
> Perfectionist- you are very reliable when it comes to your friends.

Taurus is the element of the earth. Earth and the element of fire create an eruption of emotions. This is the development of the auxiliary function. This takes place from six to twelve years of age. The emotions that aid in its development are careless, indecisive, orderly and stubborn.

Judging: Judgment/ Intuition

This is the use of your moral thought.

> Careless- you're very practical in your views concerning home life.
>
> Indecisive- when expressing emotions you are very lazy.
>
> Orderly- you are very possessive about your appearance.
>
> Stubborn- you are very stubborn in your views of the

world.

Taurus is the element of the earth. Earth and the element of air create a tornado of emotions, thrashing and trashing everything in its sight. This is the development of the third function. This takes place from twelve to twenty-five years of age. The emotions that aid in its development are creativity, independence, intuition and romantic.

Sensing: Vibes

This is the use of your analytical emotions.

> Creativity-Your very solid in your view of life shows creativity.
>
> Independence- you're very persistent about doing your job.
>
> Intuition- when it comes to money you're very trustworthy.
>
> Romantic- you're very affectionate when you feel loved.

Taurus is the element of the earth. Earth and the element of water create a flood of emotions, drowning everything in its path. This is the development of the fourth function. This takes place from twenty-five to fifty years of age. The emotions that aid in its development are accident prone, emotional, idealistic and intelligence.

Feeling: Emotions

This is the use of your moral emotions.

> Accident Prone- you are violent when you are angry.
>
> Emotional- you are greedy when in love.
>
> Idealistic- you are warm hearted when it relates to your family.
>
> Intelligence- being strong- willed is a strength you possess.

Gemini- The Element of Air

Gemini is the element of air. Air and the element of earth create a tornado of emotions, thrashing and trashing everything in its sight. This is the development of the dominant function. This takes place from birth to six years of age. The emotions that aid in its development are cunning, diplomatic, inventive and perfectionist.

Thinking: Intelligence

This is the use of analytical thought.

> Cunning- you are very cunning when you are upset.
>
> Diplomatic- when you are angry you are very devious.
>
> Inventive- you are a communicator about the way you think.
>
> Perfectionist- you can be very versatile when in love.

Gemini is the element of air. Air and the element of fire create a bonfire of emotions, rising given the temperament. This is the development of the third function. This takes place from twelve to twenty-five years of age. The emotions that aid in its development are careless, indecisive, orderly and stubborn.

Judging: Judgment/ Intuition

This is the use of moral thought.

 Careless-you are very secretive about your view of the world.

 Indecisive- you can be superficial when it pertains to money.

 Orderly-you are logical in your home life.

 Stubborn- you are inconsistent when expressing your emotions.

Gemini is the element of air. Air and the element of air create a world wind of emotions. This is the development of the auxiliary function. This takes place from six to twelve years of age. The emotions that aid in its development are creativity, independence, intuition and romantic.

Sensing: Vibes

This is the use of analytical emotions.

 Creativity- you are very energetic when it pertains to your
  friends.

 Independence- you are adaptable as it relates to your job.

 Intuition- being an intellectual is a strength possessed.

  Romantic- you are very witty when in love.

Gemini is the element of air. Air and the element of water create a hurricane of emotions. This is the development of the fourth function. This takes place from twenty-five to fifty years of age. The emotions that aid in its development are accident prone, emotional, idealistic and intelligence.

Feeling: Emotions

This is the use of moral emotions.

> Accident Prone- you are very restless when it pertains to your family.
>
> Emotional- you are nosey when you face a difficult situation.
>
> Idealistic- you are very flighty in your appearance.
>
> Intelligence- you are very spontaneous in your views of life.

Cancer- The Element of Water

Cancer is the element of water. Water and the element of earth create a flood of emotions, drowning everything in its path. This is the development of the dominant function. This takes place from birth to six years of age. The emotions that aid in its development are cunning, diplomatic, inventive and perfectionist.

Thinking: Intelligence

This is the use of analytical thought.

> Cunning- being sympathetic is a strength possessed.
>
> Diplomatic- when expressing emotions you can be over indulgent in self-pity.
>
> Inventive- you are very receptive when you think.
>
> Perfectionist- when you feel loved you can be moody.

Cancer is the element of water. Water and the element of fire create a steam of emotions. This is the development of the second function auxiliary. This takes place from six to twelve years of age. The emotions that aid in its development are careless, indecisive, orderly and stubborn.

Judging: Judgment/ Intuition

This is the use of moral thought.

Careless- you are very shrewd when you are angry.

Indecisive- your home life is very unstable.

Orderly- your appearance is changeable.

Stubborn- when upset you are unforgiving.

Cancer is the element of water. Water and the element of air create a hurricane of emotions. This is the development of the third function. This takes place from twelve to twenty-five years of age. The emotions that aid in its development are creativity, independence, intuition, and romantic.

Sensing: Vibes

This is the use of analytical emotions.

Creativity- you're very kind to your friends.

Independence- your job is very messy.

Intuition- you're very judgmental in your views of life.

Romantic- when in love you can be overly emotional.

Cancer is the element of water. Water and the element of water create a wave of emotions. This is the development of the fourth function. This takes place from twenty-five to fifty years of age. The emotions that aid in its development are accident prone, emotional, idealistic and intelligence.

Feeling: Emotions

This is the use of moral emotions.

Accident Prone-you are hyper sensitive when it pertains to family.

Emotional- when you face a difficult situation you can be very emotional.

Idealistic- you are thrifty when it pertains to money.

Intelligence- you are sensitive in your view of the world.

Leo- The Element of Fire

Leo is the element of fire. Fire and the element of earth create an eruption of emotions. This is the development of the dominant function. This takes place from birth to six years of age. The emotions that aid in its development are cunning, diplomatic, inventive and perfectionist.

Thinking: Intelligence

This is the use of your analytical thought.

Cunning- you are patronizing when it relates to your family.

Diplomatic- when you face a difficult situation you are dogmatic.

Inventive- your view of the world is creative.

Perfectionist- when it comes to money you are extravagant.

Leo is the element of fire. Fire and the element of fire create heated emotions. This is a very judgmental person. This is the development of the third function. This takes place from twelve to twenty-five years of age. The emotions that aid in its development are careless, indecisive, orderly and stubborn.

Judging: Judgment/ Intuition

This is the use of your moral thought.

    Careless- when you're angry you appear very snobbish.

    Indecisive- at your job you are very egotistical.

    Orderly- your home life is organized.

    Stubborn- when upset you are intolerant.

Leo is the element of fire. Fire and the element of air create a bonfire of emotions, rising given the temperament. This is the development of the second function auxiliary. This takes place from six to twelve years of age. The emotions that aid in its development are creativity, independence, intuition, and romantic.

Sensing: Vibes

This is the use of your analytical emotions.

    Creativity- you are very enthusiastic about life.

    Independence- you are conceited about your appearance.

    Intuition-you are very optimistic when it comes to your friends.

    Romantic- when in love you are dramatic.

Leo is the element of fire. Fire and water create a steam of emotions. This is the development of the fourth function. This takes place from twenty-five to fifty years of age. The emotions that aid in its development are accident prone, emotional, idealistic and intelligence.

Feeling: Emotions

This is the use of your moral emotions.

    Accident Prone- when expressing emotions you are attention-seeking.

    Emotional- when you feel loved you are generous.

    Idealistic- being powerful is a strength possessed.

        Intelligence- you are very broad-minded in the way you think.

Virgo- The Element of Earth

Virgo is the element of earth. Earth and the element of earth create a dusty sandstorm of emotions, blinding everyone in its path. This takes place from birth to six years of age. The emotions that aid in its development are cunning, diplomatic, inventive and perfectionist.

Thinking: Intelligence

This is the use of your analytical thought.

    Cunning- being prudish is a strength possessed.

    Diplomatic- when upset you are cranky.

Inventive- you are a busy body in your home life.

Perfectionist- you are a worrier when you feel loved.

Virgo is the element of earth. Earth and the element of fire create an eruption of emotions, burning and melting with words everyone in its path. This is the development of the second function auxiliary. This takes place from six to twelve years of age. The emotions that aid in its development are careless, indecisive, orderly and stubborn.

Judging: Judgment/ Intuition

This is the use of your moral thought.

Careless- you are neat in your appearance.

Indecisive- when angry you are grouchy.

Orderly- you are meticulous when it comes to money.

Stubborn- you are analytical in your view of family.

Virgo is the element of earth. Earth and the element of air create a tornado of emotions, thrashing and trashing everyone in its path. This is the development of the third function. This takes place from twelve to twenty-five years of age. The emotions that aid in its development are creativity, independence, intuition, and romantic.

Sensing: Vibes

This is the use of your analytical emotions.

Creativity- you are practical in the way you think.

Independence- at your job you are a workaholic.

Intuition- you are hypercritical in your view of life.

Romantic when in love you are a perfectionist.

Virgo is the element of earth. Earth and the element of water create a flood of emotions, drowning with words everyone in its path. This is the development of the fourth function. This takes place from twenty-five to fifty years of age. The emotions that aid in its development are accident prone, emotional, idealistic and intelligence.

Feeling: Emotions

This is the use of your moral emotions.

　　Accident Prone- when you face a difficult situation you are
　　　　fussy.

　　Emotional- when expressing your emotions you are pessimistic.

　　Idealistic- you are conscientious about your friends.

　　Intelligence- you are hypercritical in your view of the world.

Libra- The Element of Air

Libra is the element of air. Air and the element of earth create a tornado of emotions, thrashing and drowning with words everyone in its path. This takes place from birth to six years of age. The emotions that aid in its development are cunning, diplomatic, inventive and perfectionist.

Thinking: Intelligence

This is the use of your analytical thought.

Cunning- when you face a difficult situation you are charming.

Diplomatic- when upset you are diplomatic.

Inventive- you are changeable in your appearance.

Perfectionist- you are a seeker in harmony when it relates to the world.

Libra is the element of air. Air and the element of fire create a bonfire of emotions, rising given the words and temperament. This is the development of the second function auxiliary. This takes place from six to twelve years of age. The emotions that aid in its development are careless, indecisive, orderly and stubborn.

Judging: Judgment/ Intuition

This is the use of your moral thought.

Careless- you are extravagant when you have money.

Indecisive- when expressing emotions you are very indecisive and hard for you to make up your mind.

Orderly- your home life is orderly.

Stubborn- your view of life is easy going.

Libra is the element of air. Air and the element of air create a world wind of emotions; taking your breath away with words. This is the development of the third function. This takes place from twelve to twenty-five years of age. The emotions that aid in its development are creativity, independence, intuition, and romantic.

Sensing: Vibes

This is the use of your analytical emotions.

Creativity- when you feel loved you are flirtatious.

Independence- you are frivolous when it pertains to your
friends.

Intuition- being two faced is a strength possessed.

Romantic- when in love you are romantic.

Libra is the element of air. Air and the element of water create a
hurricane of emotions; thrashing and drowning with words
everyone in its path. This is the development of the fourth function.
This takes place from twenty-five to fifty years of age. The
emotions that aid in its development are accident prone, emotional,
idealistic and intelligence.

Feeling: Emotions

This is the use of your moral emotions.

Accident Prone- when angry you are resentful.

Emotional- you are gullible when it comes to your family.

Idealistic- your job is idealistic and you don't expect much.

Intelligence- you are refined in the way you think.

Scorpio- The Element of Water

Scorpio is the element of water. Water and the element of earth
create a flood of emotions, drowning with words everything in its
path. This takes place from birth to six years of age. The emotions
that aid in its development are cunning, diplomatic, inventive and

perfectionist.

Thinking: Intelligence

This is the use of your analytical thought.

Cunning- you are vengeful in your views of the world.

Diplomatic- when you face a difficult situation you are jealous.

Inventive- you are determined when it relates to your family.

Perfectionist- your home life is secretive.

Scorpio is the element of water. Water and the element of fire create a steam of emotions. This is the development of the second function auxiliary. This takes place from six to twelve years of age. The emotions that aid in its development are careless, indecisive, orderly and stubborn.

Judging: Judgment/ Intuition

This is the use of your moral thought.

Careless- when expressing emotions you are overly emotional.

Indecisive- you are energetic when it relates to your friends.

Orderly-being persistent is a strength possessed.

Stubborn-when upset you are stubborn.

Scorpio is the element of water. Water and the element of air create a hurricane of emotions, thrashing and drowning with words everyone in its path. This is the development of the third function. This takes place from twelve to twenty-five years of age. The emotions that aid in its development are creativity, independence, intuition, and romantic.

Sensing: Vibes

This is the use of your analytical emotions.

Creativity-you are creative in life.

Independence- you are independent in your job.

Intuition- you are very judgmental when you think.

Romantic- when in love you are passionate.

Scorpio is the element of water. Water and the element of water create a wave of emotions, crashing and drowning everyone in its path. This is the development of the fourth function. This takes place from twenty-five to fifty years of age. The emotions that aid in its development are accident prone, emotional, idealistic and intelligence.

Feeling: Emotions

This is the use of your moral emotions.

Accident Prone- you are violent when you are angry.

Emotional- when you feel loved you are emotional.

Idealistic- your appearance is practical.

Intelligence- you are very manipulative when it comes to money.

Sagittarius- The Element of Fire

Sagittarius is the element of fire. Fire and the element of earth create an eruption of emotions, burning and melting with words everyone in its path. This takes place from birth to six years of age. The emotions that aid in its development are cunning, diplomatic, inventive and perfectionist.

Thinking: Intelligence

This is the use of your analytical thought.

Cunning- when faced with a difficult situation you remain sincere.

Diplomatic-you are frivolous when you are upset.

Inventive- you are tactless in your appearance.

Perfectionist-you are undisciplined in your life.

Sagittarius is the element of fire. Fire and the element of fire create heated emotions, burning with words everything in its path. This is a very judgmental person. This is the development of the second function auxiliary. This takes place from six to twelve years of age. The emotions that aid in its development are careless, indecisive, orderly and stubborn.

Judging: Judgment/ Intuition

This is the use of your moral thought.

Careless- you are careless in the way you think.

Indecisive- when expressing emotions you are frank and give short answers.

Orderly- your home life is restless.

Stubborn- you are exaggerative when you have money.

Sagittarius is the element of fire. Fire and the element of air create a bonfire of emotions, rising given the words and temperament. This is the development of the third function. This takes place from twelve to twenty-five years of age. The emotions that aid in its development are creativity, independence, intuition, and romantic.

Sensing: Vibes

This is the use of your analytical emotions.

Creativity- you are erratic when upset.

Independence- you are free spirited in your view of the world.

Intuition- being optimistic is a strength you possess.

Romantic-when in love you are very passionate.

Sagittarius is the element of fire. Fire and the element of water create a steam of emotions, bursting with cloudy judgment toward everyone in its path. This is the development of the fourth function. This takes place from twenty-five to fifty years of age. The emotions that aid in its development are accident prone, emotional, idealistic and intelligence.

Feeling: Emotions

This is the use of your moral emotions.

Accident Prone- you are irresponsible when it pertains to family.

Emotional-when you feel loved you are ambitious.

Idealistic-you are very dependable when it pertains to friends.

Intelligence- you are energetic when it pertains to your job.

Capricorn- The Element of Earth

Capricorn is the element of earth. Earth and the element of earth create a dusty, sandstorm of emotions, blinding everyone with words in its path. This takes place from birth to six years of age. The emotions that aid in its development are cunning, diplomatic, inventive and perfectionist.

Thinking: Intelligence

This is the use of your analytical thought.

Cunning-you are opportunistic when it pertains to money.

Diplomatic- you are prudent in the way you think.

Inventive- you are reliable when it pertains to family.

Perfectionist- you are overly ordinary in your life.

Capricorn is the element of earth. Earth and the element of fire create an eruption of emotions, burning and melting with words everyone in its path. This is the development of the second function auxiliary. This takes place from six to twelve years of age. The emotions that aid in its development are careless, indecisive, orderly and stubborn.

Judging: Judgment/ Intuition

This is the use of your moral thought.

Careless- when upset you are mean.

Indecisive- when you feel loved you are determined.

Orderly- your home life is organized.

Stubborn- when you face a difficult situation you are rigid.

Capricorn is the element of earth. Earth and the element of air create a tornado of emotions, thrashing and trashing with words everyone in its sight. This is the development of the third function. This takes place from twelve to twenty-five years of age. The emotions that aid in its development are creativity, independence, intuition, and romantic.

Sensing: Vibes

This is the use of your analytical emotions.

Creativity-you are ambitious about doing your job.

Independence- you are comfortable in your appearance.

Intuition- when in love you are generous.

Romantic-you are patient in your view of the world.

Capricorn is the element of earth. Earth and the element of water create a flood of emotions, drowning with words everything in its path. This is the development of the fourth function. This takes place from twenty-five to fifty years of age. The emotions that aid in its development are accident prone, emotional, idealistic and intelligence.

Feeling: Emotions

This is the use of your moral emotions.

Accident Prone- you are a social climber when it pertains to friends.

Emotional- you are miserly at expressing emotions.

Idealistic- having a sense of humor is a strength you possess.

Intelligence- when you are angry you are a nit-picker and you pick the least important thing to argue about.

Aquarius- The Element of Air

Aquarius is the element of air. Air and the element of earth create a tornado of emotions, thrashing and trashing with words everyone in its sight. This takes place from birth to six years of age. The emotions that aid in its development are cunning, diplomatic, inventive and perfectionist.

Thinking: Intelligence

This is the use of your analytical thought.

Cunning- when angry you are unpredictable.

Diplomatic- you are human in your view of the world.

Inventive- being inventive is a strength you possess.

Perfectionist- when in love you are charismatic.

Aquarius is the element of air. Air and the element of fire create a bonfire of emotions, rising given the words and temperament. This is the development of the second function auxiliary. This takes place from six to twelve years of age. The emotions that aid in its development are careless, indecisive, orderly and stubborn.

Judging: Judgment/ Intuition

This is the use of your moral thought.

Careless- your home life is disorganized.

Indecisive- you are impulsive in your life.

Orderly- you are neat in appearance.

Stubborn- you are rebellious when you face a difficult situation.

Aquarius is the element of air. Air and the element of air create a world wind of emotions, taking your breath away with words. This is the development of the third function. This takes place from twelve to twenty-five years of age. The emotions that aid in its development are creativity, independence, intuition, and romantic.

Sensing: Vibes

This is the use of your analytical emotions.

Creativity- you are eccentric when it pertains to family and there is no one like you.

Independence- you are independent at your job.

Intuition- you are judgmental in the way you think.

Romantic-when you feel loved you are perverse.

Aquarius is the element of air. Air and the element of water create a hurricane of emotions, thrashing and drowning with words everyone in its path. This is the development of the fourth function. This takes place from twenty-five to fifty years of age. The emotions that aid in its development are accident prone, emotional, idealistic and intelligence.

Feeling: Emotions

This is the use of your moral emotions.

Accident Prone- you are tactless when it pertains to friends.

Emotional- when expressing emotions you are friendly.

Idealistic-you are idealistic when it pertains to money.

Intelligence- when upset you are intelligent.

Pisces- The Element of Water

Pisces is the element of water. Water and the element of earth create a flood of emotions, drowning with words everything in its path. This takes place from birth to six years of age. The emotions that aid in its development are cunning, diplomatic, inventive and perfectionist.

Thinking: Intelligence

This is the use of your analytical thought.

Cunning- when faced with a difficult situation you are secretive.

Diplomatic- you are compassionate in your view of the world.

Inventive-you are imaginative when it pertains to money.

Perfectionist- you are impressionable in your life.

Pisces is the element of water. Water and the element of fire create a steam of emotions; bursting with cloudy judgment toward everyone in its path. This is the development of the second function auxiliary. This takes place from six to twelve years of age. The emotions that aid in its development are careless, indecisive, orderly and stubborn.

Judging: Judgment/ Intuition

This is the use of your moral thought.

Careless- you are careless when it pertains to family.

Indecisive- when expressing emotions you are indecisive.

Orderly- you are receptive at your job.

Stubborn- when you are angry you are vague and don't reveal a lot of information as to why you feel the way you do.

Pisces is the element of water. Water and the element of air create a hurricane of emotions, thrashing and drowning with words everyone in its path. This is the development of the third function. This takes place from twelve to twenty-five years of age. The emotions that aid in its development are creativity, independence, intuition, and romantic.

Sensing: Vibes

This is the use of your analytical emotions.

Creativity- you are sensitive when it pertains to friends.

Independence- you are mysterious in your appearance.

Intuition- being judgmental is a strength possessed.

Romantic- when in love you are romantic.

Pisces is the element of water. Water and the element of water create a wave of emotions, crashing and drowning everyone in its path. This is the development of the fourth function. This takes place from twenty-five to fifty years of age. The emotions that aid in its development are accident prone, emotional, idealistic and intelligence.

Feeling: Emotions

This is the use of your moral emotions.

Accident Prone- when you feel loved you are weak-willed.

Emotional-when upset you are emotional.

Idealistic- you are compassionate in your view of the world.

Intelligence- you are unworldly in the way you think.

Chapter 7: ISTJ & ESTP
Vibes, Intelligence, Emotions, and Judgment

Masculine Sexuality Type
ISTJ (Sense as a sensor, think as an introvert, feel as a feeler and judger as a judger)

Sensing (Feminine)

Intuition- you trust what is certain, can be proven and you present information in a step-by-step manner.

Independence- you are knowledgeable of your established skills and make a judgment by the facts you gather.

Creativity- you like new ideas only if they have practical applications and tend to be specific and literal about giving a detailed description.

Romantic- you value realism and common sense and are oriented towards the present.

Behavior: Illusionist

My natural temperament of air uses the element of my vibes that I pick up on from my sight, smelling, hearing, tasting, and touching to create an attitude of being sensitive to activate the action of my perception which effects my function sensing which leads to the behavior of being an illusionist. This behavioral person is a natural liar and their work has to have some form of illusions in it or they just won't be happy.

Thinking (Masculine)

Cunning-you are private and are energized by spending time alone, you like to think things through inside your head and you share personal info with a select few people.

Inventive- you avoid being the center of attention and keep your enthusiasm to yourself.

Diplomatic- you think more than you react to any given situation and you prefer knowing more information than a little.

Perfectionist- you listen more than you talk and respond after taking the time to think things through inside your head.

Behavior: Impatient/ Rationalist

My natural temperament of earth uses the element of my intelligence to create an attitude of being intelligent to activate the action of my extroversion which effects my function of thinking which leads to the behavior of being a rationalist of impatient. This behavioral person is unable to wait patiently. They can't endure irritation for long periods of time. They have the ability to reason. They are always on a quest for truth even when the truth is laid out honestly before them. They have a natural desire to constantly search things over for truth. They believe "reason" to be the main source of knowledge and spiritual truth meaning because you have asked the question of "why" this brings about intelligence.

Feeling (Masculine)

Intelligence- you consider it important to be tactful as well as truthful. You step forward and consider the effects of your actions on others.

Idealistic- you show appreciation easily to others and believe any feeling is valid whether it makes sense or not. You naturally like to please others and may need to be encouraged to have own needs met.

Emotional- you value empathy and harmony but see the exception to the rule when it pertains to your own feelings. You make judgment based on your own feelings and values but you are people oriented and aware of others feelings. You are happiest in friendly, supportive, and cooperative environments.

Accident Prone- You may be seen as overemotional, illogical, and weak. You are an impatient person but are motivated by a desire to be appreciated.

Behavior: Patient

My natural temperament of water uses the element of my emotions to create an attitude of being emotional to activate the action of my introversion which effects my function of feeling which leads to the behavior of being patient. This behavioral person is very calm and capable of handling all. They have a high tolerance of bearing even the most difficult of challenges. They are very understanding and their for you as an individual.

Judging (Feminine)

Indecisive- Have trouble keeping on track or following directions.
Careless- you are product oriented and less likely to deal with specifics because your emphasis is on completing the task and you prefer to focus on the big picture.
Orderly- you prefer to make plans and follow them accordingly. You are usually well organized. You set goals and work toward achieving them on time and are happiest after final decisions have been made and feel satisfaction from finishing the projects.
Stubborn- you have a work ethic, work first play later, and prefer to know what you are getting into.

Behavior: Realistic
My natural temperament of fire uses the element of my judgment to created an attitude of being judgmental to activate the action of

my intuition which effects my function of judging which leads to the behavior of being realistic. This behavioral person is a natural truth teller and their work has to tell things as they naturally are or they will not be content. They love representing the truth as described.

Feminine Sexuality Type
ESTP (Sense as a perceiver, think as a thinker, feel as an extrovert and judge as a judger)

Sensing (Masculine)

Creativity- you are better at concentration exercises than fantasy or daydreaming. You have a play ethic, enjoy now and finish the job later, and enjoy exercises that allow you to learn new thing and have fun doing it. You are process oriented and your emphasis is on how the task is completed.

Intuition- you are influenced by past experiences and this is your knowledge of doing things. You don't like to brainstorm for answers and are happiest leaving your options open. You change goals as new information becomes available and prefer to not decide but continue to collect information for later usage.

Romantic-you feel satisfaction from starting projects and see time as a renewable resource and set deadlines.

Independence- you are flexible, adaptable, and change gears quickly so that you may be available for many different approaches and techniques. You have a natural curiosity and like adapting to new situations.

Behavior: Illusionist

My natural temperament of air uses the element of my vibes that I pick up on from my sight, smelling, hearing, tasting, and touching to create an attitude of being sensitive to activate the action of my perception which effects my function sensing which leads to the behavior of being an illusionist. This behavioral person is a natural liar and their work has to have some form of illusions in it or they just won't be happy.

Thinking (Feminine)

Diplomatic- You value logic, justice and fairness which to you is one standard for all. You step back and try to see the situation objectively before problem solving. You feel the need to be convinced that a specific event or activity makes sense before you will even believe.

Perfectionist- you naturally see flaws and tend to be critical of others and believe it is more important to be truthful than tactful. Believe others feelings are irrelevant to the situation at hand.

Inventive- Believe feelings are valid only if they are logical. You are motivated by a desire for achievement and accomplishment but have a hard time translating ideas into active steps.

Cunning- you may be seen as heartless, Insensitive and uncaring but are impressed by competence and the end result.

Behavior: Impatient/ Rationalist

My natural temperament of earth uses the element of my intelligence to create an attitude of being intelligent to activate the action of my extroversion which effects my function of thinking which leads to the behavior of being a rationalist of impatient. This behavioral person is unable to wait patiently. They can't endure irritation for long periods of time. They have the ability to reason. They are always on a quest for truth even when the truth is laid out honestly before them. They have a natural desire to constantly search things over for truth. They believe "reason" to be the main source of knowledge and spiritual truth meaning because you have asked the question of "why" this brings about intelligence.

Feeling (Feminine)

Emotional- being with others energizes you. You react more than you think and you communicate to others with enthusiasm.

Accident Prone- You respond quickly without hearing the whole conversation. you enjoy being the center of attention, and enjoy a fast pace.

Idealistic- you think out loud and are easier to know and read. You were your emotions on your sleeve and talk with your body language. When your emotions have been hurt you feel the need to voice your opinion and you share personal information freely and sometimes without enough forethought.

Intelligence- you talk more than you listen and prefer to know a little information rather than it all.

Behavior: <u>Patient</u>

My natural temperament of water uses the element of my emotions to create an attitude of being emotional to activate the action of my introversion which effects my function of feeling which leads to the behavior of being patient. This behavioral person is very calm and capable of handling all. They have a high tolerance of bearing even the most difficult of challenges. They are very understanding and their for you as an individual.

<u>Judging (Feminine)</u>

Indecisive- Have trouble keeping on track or following directions.

Careless- you are product oriented and less likely to deal with specifics because your emphasis is on completing the task and you prefer to focus on the big picture.

Orderly- you prefer to make plans and follow them accordingly.

You are usually well organized. You set goals and work toward achieving them on time and are happiest after final decisions have been made and feel satisfaction from finishing the projects.

Stubborn- you have a work ethic, work first play later, and prefer to know what you are getting into.

Behavior: Realistic

My natural temperament of fire uses the element of my judgment to created an attitude of being judgmental to activate the action of my intuition which effects my function of judging which leads to the behavior of being realistic. This behavioral person is a natural truth teller and their work has to tell things as they naturally are or they will not be content. They love representing the truth as described.

Aries- The Element of Fire

Aries is the element of fire. Fire and the element of Air create a bonfire of emotions, rising giving the temperaments. This is the development of the dominant function and one of your strengths. This takes place from birth to six years of age. The emotions that aid in its development are creativity, independence, intuition, and romantic.

Sensing: Vibes

This is the use of your analytical emotions.

Creativity-your optimistic as it pertains to your friends

Independence- you're courageous when you face a difficult

situation.

Intuition- you're a free spirit in your view of the world.

Romantic- your impatient when you feel loved.

Aries is the element of fire. Fire and element of earth create an eruption of emotions, burning everything and everyone, which crosses its path. This is the development of the auxiliary function. This takes place from six to twelve years of age. The four emotions, which aid in the growth of your intelligence are cunning, diplomatic, inventive and perfectionist.

Thinking: Intelligence

This is the use of your analytical thought.

Cunning- your adventuresome as it pertains to life shows cunning.

Diplomatic- your enthusiastic when experiencing love.

Inventive- your impulsive as it pertains to their appearance.

Perfectionist- you're innovative in your home life.

Aries is the element of fire. Fire and the element of water create a steam of emotions, bursting with cloudy judgment toward everyone in its path. This is the development of the third function. This takes place from twelve to twenty-five years of age. The emotions that aid in its development are accident prone, emotional, idealistic, and intelligence.

Feeling: Emotions

This is the use of your moral emotions.

Accident prone- your accident prone when your upset.

Emotional- you're quick tempered when you're angry.

Idealistic- being assertive is a strength you possess.

Intelligence- you're very tactless in the way you think.

Aries is the element of fire. Fire and the element of Fire create heated emotions. This is the development of the fourth function, which takes place from twenty five to fifty years of age. The emotions that aid in its development are careless, indecisive, orderly, and stubborn.

Judging: Judgment/ Intuition

This is the use of your moral thought.

Careless- you're a procrastinator as it relates to your family.

Indecisive- you are energetic about doing your job.

Orderly- you are selfish when it comes to money.

Stubborn- you are self-centered when expressing your emotions.

Taurus- The Element of Earth

Taurus is the element of the earth. Earth and the element of air create a tornado of emotions, thrashing and trashing everything in its sight. . This is the development of the dominant function, which takes place from birth to six years of age. The emotions that aid in its development are creativity, independence, intuition and romantic.

Sensing: Vibes

This is the use of your analytical emotions.

> Creativity-Your very solid in your view of life shows creativity.
>
> Independence- you're very persistent about doing your job.
>
> Intuition- when it comes to money you're very trustworthy.
>
> Romantic- you're very affectionate when you feel loved.

Taurus is the element of the earth. Earth and the element of earth produce a dusty sandstorm of emotions. Blinding everyone in sight. This is the development of the auxiliary function. This takes place from six to twelve years of age. The emotions that aid in its development are cunning, diplomatic, inventive and perfectionist.

Thinking: Intelligence

This is the use of your analytical thought.

> Cunning- when you face a difficult situation you're very resentful.
>
> Diplomatic- you are set in your ways when you think.
>
> Inventive- When upset you are very inflexible.
>
> Perfectionist- you are very reliable when it comes to your friends.

Taurus is the element of the earth. Earth and the element of water create a flood of emotions; drowning everything in its path. This is the development of the third function. This takes place from twelve to twenty-five years of age. The emotions that aid in its development are accident prone, emotional, idealistic and intelligence.

Feeling: Emotions

This is the use of your moral emotions.

> Accident Prone- you are violent when you are angry.
>
> Emotional- you are greedy when in love.
>
> Idealistic- you are warm hearted when it relates to your family.
>
> Intelligence- being strong- willed is a strength you possess.

Taurus is the element of the earth. Earth and the element of fire create an eruption of emotions. This is the development of the fourth function. This takes place from twenty five to fifty years of age. The emotions that aid in its development are careless, indecisive, orderly and stubborn.

Judging: Judgment/ Intuition

This is the use of your moral thought.

> Careless- you're very practical in your views concerning home life.
>
> Indecisive- when expressing emotions you are very lazy.

Orderly- you are very possessive about your
appearance.

Stubborn- you are very stubborn in your views of the
world.

Gemini- The Element of Air

Gemini is the element of air. Air and the element of air create a
world wind of emotions. This is the development of the dominant
function. This takes place from birth to six years of age. The
emotions that aid in its development are creativity, independence,
intuition and romantic.

Sensing: Vibes

This is the use of analytical emotions.

Creativity- you are very energetic when it pertains to your
friends.

Independence- you are adaptable as it relates to your job.

Intuition- being an intellectual is a strength possessed.

Romantic- you are very witty when in love.

Gemini is the element of air. Air and the element of earth create a
tornado of emotions, thrashing and trashing everything in its sight.
This is the development of the auxiliary function. This takes place
from six to twelve years of age. The emotions that aid in its
development are cunning, diplomatic, inventive and perfectionist.

Thinking: Intelligence

This is the use of analytical thought.

Cunning- you are very cunning when you are upset.

Diplomatic- when you are angry you are very devious.

Inventive- you are a communicator about the way you think.

Perfectionist- you can be very versatile when in love.

Gemini is the element of air. Air and the element of water create a hurricane of emotions. This is the development of the third function. This takes place from twelve to twenty-five years of age. The emotions that aid in its development are accident prone, emotional, idealistic and intelligence.

Feeling: Emotions

This is the use of moral emotions.

Accident Prone- you are very restless when it pertains to your family.

Emotional- you are nosey when you face a difficult situation.

Idealistic- you are very flighty in your appearance.

Intelligence- you are very spontaneous in your views of life.

Gemini is the element of air. Air and the element of fire create a bonfire of emotions, rising given the temperament. This is the development of the fourth function. This takes place from twenty five to fifty years of age. The emotions that aid in its development

are careless, indecisive, orderly and stubborn.

Judging: Judgment/ Intuition

This is the use of moral thought.

Careless-you are very secretive about your view of the world.

Indecisive- you can be superficial when it pertains to money.

Orderly-you are logical in your home life.

Stubborn- you are inconsistent when expressing your emotions.

Cancer- The Element of Water

Cancer is the element of water. Water and the element of air create a hurricane of emotions. . This is the development of the dominant function. This takes place from birth to six years of age. The emotions that aid in its development are creativity, independence, intuition, and romantic.

Sensing: Vibes

This is the use of analytical emotions.

Creativity- you're very kind to your friends.

Independence- your job is very messy.

Intuition- you're very judgmental in your views of life.

Romantic- when in love you can be overly emotional.

Cancer is the element of water. Water and the element of earth create a flood of emotions, drowning everything in its path. This is the development of the second function auxiliary. This takes place from six to twelve years of age. The emotions that aid in its

development are cunning, diplomatic, inventive and perfectionist.

Thinking: Intelligence

This is the use of analytical thought.

Cunning- being sympathetic is a strength possessed.

Diplomatic- when expressing emotions you can be over indulgent in self-pity.

Inventive- you are very receptive when you think.

Perfectionist- when you feel loved you can be moody.

Cancer is the element of water. Water and the element of water create a wave of emotions This is the development of the third function. This takes place from twelve to twenty-five years of age. The emotions that aid in its development are accident prone, emotional, idealistic and intelligence.

Feeling: Emotions

This is the use of moral emotions.

Accident Prone-you are hyper sensitive when it pertains to family.

Emotional- when you face a difficult situation you can be very emotional.

Idealistic- you are thrifty when it pertains to money.

Intelligence- you are sensitive in your view of the world.

Cancer is the element of water. Water and the element of fire create a steam of emotions. This is the development of the fourth function. This takes place from twenty five to fifty years of age. The emotions that aid in its development are careless, indecisive, orderly and stubborn.

Judging: Judgment/ Intuition

This is the use of moral thought.

    Careless- you are very shrewd when you are angry.

    Indecisive- your home life is very unstable.

    Orderly- your appearance is changeable.

    Stubborn- when upset you are unforgiving.

Leo- The Element of Fire

Leo is the element of fire. Fire and the element of air create a bonfire of emotions, rising given the temperament. This is the development of the dominant function. This takes place from birth to six years of age. The emotions that aid in its development are creativity, independence, intuition, and romantic.

Sensing: Vibes

This is the use of your analytical emotions.

    Creativity- you are very enthusiastic about life.

    Independence- you are conceited about your appearance.

    Intuition-you are very optimistic when it comes to your friends.

    Romantic- when in love you are dramatic.

Leo is the element of fire. Fire and the element of earth create an eruption of emotions. This is the development of the second function auxiliary. This takes place from six to twelve years of age. The emotions that aid in its development are cunning, diplomatic, inventive and perfectionist.

Thinking: Intelligence

This is the use of your analytical thought.

Cunning- you are patronizing when it relates to your family.

Diplomatic- when you face a difficult situation you are dogmatic.

Inventive- your view of the world is creative.

Perfectionist- when it comes to money you are extravagant.

Leo is the element of fire. Fire and water create a steam of emotions. This is the development of the third function. This takes place from twelve to twenty-five years of age. The emotions that aid in its development are accident prone, emotional, idealistic and intelligence.

Feeling: Emotions

This is the use of your moral emotions.

Accident Prone- when expressing emotions you are attention-seeking.

Emotional- when you feel loved you are generous.

Idealistic- being powerful is a strength possessed.

Intelligence- you are very broad-minded in the way you think.

Leo is the element of fire. Fire and the element of fire create heated emotions. This is a very judgmental person. This is the development of the fourth function. This takes place from twenty five to fifty years of age. The emotions that aid in its development are careless, indecisive, orderly and stubborn.

Judging: Judgment/ Intuition

This is the use of your moral thought.

Careless- when you're angry you appear very snobbish.

Indecisive- at your job you are very egotistical.

Orderly- your home life is organized.

Stubborn- when upset you are intolerant.

Virgo- The Element of Earth

Virgo is the element of earth. Earth and the element of air create a tornado of emotions, thrashing and trashing everyone in its path. This is the development of the dominant function. This takes place from birth to six years of age. The emotions that aid in its development are creativity, independence, intuition, and romantic.

Sensing: Vibes

This is the use of your analytical emotions.

Creativity- you are practical in the way you think.

Independence- at your job you are a workaholic.

Intuition- you are hypercritical in your view of life.

Romantic- when in love you are a perfectionist.

Virgo is the element of earth. Earth and the element of earth create a dusty sandstorm of emotions, blinding everyone in its path. This is the development of the second function auxiliary. This takes place from six to twelve years of age. The emotions that aid in its development are cunning, diplomatic, inventive and perfectionist.

Thinking: Intelligence

This is the use of your analytical thought.

Cunning- being prudish is a strength possessed.

Diplomatic- when upset you are cranky.

Inventive- you are a busy body in your home life.

Perfectionist- you are a worrier when you feel loved.

Virgo is the element of earth. Earth and the element of water create a flood of emotions, drowning with words everyone in its path. This is the development of the third function. This takes place from twelve to twenty-five years of age. The emotions that aid in its development are accident prone, emotional, idealistic and intelligence.

Feeling: Emotions

This is the use of your moral emotions.

Accident Prone- when you face a difficult situation you are fussy.

Emotional- when expressing your emotions you are pessimistic.

Idealistic- you are conscientious about your friends.

Intelligence- you are hypercritical in your view of the world.

Virgo is the element of earth. Earth and the element of fire create an eruption of emotions, burning and melting with words everyone in its path. This is the development of the fourth function. This takes place from birth to six years of age. The emotions that aid in its development are careless, indecisive, orderly and stubborn.

Judging: Judgment/ Intuition

This is the use of your moral thought.

Careless- you are neat in your appearance.

Indecisive- when angry you are grouchy.

Orderly- you are meticulous when it comes to money.

Stubborn- you are analytical in your view of family.

Libra- The Element of Air

Libra is the element of air. Air and the element of air create a world wind of emotions; taking your breath away with words. This is the development of the dominant function. This takes place from birth to six years of age. The emotions that aid in its development are creativity, independence, intuition, and romantic.

Sensing: Vibes

This is the use of your analytical emotions.

Creativity- when you feel loved you are flirtatious.

Independence- you are frivolous when it pertains to your friends.

Intuition- being two faced is a strength possessed.

Romantic- when in love you are romantic.

Libra is the element of air. Air and the element of earth create a tornado of emotions, thrashing and drowning with words everyone in its path. This is the development of the second function auxiliary. This takes place from six to twelve years of age. The emotions that aid in its development are cunning, diplomatic, inventive and perfectionist.

Thinking: Intelligence

This is the use of your analytical thought.

Cunning- when you face a difficult situation you are charming.

Diplomatic- when upset you are diplomatic.

Inventive- you are changeable in your appearance.

Perfectionist- you are a seeker in harmony when it relates to the world.

Libra is the element of air. Air and the element of water create a hurricane of emotions; thrashing and drowning with words everyone in its path. This is the development of the third function. This takes place from twelve to twenty-five years of age. The emotions that aid in its development are accident prone, emotional, idealistic and intelligence.

Feeling: Emotions

This is the use of your moral emotions.

Accident Prone- when angry you are resentful.

Emotional- you are gullible when it comes to your family.

Idealistic- your job is idealistic and you don't expect much.

Intelligence- you are refined in the way you think.

Libra is the element of air. Air and the element of fire create a bonfire of emotions, rising given the words and temperament. This is the development of the fourth function. This takes place from twenty five to fifty years of age. The emotions that aid in its development are careless, indecisive, orderly and stubborn.

Judging: Judgment/ Intuition

This is the use of your moral thought.

Careless- you are extravagant when you have money.

Indecisive- when expressing emotions you are very indecisive and hard for you to make up your mind.

Orderly- your home life is orderly.

Stubborn- your view of life is easy going.

Scorpio- The Element of Water

Scorpio is the element of water. Water and the element of air create a hurricane of emotions, thrashing and drowning with words everyone in its path. This is the development of the dominant function. This takes place from birth to six years of age. The emotions that aid in its development are creativity, independence, intuition, and romantic.

Sensing: Vibes

This is the use of your analytical emotions.

Creativity-you are creative in life.

Independence- you are independent in your job.

Intuition- you are very judgmental when you think.

Romantic- when in love you are passionate.

Scorpio is the element of water. Water and the element of earth create a flood of emotions, drowning with words everything in its path. This is the development of the second function auxiliary. This takes place from six to twelve years of age. The emotions that aid in its development are cunning, diplomatic, inventive and perfectionist.

Thinking: Intelligence

This is the use of your analytical thought.

Cunning- you are vengeful in your views of the world.

Diplomatic- when you face a difficult situation you are jealous.

Inventive- you are determined when it relates to your family.

Perfectionist- your home life is secretive.

Scorpio is the element of water. Water and the element of water create a wave of emotions, crashing and drowning everyone in its path. This is the development of the third function. This takes place from twelve to twenty-five years of age. The emotions that aid in its development are accident prone, emotional, idealistic and intelligence.

Feeling: Emotions

This is the use of your moral emotions.

Accident Prone- you are violent when you are angry.

Emotional- when you feel loved you are emotional.

Idealistic- your appearance is practical.

Intelligence- you are very manipulative when it comes to money.

Scorpio is the element of water. Water and the element of fire create a steam of emotions. This is the development of the fourth function. This takes place from twenty five to fifty years of age. The emotions that aid in its development are careless, indecisive, orderly and stubborn.

Judging: Judgment/ Intuition

This is the use of your moral thought.

Careless- when expressing emotions you are overly emotional.

Indecisive- you are energetic when it relates to your friends.

Orderly-being persistent is a strength possessed.

Stubborn-when upset you are stubborn.

Sagittarius- The Element of Fire

Sagittarius is the element of fire. Fire and the element of air create a bonfire of emotions, rising given the words and temperament. This is the development of the dominant function. This takes place from birth to six years of age. The emotions that aid in its development are creativity, independence, intuition, and romantic.

Sensing: Vibes

This is the use of your analytical emotions.

Creativity- you are erratic when upset.

Independence- you are free spirited in your view of the world.

Intuition- being optimistic is a strength you possess.

Romantic-when in love you are very passionate.

Sagittarius is the element of fire. Fire and the element of earth create an eruption of emotions, burning and melting with words everyone in its path. This is the development of the second function auxiliary. This takes place from six to twelve years of age. The emotions that aid in its development are cunning, diplomatic, inventive and perfectionist.

Thinking: Intelligence

This is the use of your analytical thought.

Cunning- when faced with a difficult situation you remain sincere.

Diplomatic-you are frivolous when you are upset.

Inventive- you are tactless in your appearance.

Perfectionist-you are undisciplined in your life.

Sagittarius is the element of fire. Fire and the element of water create a steam of emotions, bursting with cloudy judgment toward everyone in its path. This is the development of the third function. This takes place from twelve to twenty-five years of age. The emotions that aid in its development are accident prone, emotional, idealistic and intelligence.

Feeling: Emotions

This is the use of your moral emotions.

Accident Prone- you are irresponsible when it pertains to family.

Emotional-when you feel loved you are ambitious.

Idealistic-you are very dependable when it pertains to friends.

Intelligence- you are energetic when it pertains to your job.

Sagittarius is the element of fire. Fire and the element of fire create heated emotions, burning with words everything in its path. This is a very judgmental person. This is the development of the fourth function. This takes place from twenty five to fifty years of age. The emotions that aid in its development are careless, indecisive, orderly and stubborn.

Judging: Judgment/ Intuition

This is the use of your moral thought.

Careless- you are careless in the way you think.

Indecisive- when expressing emotions you are frank and give short answers.

Orderly- your home life is restless.

Stubborn- you are exaggerative when you have money.

Capricorn- The Element of Earth

Capricorn is the element of earth. Earth and the element of air create a tornado of emotions, thrashing and trashing with words everyone in its sight. This is the development of the dominant function. This takes place from birth to six years of age. The emotions that aid in its development are creativity, independence, intuition, and romantic.

Sensing: Vibes

This is the use of your analytical emotions.

Creativity-you are ambitious about doing your job.

Independence- you are comfortable in your appearance.

Intuition- when in love you are generous.

Romantic-you are patient in your view of the world.

Capricorn is the element of earth. Earth and the element of earth create a dusty, sandstorm of emotions, blinding everyone with words in its path. This is the development of the second function auxiliary. This takes place from six to twelve years of age. The emotions that aid in its development are cunning, diplomatic, inventive and perfectionist.

Thinking: Intelligence

This is the use of your analytical thought.

Cunning-you are opportunistic when it pertains to money.

Diplomatic- you are prudent in the way you think.

Inventive- you are reliable when it pertains to family.

Perfectionist- you are overly ordinary in your life.

Capricorn is the element of earth. Earth and the element of water create a flood of emotions, drowning with words everything in its path. This is the development of the third function. This takes place from twelve to twenty-five years of age. The emotions that aid in its development are accident prone, emotional, idealistic and intelligence.

Feeling: Emotions

This is the use of your moral emotions.

Accident Prone- you are a social climber when it pertains to friends.

Emotional- you are miserly at expressing emotions.

Idealistic- having a sense of humor is a strength you possess.

Intelligence- when you are angry you are a nit-picker and you pick the least important thing to argue about.

Capricorn is the element of earth. Earth and the element of fire create an eruption of emotions, burning and melting with words everyone in its path. This is the development of the fourth function. This takes place from twenty five to fifty years of age. The emotions that aid in its development are careless, indecisive, orderly and stubborn.

Judging: Judgment/ Intuition

This is the use of your moral thought.

Careless- when upset you are mean.

Indecisive- when you feel loved you are determined.

Orderly- your home life is organized.

Stubborn- when you face a difficult situation you are rigid.

Aquarius- The Element of Air

Aquarius is the element of air. Air and the element of air create a wurl wind of emotions, taking your breath away with words. This is the development of the dominant function. This takes place from birth to six years of age. The emotions that aid in its development are creativity, independence, intuition, and romantic.

Sensing: Vibes

This is the use of your analytical emotions.

Creativity- you are eccentric when it pertains to family and there is no one like you.

Independence- you are independent at your job.

Intuition- you are judgmental in the way you think.

Romantic-when you feel loved you are perverse.

Aquarius is the element of air. Air and the element of earth create a tornado of emotions, thrashing and trashing with words everyone in its sight. This is the development of the second function auxiliary. This takes place from six to twelve years of age. The emotions that aid in its development are cunning, diplomatic, inventive and perfectionist.

Thinking: Intelligence

This is the use of your analytical thought.

Cunning- when angry you are unpredictable.

Diplomatic- you are human in your view of the world.

Inventive- being inventive is a strength you possess.

Perfectionist- when in love you are charismatic.

Aquarius is the element of air. Air and the element of water create a hurricane of emotions, thrashing and drowning with words everyone in its path. This is the development of the third function. This takes place from twelve to twenty-five years of age. The emotions that aid in its development are accident prone, emotional, idealistic and intelligence.

Feeling: Emotions

This is the use of your moral emotions.

Accident Prone- you are tactless when it pertains to friends.

Emotional- when expressing emotions you are friendly.

Idealistic-you are idealistic when it pertains to money.

Intelligence- when upset you are intelligent.

Aquarius is the element of air. Air and the element of fire create a bonfire of emotions, rising given the words and temperament. This is the development of the fourth function. This takes place from twenty five to fifty years of age. The emotions that aid in its development are careless, indecisive, orderly and stubborn.

Judging: Judgment/ Intuition

This is the use of your moral thought.

Careless- your home life is disorganized.

Indecisive- you are impulsive in your life.

Orderly- you are neat in appearance.

Stubborn- you are rebellious when you face a difficult situation.

Pisces- The Element of Water

Pisces is the element of water. Water and the element of air create a hurricane of emotions, thrashing and drowning with words everyone in its path. This is the development of the dominant function. This takes place from birth to six years of age. The emotions that aid in its development are creativity, independence, intuition, and romantic.

Sensing: Vibes

This is the use of your analytical emotions.

Creativity- you are sensitive when it pertains to friends.

Independence- you are mysterious in your appearance.

Intuition- being judgmental is a strength possessed.

Romantic- when in love you are romantic.

Pisces is the element of water. Water and the element of earth create a flood of emotions, drowning with words everything in its path. This is the development of the second function auxiliary. This takes place from six to twelve years of age. The emotions that aid in its development are cunning, diplomatic, inventive and perfectionist.

Thinking: Intelligence

This is the use of your analytical thought.

Cunning- when faced with a difficult situation you are secretive.

Diplomatic- you are compassionate in your view of the world.

Inventive-you are imaginative when it pertains to money.

Perfectionist- you are impressionable in your life.

Pisces is the element of water. Water and the element of water create a wave of emotions, crashing and drowning everyone in its path. This is the development of the third function. This takes place from twelve to twenty-five years of age. The emotions that aid in its development are accident prone, emotional, idealistic and intelligence.

Feeling: Emotions

This is the use of your moral emotions.

Accident Prone- when you feel loved you are weak-willed.

Emotional-when upset you are emotional.

Idealistic- you are compassionate in your view of the world.

Intelligence- you are unworldly in the way you think.

Pisces is the element of water. Water and the element of fire create a steam of emotions; bursting with cloudy judgment toward everyone in its path. This is the development of the fourth function. This takes place from twenty five to fifty years of age. The emotions that aid in its development are careless, indecisive, orderly and stubborn.

Judging: Judgment/ Intuition

This is the use of your moral thought.

Careless- you are careless when it pertains to family.

Indecisive- when expressing emotions you are indecisive.

Orderly- you are receptive at your job.

Stubborn- when you are angry you are vague and don't reveal a
lot of information as to why you feel the way you do.

Chapter 8: INTJ & ENTP

Judgment, Intelligence, Emotions, and Vibes

Masculine Sexuality Type

INTJ (Judge as an intuitive, think as an introvert, feel as a feeler, and sense as a sensor)

<u>**Judging**</u> **(Masculine)**

Stubborn- you trust inspiration, spiritual guidance, and fiction and are oriented towards the future.

Careless- you like new ideas for your own sake, value imagination and innovation but tend to be general and figurative by using metaphors and analogies.

Indecisive- you enjoy learning new skills and get bored easily after mastering them. You present information through leaps and hurdles in a round about manner and are uncertain about your skills but make a judgment based on your own feelings.

Behavior: <u>Realistic</u>

My natural temperament of fire uses the element of my judgment to created an attitude of being judgmental to activate the action of

my intuition which effects my function of judging which leads to the behavior of being realistic. This behavioral person is a natural truth teller and their work has to tell things as they naturally are or they will not be content. They love representing the truth as described.

Thinking (Masculine)

Cunning-you are private and are energized by spending time alone, you like to think things through inside your head and you share personal info with a select few people.

Inventive- you avoid being the center of attention and keep your enthusiasm to yourself.

Diplomatic- you think more than you react to any given situation and you prefer knowing more information than a little.

Perfectionist- you listen more than you talk and respond after taking the time to think things through inside your head.

Behavior: Impatient/ Rationalist

My natural temperament of earth uses the element of my intelligence to create an attitude of being intelligent to activate the action of my extroversion which effects my function of thinking which leads to the behavior of being a rationalist of impatient. This behavioral person is unable to wait patiently. They can't endure irritation for long periods of time. They have the ability to reason. They are always on a quest for truth even when the truth is laid out honestly before them. They have a natural desire to constantly search things over for truth. They believe "reason" to be the main source of knowledge and spiritual truth meaning because you have asked the question of "why" this brings about intelligence.

Feeling (Masculine)

Intelligence- you consider it important to be tactful as well as truthful. You step forward and consider the effects of your actions on others.

Idealistic- you show appreciation easily to others and believe any feeling is valid whether it makes sense or not. You naturally like to please others and may need to be encouraged to have own needs met.

Emotional- you value empathy and harmony but see the exception to the rule when it pertains to your own feelings. You make judgment based on your own feelings and values but you are people oriented and aware of others feelings. You are happiest in friendly, supportive, and cooperative environments.

Accident Prone- You may be seen as overemotional, illogical, and weak. You are an impatient person but are motivated by a desire to be appreciated.

Behavior: Patient

My natural temperament of water uses the element of my emotions to create an attitude of being emotional to activate the action of my introversion which effects my function of feeling which leads to the behavior of being patient. This behavioral person is very calm and capable of handling all. They have a high tolerance of bearing even the most difficult of challenges. They are very understanding and their for you as an individual.

Sensing (Feminine)

Intuition- you trust what is certain, can be proven and you present information in a step-by-step manner.

Independence- you are knowledgeable of your established skills and make a judgment by the facts you gather.

Creativity- you like new ideas only if they have practical applications and tend to be specific and literal about giving a detailed description.

Romantic- you value realism and common sense and are oriented towards the present.

Behavior: Illusionist

My natural temperament of air uses the element of my vibes that I pick up on from my sight, smelling, hearing, tasting, and touching to create an attitude of being sensitive to activate the action of my perception which effects my function sensing which leads to the behavior of being an illusionist. This behavioral person is a natural liar and their work has to have some form of illusions in it or they just won't be happy.

Feminine Sexuality Type

ENTP (Judge as an intuitive, think as a thinker, feel as an extrovert, and sense as a perceiver)

Judging (Masculine)

Stubborn- you trust inspiration, spiritual guidance, and fiction and are oriented towards the future.

Careless- you like new ideas for your own sake, value imagination and innovation but tend to be general and figurative by using metaphors and analogies.

Indecisive- you enjoy learning new skills and get bored easily after mastering them. You present information through leaps and hurdles in a round about manner and are uncertain about your skills but make a judgment based on your own feelings.

Behavior: Realistic

My natural temperament of fire uses the element of my judgment to created an attitude of being judgmental to activate the action of my intuition which effects my function of judging which leads to the

290

behavior of being realistic. This behavioral person is a natural truth teller and their work has to tell things as they naturally are or they will not be content. They love representing the truth as described.

Thinking (Feminine)

Diplomatic- You value logic, justice and fairness which to you is one standard for all. You step back and try to see the situation objectively before problem solving. You feel the need to be convinced that a specific event or activity makes sense before you will even believe.

Perfectionist- you naturally see flaws and tend to be critical of others and believe it is more important to be truthful than tactful. Believe others feelings are irrelevant to the situation at hand.

Inventive- Believe feelings are valid only if they are logical. You are motivated by a desire for achievement and accomplishment but have a hard time translating ideas into active steps.

Cunning- you may be seen as heartless, insensitive and uncaring but are impressed by competence and the end result.

Behavior: Impatient/ Rationalist

My natural temperament of earth uses the element of my intelligence to create an attitude of being intelligent to activate the action of my extroversion which effects my function of thinking which leads to the behavior of being a rationalist of impatient. This behavioral person is unable to wait patiently. They can't endure irritation for long periods of time. They have the ability to reason. They are always on a quest for truth even when the truth is laid out honestly before them. They have a natural desire to constantly search things over for truth. They believe "reason" to be the main source of knowledge and spiritual truth meaning because you have asked the question of "why" this brings about intelligence.

Feeling (Feminine)

Emotional- being with others energizes you. You react more than you think and you communicate to others with enthusiasm.

Accident Prone- You respond quickly without hearing the whole conversation. you enjoy being the center of attention, and enjoy a fast pace.

Idealistic- you think out loud and are easier to know and read. You were your emotions on your sleeve and talk with your body language. When your emotions have been hurt you feel the need to voice your opinion and you share personal information freely and sometimes without enough forethought.

Intelligence- you talk more than you listen and prefer to know a little information rather than it all.

Behavior: Patient

My natural temperament of water uses the element of my emotions to create an attitude of being emotional to activate the action of my introversion which effects my function of feeling which leads to the behavior of being patient. This behavioral person is very calm and capable of handling all. They have a high tolerance of bearing even the most difficult of challenges. They are very understanding and their for you as an individual.

Sensing (Masculine)

Creativity- you are better at concentration exercises than fantasy or daydreaming. You have a play ethic, enjoy now and finish the job later, and enjoy exercises that allow you to learn new thing and have fun doing it. You are process oriented and your emphasis is on how the task is completed.

Intuition- you are influenced by past experiences and this is your knowledge of doing things. You don't like to brainstorm for answers and are happiest leaving your options open. You change goals as new information becomes available and prefer to not decide but continue to collect information for later usage.

Romantic-you feel satisfaction from starting projects and see time as a renewable resource and set deadlines.

Independence- you are flexible, adaptable, and change gears quickly so that you may be available for many different approaches and techniques. You have a natural curiosity and like adapting to new situations.

Behavior: Illusionist

My natural temperament of air uses the element of my vibes that I pick up on from my sight, smelling, hearing, tasting, and touching to create an attitude of being sensitive to activate the action of my perception which effects my function sensing which leads to the behavior of being an illusionist. This behavioral person is a natural liar and their work has to have some form of illusions in it or they just won't be happy.

Aries- The Element of Fire

Aries is the element of fire. Fire and the element of Fire create heated emotions. This is the development of the dominant function and one of your strengths. This takes place from birth to six years of age. The emotions that aid in its development are careless, indecisive, orderly, and stubborn.

Judging: Judgment/ Intuition

This is the use of your moral thought.

> Careless- you're a procrastinator as it relates to your family.
> Indecisive- you are energetic about doing your job.
> Orderly- you are selfish when it comes to money.
> Stubborn- you are self-centered when expressing your emotions.

Aries is the element of fire. Fire and element of earth create an eruption of emotions, burning everything and everyone, which crosses its path. This is the development of the auxiliary function. This takes place from six to twelve years of age. The four emotions, which aid in the growth of your intelligence are cunning, diplomatic, inventive and perfectionist.

Thinking: Intelligence

This is the use of your analytical thought.

    Cunning- your adventuresome as it pertains to life shows cunning.

    Diplomatic- your enthusiastic when experiencing love.

    Inventive- your impulsive as it pertains to their appearance.

    Perfectionist- you're innovative in your home life.

Aries is the element of fire. Fire and the element of water create a steam of emotions, bursting with cloudy judgment toward everyone in its path. This is the development of the third function. This takes place from twelve to twenty-five years of age. The emotions that aid in its development are accident prone, emotional, idealistic, and intelligence.

Feeling: Emotions

This is the use of your moral emotions.

    Accident prone- your accident prone when your upset.

    Emotional- you're quick tempered when you're angry.

Idealistic- being assertive is a strength you possess.

Intelligence- you're very tactless in the way you think.

Aries is the element of fire. Fire and the element of Air create a bonfire of emotions, rising giving the temperaments. This is the development of the fourth function, which takes place from twenty five to fifty years of age. The emotions that aid in its development are creativity, independence, intuition, and romantic.

Sensing: Vibes

This is the use of your analytical emotions.

Creativity-your optimistic as it pertains to your friends

Independence- you're courageous when you face a difficult situation.

Intuition- you're a free spirit in your view of the world.

Romantic- your impatient when you feel loved.

Taurus- The Element of Earth

Taurus is the element of the earth. Earth and the element of fire create an eruption of emotions. This is the development of the dominant function, which takes place from birth to six years of age. The emotions that aid in its development are careless, indecisive, orderly and stubborn.

Judging: Judgment/ Intuition

This is the use of your moral thought.

Careless- you're very practical in your views concerning

home life.

Indecisive- when expressing emotions you are very lazy.

Orderly- you are very possessive about your appearance.

Stubborn- you are very stubborn in your views of the world.

Taurus is the element of the earth. Earth and the element of earth produce a dusty sandstorm of emotions. Blinding everyone in sight. This is the development of the auxiliary function. This takes place from six to twelve years of age. The emotions that aid in its development are cunning, diplomatic, inventive and perfectionist.

Thinking: Intelligence

This is the use of your analytical thought.

Cunning- when you face a difficult situation you're very resentful.

Diplomatic- you are set in your ways when you think.

Inventive- When upset you are very inflexible.

Perfectionist- you are very reliable when it comes to your friends.

Taurus is the element of the earth. Earth and the element of water create a flood of emotions; drowning everything in its path. This is the development of the third function. This takes place from twelve to twenty-five years of age. The emotions that aid in its development are accident prone, emotional, idealistic and intelligence.

Feeling: Emotions

This is the use of your moral emotions.

> Accident Prone- you are violent when you are angry.
>
> Emotional- you are greedy when in love.
>
> Idealistic- you are warm hearted when it relates to your family.
>
> Intelligence- being strong- willed is a strength you possess.

Taurus is the element of the earth. Earth and the element of air create a tornado of emotions, thrashing and trashing everything in its sight. This is the development of the fourth function. This takes place from twenty five to fifty years of age. The emotions that aid in its development are creativity, independence, intuition and romantic.

Sensing: Vibes

This is the use of your analytical emotions.

> Creativity-Your very solid in your view of life shows creativity.
>
> Independence- you're very persistent about doing your job.
>
> Intuition- when it comes to money you're very trustworthy.

Romantic- you're very affectionate when you feel loved.

Gemini- The Element of Air

Gemini is the element of air. Air and the element of fire create a bonfire of emotions, rising given the temperament. This is the development of the dominant function. This takes place from birth to six years of age. The emotions that aid in its development are careless, indecisive, orderly and stubborn.

Judging: Judgment/ Intuition

This is the use of moral thought.

Careless-you are very secretive about your view of the world.

Indecisive- you can be superficial when it pertains to money.

Orderly-you are logical in your home life.

Stubborn- you are inconsistent when expressing your emotions.

Gemini is the element of air. Air and the element of earth create a tornado of emotions, thrashing and trashing everything in its sight. This is the development of the auxiliary function. This takes place from six to twelve years of age. The emotions that aid in its development are cunning, diplomatic, inventive and perfectionist.

Thinking: Intelligence

This is the use of analytical thought.

Cunning- you are very cunning when you are upset.

Diplomatic- when you are angry you are very devious.

Inventive- you are a communicator about the way you think.

Perfectionist- you can be very versatile when in love.

Gemini is the element of air. Air and the element of water create a hurricane of emotions. This is the development of the third function. This takes place from twelve to twenty-five years of age. The emotions that aid in its development are accident prone, emotional, idealistic and intelligence.

Feeling: Emotions

This is the use of moral emotions.

> Accident Prone- you are very restless when it pertains to your family.
>
> Emotional- you are nosey when you face a difficult situation.
>
> Idealistic- you are very flighty in your appearance.
>
> Intelligence- you are very spontaneous in your views of life.

Gemini is the element of air. Air and the element of air create a world wind of emotions. This is the development of the fourth function. This takes place from twenty five to fifty years of age. The emotions that aid in its development are creativity, independence, intuition and romantic.

Sensing: Vibes

This is the use of analytical emotions.

Creativity- you are very energetic when it pertains to your

friends.

Independence- you are adaptable as it relates to your job.

Intuition- being an intellectual is a strength possessed.

Romantic- you are very witty when in love.

Cancer- The Element of Water

Cancer is the element of water. Water and the element of fire create a steam of emotions. This is the development of the dominant function. This takes place from birth to six years of age. The emotions that aid in its development are careless, indecisive, orderly and stubborn.

Judging: Judgment/ Intuition

This is the use of moral thought.

Careless- you are very shrewd when you are angry.

Indecisive- your home life is very unstable.

Orderly- your appearance is changeable.

Stubborn- when upset you are unforgiving.

Cancer is the element of water. Water and the element of earth create a flood of emotions, drowning everything in its path. This is the development of the second function auxiliary. This takes place from six to twelve years of age. The emotions that aid in its development are cunning, diplomatic, inventive and perfectionist.

Thinking: Intelligence

This is the use of analytical thought.

Cunning- being sympathetic is a strength possessed.

Diplomatic- when expressing emotions you can be over indulgent in self-pity.

Inventive- you are very receptive when you think.

Perfectionist- when you feel loved you can be moody.

Cancer is the element of water. Water and the element of water create a wave of emotions. This is the development of the third function. This takes place from twelve to twenty-five years of age. The emotions that aid in its development are accident prone, emotional, idealistic and intelligence.

Feeling: Emotions

This is the use of moral emotions.

Accident Prone-you are hyper sensitive when it pertains to family.

Emotional- when you face a difficult situation you can be very emotional.

Idealistic- you are thrifty when it pertains to money.

Intelligence- you are sensitive in your view of the world.

Cancer is the element of water. Water and the element of air create a hurricane of emotions. This is the development of the fourth function. This takes place from twenty five to fifty years of age. The emotions that aid in its development are creativity, independence, intuition, and romantic.

Sensing: Vibes

This is the use of analytical emotions.

Creativity- you're very kind to your friends.

Independence- your job is very messy.

Intuition- you're very judgmental in your views of life.

Romantic- when in love you can be overly emotional.

Leo- The Element of Fire

Leo is the element of fire. Fire and the element of fire create heated emotions. This is a very judgmental person. This is the development of the dominant function. This takes place from birth to six years of age. The emotions that aid in its development are careless, indecisive, orderly and stubborn.

Judging: Judgment/ Intuition

This is the use of your moral thought.

Careless- when you're angry you appear very snobbish.

Indecisive- at your job you are very egotistical.

Orderly- your home life is organized.

Stubborn- when upset you are intolerant.

Leo is the element of fire. Fire and the element of earth create an eruption of emotions. This is the development of the second function auxiliary. This takes place from six to twelve years of age. The emotions that aid in its development are cunning, diplomatic, inventive and perfectionist.

Thinking: Intelligence

This is the use of your analytical thought.

Cunning- you are patronizing when it relates to your family.

Diplomatic- when you face a difficult situation you are dogmatic.

Inventive- your view of the world is creative.

Perfectionist- when it comes to money you are extravagant.

Leo is the element of fire. Fire and water create a steam of emotions. This is the development of the third function. This takes place from twelve to twenty-five years of age. The emotions that aid in its development are accident prone, emotional, idealistic and intelligence.

Feeling: Emotions

This is the use of your moral emotions.

Accident Prone- when expressing emotions you are attention-seeking.

Emotional- when you feel loved you are generous.

Idealistic- being powerful is a strength possessed.

Intelligence- you are very broad-minded in the way you think.

Leo is the element of fire. Fire and the element of air create a bonfire of emotions, rising given the temperament. This is the development of the fourth function. This takes place from twenty five to fifty years of age. The emotions that aid in its development are creativity, independence, intuition, and romantic.

Sensing: Vibes

This is the use of your analytical emotions.

Creativity- you are very enthusiastic about life.

Independence- you are conceited about your appearance.

Intuition-you are very optimistic when it comes to your friends.

Romantic- when in love you are dramatic.

Virgo- The Element of Earth

Virgo is the element of earth. Earth and the element of fire create an eruption of emotions, burning and melting with words everyone in its path. This is the development of the dominant function. This takes place from birth to six years of age. The emotions that aid in its development are careless, indecisive, orderly and stubborn.

Judging: Judgment/ Intuition

This is the use of your moral thought.

Careless- you are neat in your appearance.

Indecisive- when angry you are grouchy.

Orderly- you are meticulous when it comes to money.

Stubborn- you are analytical in your view of family.

Virgo is the element of earth. Earth and the element of earth create a dusty sandstorm of emotions, blinding everyone in its path. This is the development of the second function auxiliary. This takes place from six to twelve years of age. The emotions that aid in its

development are cunning, diplomatic, inventive and perfectionist.

Thinking: Intelligence

This is the use of your analytical thought.

Cunning- being prudish is a strength possessed.

Diplomatic- when upset you are cranky.

Inventive- you are a busy body in your home life.

Perfectionist- you are a worrier when you feel loved.

Virgo is the element of earth. Earth and the element of water create a flood of emotions, drowning with words everyone in its path. This is the development of the third function. This takes place from twelve to twenty-five years of age. The emotions that aid in its development are accident prone, emotional, idealistic and intelligence.

Feeling: Emotions

This is the use of your moral emotions.

Accident Prone- when you face a difficult situation you are fussy.

Emotional- when expressing your emotions you are pessimistic.

Idealistic- you are conscientious about your friends.

Intelligence- you are hypercritical in your view of the world.

Virgo is the element of earth. Earth and the element of air create a tornado of emotions, thrashing and trashing everyone in its path. This is the development of the fourth function. This takes place from birth to six years of age. The emotions that aid in its development are creativity, independence, intuition, and romantic.

Sensing: Vibes

This is the use of your analytical emotions.

Creativity- you are practical in the way you think.

Independence- at your job you are a workaholic.

Intuition- you are hypercritical in your view of life.

Romantic- when in love you are a perfectionist.

Libra- The Element of Air

Libra is the element of air. Air and the element of fire create a bonfire of emotions, rising given the words and temperament. This is the development of the dominant function. This takes place from birth to six years of age. The emotions that aid in its development are careless, indecisive, orderly and stubborn.

Judging: Judgment/ Intuition

This is the use of your moral thought.

Careless- you are extravagant when you have money.

Indecisive- when expressing emotions you are very indecisive and hard for you to make up your mind.

Orderly- your home life is orderly.

Stubborn- your view of life is easy going.

Libra is the element of air. Air and the element of earth create a tornado of emotions, thrashing and drowning with words everyone in its path. This is the development of the second function auxiliary. This takes place from six to twelve years of age. The emotions that aid in its development are cunning, diplomatic, inventive and perfectionist.

Thinking: Intelligence

This is the use of your analytical thought.

Cunning- when you face a difficult situation you are charming.

Diplomatic- when upset you are diplomatic.

Inventive- you are changeable in your appearance.

Perfectionist- you are a seeker in harmony when it relates to the world.

Libra is the element of air. Air and the element of water create a hurricane of emotions; thrashing and drowning with words everyone in its path. This is the development of the third function. This takes place from twelve to twenty-five years of age. The emotions that aid in its development are accident prone, emotional, idealistic and intelligence.

Feeling: Emotions

This is the use of your moral emotions.

Accident Prone- when angry you are resentful.

Emotional- you are gullible when it comes to your family.

Idealistic- your job is idealistic and you don't expect much.

Intelligence- you are refined in the way you think.

Libra is the element of air. Air and the element of air create a world wind of emotions; taking your breath away with words. This is the development of the fourth function. This takes place from twenty five to fifty years of age. The emotions that aid in its development are creativity, independence, intuition, and romantic.

Sensing: Vibes

This is the use of your analytical emotions.

Creativity- when you feel loved you are flirtatious.

Independence- you are frivolous when it pertains to your friends.

Intuition- being two faced is a strength possessed.

Romantic- when in love you are romantic.

Scorpio- The Element of Water

Scorpio is the element of water. Water and the element of fire create a steam of emotions. This is the development of the dominant function. This takes place from birth to six years of age. The emotions that aid in its development are careless, indecisive, orderly and stubborn.

Judging: Judgment/ Intuition

This is the use of your moral thought.

Careless- when expressing emotions you are overly emotional.

Indecisive- you are energetic when it relates to your friends.

Orderly-being persistent is a strength possessed.

Stubborn-when upset you are stubborn.

Scorpio is the element of water. Water and the element of earth create a flood of emotions, drowning with words everything in its path. This is the development of the second function auxiliary. This takes place from six to twelve years of age. The emotions that aid in its development are cunning, diplomatic, inventive and perfectionist.

Thinking: Intelligence

This is the use of your analytical thought.

Cunning- you are vengeful in your views of the world.

Diplomatic- when you face a difficult situation you are jealous.

Inventive- you are determined when it relates to your family.

Perfectionist- your home life is secretive.

Scorpio is the element of water. Water and the element of water create a wave of emotions, crashing and drowning everyone in its path. This is the development of the third function. This takes place from twelve to twenty-five years of age. The emotions that aid in its development are accident prone, emotional, idealistic and intelligence.

Feeling: Emotions

This is the use of your moral emotions.

Accident Prone- you are violent when you are angry.

Emotional- when you feel loved you are emotional.

Idealistic- your appearance is practical.

Intelligence- you are very manipulative when it comes to money.

Scorpio is the element of water. Water and the element of air create a hurricane of emotions, thrashing and drowning with words everyone in its path. This is the development of the fourth function. This takes place from twenty five to fifty years of age. The emotions that aid in its development are creativity, independence, intuition, and romantic.

Sensing: Vibes

This is the use of your analytical emotions.

Creativity-you are creative in life.

Independence- you are independent in your job.

Intuition- you are very judgmental when you think.

Romantic- when in love you are passionate.

Sagittarius- The Element of Fire

Sagittarius is the element of fire. Fire and the element of fire create heated emotions, burning with words everything in its path. This is a very judgmental person. This is the development of the dominant function. This takes place from birth to six years of age. The emotions that aid in its development are careless, indecisive, orderly and stubborn.

Judging: Judgment/ Intuition

This is the use of your moral thought.

Careless- you are careless in the way you think.

Indecisive- when expressing emotions you are frank and give short answers.

Orderly- your home life is restless.

Stubborn- you are exaggerative when you have money.

Sagittarius is the element of fire. Fire and the element of earth create an eruption of emotions, burning and melting with words everyone in its path. This is the development of the second function auxiliary. This takes place from six to twelve years of age. The emotions that aid in its development are cunning, diplomatic, inventive and perfectionist.

Thinking: Intelligence

This is the use of your analytical thought.

Cunning- when faced with a difficult situation you remain sincere.

Diplomatic-you are frivolous when you are upset.

Inventive- you are tactless in your appearance.

Perfectionist-you are undisciplined in your life.

Sagittarius is the element of fire. Fire and the element of water create a steam of emotions, bursting with cloudy judgment toward everyone in its path. This is the development of the third function. This takes place from twelve to twenty-five years of age. The emotions that aid in its development are accident prone, emotional, idealistic and intelligence.

Feeling: Emotions

This is the use of your moral emotions.

Accident Prone- you are irresponsible when it pertains to family.

Emotional-when you feel loved you are ambitious.

Idealistic-you are very dependable when it pertains to friends.

Intelligence- you are energetic when it pertains to your job.

Sagittarius is the element of fire. Fire and the element of air create a bonfire of emotions, rising given the words and temperament. This is the development of the fourth function. This takes place from twenty five to fifty years of age. The emotions that aid in its development are creativity, independence, intuition, and romantic.

Sensing: Vibes

This is the use of your analytical emotions.

Creativity- you are erratic when upset.

Independence- you are free spirited in your view of the world.

Intuition- being optimistic is a strength you possess.

Romantic-when in love you are very passionate.

Capricorn- The Element of Earth

Capricorn is the element of earth. Earth and the element of fire create an eruption of emotions, burning and melting with words everyone in its path. This is the development of the dominant function. This takes place from birth to six years of age. The emotions that aid in its development are careless, indecisive, orderly and stubborn.

Judging: Judgment/ Intuition

This is the use of your moral thought.

Careless- when upset you are mean.

Indecisive- when you feel loved you are determined.

Orderly- your home life is organized.

Stubborn- when you face a difficult situation you are rigid.

Capricorn is the element of earth. Earth and the element of earth create a dusty, sandstorm of emotions, blinding everyone with words in its path. This is the development of the second function auxiliary. This takes place from six to twelve years of age. The emotions that aid in its development are cunning, diplomatic, inventive and perfectionist.

Thinking: Intelligence

This is the use of your analytical thought.

Cunning-you are opportunistic when it pertains to money.

Diplomatic- you are prudent in the way you think.

Inventive- you are reliable when it pertains to family.

Perfectionist- you are overly ordinary in your life.

Capricorn is the element of earth. Earth and the element of water create a flood of emotions, drowning with words everything in its path. This is the development of the third function. This takes place from twelve to twenty-five years of age. The emotions that aid in its development are accident prone, emotional, idealistic and intelligence.

Feeling: Emotions

This is the use of your moral emotions.

Accident Prone- you are a social climber when it pertains to friends.

Emotional- you are miserly at expressing emotions.

Idealistic- having a sense of humor is a strength you possess.

Intelligence- when you are angry you are a nit-picker and you pick the least important thing to argue about.

Capricorn is the element of earth. Earth and the element of air create a tornado of emotions, thrashing and trashing with words everyone in its sight. This is the development of the fourth function. This takes place from twenty five to fifty years of age. The emotions that aid in its development are creativity, independence, intuition, and romantic.

Sensing: Vibes

This is the use of your analytical emotions.

Creativity-you are ambitious about doing your job.

Independence- you are comfortable in your appearance.

Intuition- when in love you are generous.

Romantic-you are patient in your view of the world.

Aquarius- The Element of Air

Aquarius is the element of air. Air and the element of fire create a bonfire of emotions, rising given the words and temperament. This is the development of the dominant function. This takes place from birth to six years of age. The emotions that aid in its development are careless, indecisive, orderly and stubborn.

Judging: Judgment/ Intuition

This is the use of your moral thought.

Careless- your home life is disorganized.

Indecisive- you are impulsive in your life.

Orderly- you are neat in appearance.

Stubborn- you are rebellious when you face a difficult situation.

Aquarius is the element of air. Air and the element of earth create a tornado of emotions, thrashing and trashing with words everyone in its sight. This is the development of the second function auxiliary. This takes place from six to twelve years of age. The emotions that aid in its development are cunning, diplomatic, inventive and perfectionist.

Thinking: Intelligence

This is the use of your analytical thought.

Cunning- when angry you are unpredictable.

Diplomatic- you are human in your view of the world.

Inventive- being inventive is a strength you possess.

Perfectionist- when in love you are charismatic.

Aquarius is the element of air. Air and the element of water create a hurricane of emotions, thrashing and drowning with words everyone in its path. This is the development of the third function. This takes place from twelve to twenty-five years of age. The emotions that aid in its development are accident prone, emotional, idealistic and intelligence.

Feeling: Emotions

This is the use of your moral emotions.

Accident Prone- you are tactless when it pertains to friends.

Emotional- when expressing emotions you are friendly.

Idealistic-you are idealistic when it pertains to money.

Intelligence- when upset you are intelligent.

Aquarius is the element of air. Air and the element of air create a world wind of emotions, taking your breath away with words. This is the development of the fourth function. This takes place from twenty five to fifty years of age. The emotions that aid in its development are creativity, independence, intuition, and romantic.

Sensing: Vibes

This is the use of your analytical emotions.

Creativity- you are eccentric when it pertains to family and there is no one like you.

Independence- you are independent at your job.

Intuition- you are judgmental in the way you think.

Romantic-when you feel loved you are perverse.

Pisces- The Element of Water

Pisces is the element of water. Water and the element of fire create a steam of emotions; bursting with cloudy judgment toward everyone in its path. This is the development of the dominant function. This takes place from birth to six years of age. The emotions that aid in its development are careless, indecisive, orderly and stubborn.

Judging: Judgment/ Intuition

This is the use of your moral thought.

Careless- you are careless when it pertains to family.

Indecisive- when expressing emotions you are indecisive.

Orderly- you are receptive at your job.

Stubborn- when you are angry you are vague and don't reveal a lot of information as to why you feel the way you do.

Pisces is the element of water. Water and the element of earth create a flood of emotions, drowning with words everything in its path. This is the development of the second function auxiliary. This takes place from six to twelve years of age. The emotions that aid in its development are cunning, diplomatic, inventive and perfectionist.

Thinking: Intelligence

This is the use of your analytical thought.

Cunning when faced with a difficult situation you are secretive.

Diplomatic- you are compassionate in your view of the world.

Inventive-you are imaginative when it pertains to money.

Perfectionist- you are impressionable in your life.

Pisces is the element of water. Water and the element of water create a wave of emotions, crashing and drowning everyone in its path. This is the development of the third function. This takes place from twelve to twenty-five years of age. The emotions that aid in its development are accident prone, emotional, idealistic and intelligence.

Feeling: Emotions

This is the use of your moral emotions.

Accident Prone- when you feel loved you are weak-willed.

Emotional-when upset you are emotional.

Idealistic- you are compassionate in your view of the world.

Intelligence- you are unworldly in the way you think.

Pisces is the element of water. Water and the element of air create a hurricane of emotions, thrashing and drowning with words everyone in its path. This is the development of the fourth function. This takes place from twenty five to fifty years of age. The emotions that aid in its development are creativity, independence, intuition, and romantic.

Sensing: Vibes

This is the use of your analytical emotions.

Creativity- you are sensitive when it pertains to friends.

Independence- you are mysterious in your appearance.

Intuition- being judgmental is a strength possessed.

Romantic- when in love you are romantic.

Chapter 9: ISFJ & ESFP
Vibes, Emotions, Intelligence, and Judgment

Masculine Sexuality Type

ISFJ (Sense as a sensor, feel as a feeler, think introverted and judge as a judger)

Sensing (Feminine)

Intuition- you trust what is certain, can be proven and you present information in a step-by-step manner.

Independence- you are knowledgeable of your established skills and make a judgment by the facts you gather.

Creativity- you like new ideas only if they have practical applications and tend to be specific and literal about giving a detailed description.

Romantic- you value realism and common sense and are oriented towards the present.

Behavior: Illusionist

My natural temperament of air uses the element of my vibes that I pick up on from my sight, smelling, hearing, tasting, and touching to create an attitude of being sensitive to activate the action of my perception which effects my function sensing which leads to the behavior of being an illusionist. This behavioral person is a natural liar and their work has to have some form of illusions in it or they just won't be happy.

Feeling (Masculine)

Intelligence- you consider it important to be tactful as well as truthful. You step forward and consider the effects of your actions on others.

Idealistic- you show appreciation easily to others and believe any feeling is valid whether it makes sense or not. You naturally like to please others and may need to be encouraged to have own needs met.

 Emotional- you value empathy and harmony but see the exception to the rule when it pertains to your own feelings. You make judgment based on your own feelings and values but you are people oriented and aware of others feelings. You are happiest in friendly, supportive, and cooperative environments.

 Accident Prone- You may be seen as overemotional, illogical, and weak. You are an impatient person but are motivated by a desire to be appreciated.

Behavior: Patient

My natural temperament of water uses the element of my emotions to create an attitude of being emotional to activate the action of my introversion which effects my function of feeling which leads to the behavior of being patient. This behavioral person is very calm and capable of handling all. They have a high tolerance of bearing even the most difficult of challenges. They are very understanding and their for you as an individual.

Thinking (Masculine)

Cunning-you are private and are energized by spending time alone, you like to think things through inside your head and you share personal info with a select few people.

Inventive- you avoid being the center of attention and keep your enthusiasm to yourself.

Diplomatic- you think more than you react to any given situation and you prefer knowing more information than a little.

Perfectionist- you listen more than you talk and respond after taking the time to think things through inside your head.

Behavior: Impatient/ Rationalist

My natural temperament of earth uses the element of my intelligence to create an attitude of being intelligent to activate the action of my extroversion which effects my function of thinking which leads to the behavior of being a rationalist of impatient. This behavioral person is unable to wait patiently. They can't endure irritation for long periods of time. They have the ability to reason. They are always on a quest for truth even when the truth is laid out honestly before them. They have a natural desire to constantly search things over for truth. They believe "reason" to be the main source of knowledge and spiritual truth meaning because you have asked the question of "why" this brings about intelligence.

Judging (Feminine)

Indecisive- Have trouble keeping on track or following directions.
Careless- you are product oriented and less likely to deal with specifics because your emphasis is on completing the task and you prefer to focus on the big picture.
Orderly- you prefer to make plans and follow them accordingly. You are usually well organized. You set goals and work toward achieving them on time and are happiest after final decisions have been made and feel satisfaction from finishing the projects.
 Stubborn- you have a work ethic, work first play later, and prefer to know what you are getting into.

Behavior: Realistic

My natural temperament of fire uses the element of my judgment to created an attitude of being judgmental to activate the action of my intuition which effects my function of judging which leads to the

behavior of being realistic. This behavioral person is a natural truth teller and their work has to tell things as they naturally are or they will not be content. They love representing the truth as described.

Feminine Sexuality Type
ESFP (Sense as a perceiver, feel as an extrovert, think as a thinker and judge as a judger)

<u>**Sensing (Masculine)**</u>

Creativity- you are better at concentration exercises than fantasy or daydreaming. You have a play ethic, enjoy now and finish the job later, and enjoy exercises that allow you to learn new thing and have fun doing it. You are process oriented and your emphasis is on how the task is completed.

Intuition- you are influenced by past experiences and this is your knowledge of doing things. You don't like to brainstorm for answers and are happiest leaving your options open. You change goals as new information becomes available and prefer to not decide but continue to collect information for later usage.

Romantic-you feel satisfaction from starting projects and see time as a renewable resource and set deadlines.

Independence- you are flexible, adaptable, and change gears quickly so that you may be available for many different approaches and techniques. You have a natural curiosity and like adapting to new situations.

Behavior: <u>Illusionist</u>

My natural temperament of air uses the element of my vibes that I pick up on from my sight, smelling, hearing, tasting, and touching to create an attitude of being sensitive to activate the action of my perception which effects my function sensing which leads to the behavior of being an illusionist. This behavioral person is a natural liar and their work has to have some form of illusions in it or they just won't be happy.

Feeling (Feminine)

Emotional- being with others energizes you. You react more than you think and you communicate to others with enthusiasm.

Accident Prone- You respond quickly without hearing the whole conversation. you enjoy being the center of attention, and enjoy a fast pace.

Idealistic- you think out loud and are easier to know and read. You were your emotions on your sleeve and talk with your body language. When your emotions have been hurt you feel the need to voice your opinion and you share personal information freely and sometimes without enough forethought.

Intelligence- you talk more than you listen and prefer to know a little information rather than it all.

Behavior: <u>Patient</u>

My natural temperament of water uses the element of my emotions to create an attitude of being emotional to activate the action of my introversion which effects my function of feeling which leads to the behavior of being patient. This behavioral person is very calm and capable of handling all. They have a high tolerance of bearing even the most difficult of challenges. They are very understanding and their for you as an individual.

<u>Thinking (Feminine)</u>

Diplomatic- You value logic, justice and fairness which to you is one standard for all. You step back and try to see the situation objectively before problem solving. You feel the need to be convinced that a specific event or activity makes sense before you will even believe.

Perfectionist- you naturally see flaws and tend to be critical of others and believe it is more important to be truthful than tactful. Believe others feelings are irrelevant to the situation at hand.

Inventive- Believe feelings are valid only if they are logical. You are motivated by a desire for achievement and accomplishment but have a hard time translating ideas into active steps.

Cunning- you may be seen as heartless, insensitive and uncaring but are impressed by competence and the end result.

Behavior: Impatient/ Rationalist

My natural temperament of earth uses the element of my intelligence to create an attitude of being intelligent to activate the action of my extroversion which effects my function of thinking which leads to the behavior of being a rationalist of impatient. This behavioral person is unable to wait patiently. They can't endure irritation for long periods of time. They have the ability to reason. They are always on a quest for truth even when the truth is laid out honestly before them. They have a natural desire to constantly search things over for truth. They believe "reason" to be the main source of knowledge and spiritual truth meaning because you have asked the question of "why" this brings about intelligence.

Judging (Feminine)

Indecisive- Have trouble keeping on track or following directions.
Careless- you are product oriented and less likely to deal with specifics because your emphasis is on completing the task and you prefer to focus on the big picture.
Orderly- you prefer to make plans and follow them accordingly. You are usually well organized. You set goals and work toward achieving them on time and are happiest after final decisions have been made and feel satisfaction from finishing the projects.

Stubborn- you have a work ethic, work first play later, and prefer to know what you are getting into.

Behavior: Realistic

My natural temperament of fire uses the element of my judgment to created an attitude of being judgmental to activate the action of my intuition which effects my function of judging which leads to the behavior of being realistic. This behavioral person is a natural truth teller and their work has to tell things as they naturally are or they will not be content. They love representing the truth as described.

Aries- The Element of Fire

Aries is the element of fire. Fire and the element of Air create a bonfire of emotions, rising giving the temperaments. This is the development of the dominant function and one of your strengths. This takes place from birth to six years of age. The emotions that aid in its development are creativity, independence, intuition, and romantic.

Sensing: Vibes

This is the use of your analytical emotions.

Creativity-your optimistic as it pertains to your friends

Independence- you're courageous when you face a difficult situation.

Intuition- you're a free spirit in your view of the world.

Romantic- your impatient when you feel loved.

Aries is the element of fire. Fire and the element of water create a steam of emotions, bursting with cloudy judgment toward everyone in its path. This is the development of the auxiliary function. This takes place from six to twelve years of age. The emotions that aid in its development are accident prone, emotional, idealistic, and intelligence.

Feeling: Emotions

This is the use of your moral emotions.

Accident prone- your accident prone when your upset.

Emotional- you're quick tempered when you're angry.

Idealistic- being assertive is a strength you possess.

Intelligence- you're very tactless in the way you think.

Aries is the element of fire. Fire and element of earth create an eruption of emotions, burning everything and everyone, which crosses its path. This is the development of the third function. This takes place from twelve to twenty-five years of age. The four emotions, which aid in the growth of your intelligence are cunning, diplomatic, inventive and perfectionist.

Thinking: Intelligence

This is the use of your analytical thought.

Cunning- your adventuresome as it pertains to life shows cunning.

Diplomatic- your enthusiastic when experiencing love.

Inventive- your impulsive as it pertains to their appearance.

Perfectionist- you're innovative in your home life.

Aries is the element of fire. Fire and the element of Fire create heated emotions. This is the development of the fourth function, which takes place from twenty five to fifty years of age. The emotions that aid in its development are careless, indecisive, orderly, and stubborn.

Judging: Judgment/ Intuition

This is the use of your moral thought.

> Careless- you're a procrastinator as it relates to your family.
>
> Indecisive- you are energetic about doing your job.
>
> Orderly- you are selfish when it comes to money.
>
> Stubborn- you are self-centered when expressing your emotions.

Taurus- The Element of Earth

Taurus is the element of the earth. Earth and the element of air create a tornado of emotions, thrashing and trashing everything in its sight. . This is the development of the dominant function, which takes place from birth to six years of age. The emotions that aid in its development are creativity, independence, intuition and romantic.

Sensing: Vibes

This is the use of your analytical emotions.

Creativity-Your very solid in your view of life shows
creativity.

Independence- you're very persistent about doing your
job.

Intuition- when it comes to money you're very
trustworthy.

Romantic- you're very affectionate when you feel loved.

Taurus is the element of the earth. Earth and the element of water create a flood of emotions, drowning everything in its path. This is the development of the auxiliary function. This takes place from six to twelve years of age. The emotions that aid in its development are accident prone, emotional, idealistic and intelligence.

Feeling: Emotions

This is the use of your moral emotions.

Accident Prone- you are violent when you are angry.

Emotional- you are greedy when in love.

Idealistic- you are warm hearted when it relates to your
family.

Intelligence- being strong- willed is a strength you
possess.

Taurus is the element of the earth. Earth and the element of earth produce a dusty sandstorm of emotions. Blinding everyone in sight. This is the development of the third function. This takes place from twelve to twenty-five years of age. The emotions that aid in its development arc cunning, diplomatic, inventive and perfectionist.

Thinking: Intelligence

This is the use of your analytical thought.

> Cunning- when you face a difficult situation you're very resentful.
>
> Diplomatic- you are set in your ways when you think.
>
> Inventive- When upset you are very inflexible.
>
> Perfectionist- you are very reliable when it comes to your friends.

Taurus is the element of the earth. Earth and the element of fire create an eruption of emotions. This is the development of the fourth function. This takes place from twenty five to fifty years of age. The emotions that aid in its development are careless, indecisive, orderly and stubborn.

Judging: Judgment/ Intuition

This is the use of your moral thought.

> Careless- you're very practical in your views concerning home life.
>
> Indecisive- when expressing emotions you are very lazy.
>
> Orderly- you are very possessive about your appearance.
>
> Stubborn- you are very stubborn in your views of the world.

Gemini- The Element of Air

Gemini is the element of air. Air and the element of air create a world wind of emotions. This is the development of the dominant function. This takes place from birth to six years of age. The emotions that aid in its development are creativity, independence, intuition and romantic.

Sensing: Vibes

This is the use of analytical emotions.

Creativity- you are very energetic when it pertains to your friends.

Independence- you are adaptable as it relates to your job.

Intuition- being an intellectual is a strength possessed.

Romantic- you are very witty when in love.

Gemini is the element of air. Air and the element of water create a hurricane of emotions. This is the development of the auxiliary function. This takes place from six to twelve years of age. The emotions that aid in its development are accident prone, emotional, idealistic and intelligence.

Feeling: Emotions

This is the use of moral emotions.

Accident Prone- you are very restless when it pertains to your family.

Emotional- you are nosey when you face a difficult

situation.

Idealistic- you are very flighty in your appearance.

Intelligence- you are very spontaneous in your views of
life.

Gemini is the element of air. Air and the element of earth create a tornado of emotions, thrashing and trashing everything in its sight. This is the development of the third function. This takes place from twelve to twenty-five years of age. The emotions that aid in its development are cunning, diplomatic, inventive and perfectionist.

Thinking: Intelligence

This is the use of analytical thought.

Cunning- you are very cunning when you are upset.

Diplomatic- when you are angry you are very devious.

Inventive- you are a communicator about the way you think.

Perfectionist- you can be very versatile when in love.

Gemini is the element of air. Air and the element of fire create a bonfire of emotions, rising given the temperament. This is the development of the fourth function. This takes place from twenty five to fifty years of age. The emotions that aid in its development are careless, indecisive, orderly and stubborn.

Judging: Judgment/ Intuition

This is the use of moral thought.

Careless-you are very secretive about your view of the world.

Indecisive- you can be superficial when it pertains to money.

Orderly-you are logical in your home life.

Stubborn- you are inconsistent when expressing your emotions.

Cancer- The Element of Water

Cancer is the element of water. Water and the element of air create a hurricane of emotions. . This is the development of the dominant function. This takes place from birth to six years of age. The emotions that aid in its development are creativity, independence, intuition, and romantic.

Sensing: Vibes

This is the use of analytical emotions.

Creativity- you're very kind to your friends.

Independence- your job is very messy.

Intuition- you're very judgmental in your views of life.

Romantic- when in love you can be overly emotional.

Cancer is the element of water. Water and the element of water create a wave of emotions. This is the development of the second function auxiliary. This takes place from six to twelve years of age. The emotions that aid in its development are accident prone, emotional, idealistic and intelligence.

Feeling: Emotions

This is the use of moral emotions.

Accident Prone-you are hyper sensitive when it pertains to

family.

Emotional- when you face a difficult situation you can be very emotional.

Idealistic- you are thrifty when it pertains to money.

Intelligence- you are sensitive in your view of the world.

Cancer is the element of water. Water and the element of earth create a flood of emotions, drowning everything in its path. This is the development of the third function. This takes place from twelve to twenty-five years of age. The emotions that aid in its development are cunning, diplomatic, inventive and perfectionist.

Thinking: Intelligence

This is the use of analytical thought.

Cunning- being sympathetic is a strength possessed.

Diplomatic- when expressing emotions you can be over indulgent in self-pity.

Inventive- you are very receptive when you think.

Perfectionist- when you feel loved you can be moody.

Cancer is the element of water. Water and the element of fire create a steam of emotions. This is the development of the fourth function. This takes place from twenty five to fifty years of age. The emotions that aid in its development are careless, indecisive, orderly and stubborn.

Judging: Judgment/ Intuition

This is the use of moral thought.

Careless- you are very shrewd when you are angry.

Indecisive- your home life is very unstable.

Orderly- your appearance is changeable.

Stubborn- when upset you are unforgiving.

Leo- The Element of Fire

Leo is the element of fire. Fire and the element of air create a bonfire of emotions, rising given the temperament. This is the development of the dominant function. This takes place from birth to six years of age. The emotions that aid in its development are creativity, independence, intuition, and romantic.

Sensing: Vibes

This is the use of your analytical emotions.

Creativity- you are very enthusiastic about life.

Independence- you are conceited about your appearance.

Intuition-you are very optimistic when it comes to your friends.

Romantic- when in love you are dramatic.

Leo is the element of fire. Fire and water create a steam of emotions. This is the development of the second function auxiliary. This takes place from six to twelve years of age. The emotions that aid in its development are accident prone, emotional, idealistic and intelligence.

Feeling: Emotions

This is the use of your moral emotions.

    Accident Prone- when expressing emotions you are attention-
        seeking.

    Emotional- when you feel loved you are generous.

    Idealistic- being powerful is a strength possessed.

    Intelligence- you are very broad-minded in the way you think.

Leo is the element of fire. Fire and the element of earth create an eruption of emotions. This is the development of the third function. This takes place from twelve to twenty-five years of age. The emotions that aid in its development are cunning, diplomatic, inventive and perfectionist.

Thinking: Intelligence

This is the use of your analytical thought.

    Cunning- you are patronizing when it relates to your family.

    Diplomatic- when you face a difficult situation you are dogmatic.

    Inventive- your view of the world is creative.

    Perfectionist- when it comes to money you are extravagant.

Leo is the element of fire. Fire and the element of fire create heated emotions. This is a very judgmental person. This is the development of the fourth function. This takes place from twenty five to fifty years of age. The emotions that aid in its development

are careless, indecisive, orderly and stubborn.

Judging: Judgment/ Intuition

This is the use of your moral thought.

Careless- when you're angry you appear very snobbish.

Indecisive- at your job you are very egotistical.

Orderly- your home life is organized.

Stubborn- when upset you are intolerant.

Virgo- The Element of Earth

Virgo is the element of earth. Earth and the element of air create a tornado of emotions, thrashing and trashing everyone in its path. This is the development of the dominant function. This takes place from birth to six years of age. The emotions that aid in its development are creativity, independence, intuition, and romantic.

Sensing: Vibes

This is the use of your analytical emotions.

Creativity- you are practical in the way you think.

Independence- at your job you are a workaholic.

Intuition- you are hypercritical in your view of life.

Romantic- when in love you are a perfectionist.

Virgo is the element of earth. Earth and the element of water create a flood of emotions, drowning with words everyone in its path. This is the development of the second function auxiliary. This takes place from six to twelve years of age. The emotions that aid in its development are accident prone, emotional, idealistic and intelligence.

Feeling: Emotions

This is the use of your moral emotions.

  Accident Prone- when you face a difficult situation you are
    fussy.

  Emotional- when expressing your emotions you are pessimistic.

  Idealistic- you are conscientious about your friends.

  Intelligence- you are hypercritical in your view of the world.

Virgo is the element of earth. Earth and the element of earth create a dusty sandstorm of emotions, blinding everyone in its path. This is the development of the third function. This takes place from twelve to twenty-five years of age. The emotions that aid in its development are cunning, diplomatic, inventive and perfectionist.

Thinking: Intelligence

This is the use of your analytical thought.

  Cunning- being prudish is a strength possessed.

  Diplomatic- when upset you are cranky.

  Inventive- you are a busy body in your home life.

  Perfectionist- you are a worrier when you feel loved.

Virgo is the element of earth. Earth and the element of fire create an eruption of emotions, burning and melting with words everyone in its path. This is the development of the fourth function. This takes place from birth to six years of age. The emotions that aid in its development are careless, indecisive, orderly and stubborn.

Judging: Judgment/ Intuition

This is the use of your moral thought.

Careless- you are neat in your appearance.

Indecisive- when angry you are grouchy.

Orderly- you are meticulous when it comes to money.

Stubborn- you are analytical in your view of family.

Libra- The Element of Air

Libra is the element of air. Air and the element of air create a world wind of emotions; taking your breath away with words. This is the development of the dominant function. This takes place from birth to six years of age. The emotions that aid in its development are creativity, independence, intuition, and romantic.

Sensing: Vibes

This is the use of your analytical emotions.

Creativity- when you feel loved you are flirtatious.

Independence- you are frivolous when it pertains to your
friends.

Intuition- being two faced is a strength possessed.

Romantic- when in love you are romantic.

Libra is the element of air. Air and the element of water create a hurricane of emotions; thrashing and drowning with words everyone in its path. This is the development of the second function auxiliary. This takes place from six to twelve years of age. The emotions that aid in its development are accident prone, emotional, idealistic and intelligence.

Feeling: Emotions

This is the use of your moral emotions.

Accident Prone- when angry you are resentful.

Emotional- you are gullible when it comes to your family.

Idealistic- your job is idealistic and you don't expect much.

Intelligence- you are refined in the way you think.

Libra is the element of air. Air and the element of earth create a tornado of emotions, thrashing and drowning with words everyone in its path. This is the development of the third function. This takes place from twelve to twenty-five years of age. The emotions that aid in its development are cunning, diplomatic, inventive and perfectionist.

Thinking: Intelligence

This is the use of your analytical thought.

Cunning- when you face a difficult situation you are charming.

Diplomatic- when upset you are diplomatic.

Inventive- you are changeable in your appearance.

Perfectionist- you are a seeker in harmony when it relates to the world.

Libra is the element of air. Air and the element of fire create a bonfire of emotions, rising given the words and temperament. This is the development of the fourth function. This takes place from twenty five to fifty years of age. The emotions that aid in its development are careless, indecisive, orderly and stubborn.

Judging: Judgment/ Intuition

This is the use of your moral thought.

Careless- you are extravagant when you have money.

Indecisive- when expressing emotions you are very indecisive and hard for you to make up your mind.

Orderly- your home life is orderly.

Stubborn- your view of life is easy going.

Scorpio- The Element of Water

Scorpio is the element of water. Water and the element of air create a hurricane of emotions, thrashing and drowning with words everyone in its path. This is the development of the dominant function. This takes place from birth to six years of age. The emotions that aid in its development are creativity, independence, intuition, and romantic.

Sensing: Vibes

This is the use of your analytical emotions.

Creativity-you are creative in life.

Independence- you are independent in your job.

Intuition- you are very judgmental when you think.

Romantic- when in love you are passionate.

Scorpio is the element of water. Water and the element of water create a wave of emotions, crashing and drowning everyone in its path. This is the development of the second function auxiliary. This takes place from six to twelve years of age. The emotions that aid in its development are accident prone, emotional, idealistic and intelligence.

Feeling: Emotions

This is the use of your moral emotions.

Accident Prone- you are violent when you are angry.

Emotional- when you feel loved you are emotional.

Idealistic- your appearance is practical.

Intelligence- you are very manipulative when it comes to money.

Scorpio is the element of water. Water and the element of earth create a flood of emotions, drowning with words everything in its path. This is the development of the third function. This takes place from twelve to twenty-five years of age. The emotions that aid in its development are cunning, diplomatic, inventive and perfectionist.

Thinking: Intelligence

This is the use of your analytical thought.

Cunning- you are vengeful in your views of the world.

Diplomatic- when you face a difficult situation you are jealous.

Inventive- you are determined when it relates to your family.

Perfectionist- your home life is secretive.

Scorpio is the element of water. Water and the element of fire create a steam of emotions. This is the development of the fourth function. This takes place from twenty five to fifty years of age. The emotions that aid in its development are careless, indecisive, orderly and stubborn.

Judging: Judgment/ Intuition

This is the use of your moral thought.

Careless- when expressing emotions you are overly emotional.

Indecisive- you are energetic when it relates to your friends.

Orderly-being persistent is a strength possessed.

Stubborn-when upset you are stubborn.

Sagittarius- The Element of Fire

Sagittarius is the element of fire. Fire and the element of air create a bonfire of emotions, rising given the words and temperament. This is the development of the dominant function. This takes place from birth to six years of age. The emotions that aid in its development are creativity, independence, intuition, and romantic.

Sensing: Vibes

This is the use of your analytical emotions.

Creativity- you are erratic when upset.

Independence- you are free spirited in your view of the world.

Intuition- being optimistic is a strength you possess.

Romantic-when in love you are very passionate.

Sagittarius is the element of fire. Fire and the element of water create a steam of emotions, bursting with cloudy judgment toward everyone in its path. This is the development of the second function auxiliary. This takes place from six to twelve years of age. The emotions that aid in its development are accident prone, emotional, idealistic and intelligence.

Feeling: Emotions

This is the use of your moral emotions.

Accident Prone- you are irresponsible when it pertains to family.

Emotional-when you feel loved you are ambitious.

Idealistic-you are very dependable when it pertains to friends.

Intelligence- you are energetic when it pertains to your job.

Sagittarius is the element of fire. Fire and the element of earth create an eruption of emotions, burning and melting with words everyone in its path. This is the development of the third function. This takes place from twelve to twenty-five years of age. The emotions that aid in its development are cunning, diplomatic, inventive and perfectionist.

Thinking: Intelligence

This is the use of your analytical thought.

Cunning- when faced with a difficult situation you remain
  sincere.

Diplomatic-you are frivolous when you are upset.

Inventive- you are tactless in your appearance.

Perfectionist-you are undisciplined in your life.

Sagittarius is the element of fire. Fire and the element of fire create heated emotions, burning with words everything in its path. This is a very judgmental person. This is the development of the fourth function. This takes place from twenty five to fifty years of age. The emotions that aid in its development are careless, indecisive, orderly and stubborn.

Judging: Judgment/ Intuition

This is the use of your moral thought.

  Careless- you are careless in the way you think.

  Indecisive- when expressing emotions you are frank and give
    short answers.

  Orderly- your home life is restless.

  Stubborn- you are exaggerative when you have money.

Capricorn- The Element of Earth

Capricorn is the element of earth. Earth and the element of air create a tornado of emotions, thrashing and trashing with words everyone in its sight. This is the development of the dominant function. This takes place from birth to six years of age. The emotions that aid in its development are creativity, independence, intuition, and romantic.

Sensing: Vibes

This is the use of your analytical emotions.

Creativity-you are ambitious about doing your job.

Independence- you are comfortable in your appearance.

Intuition- when in love you are generous.

Romantic-you are patient in your view of the world.

Perfectionist- you are overly ordinary in your life.

Capricorn is the element of earth. Earth and the element of water create a flood of emotions, drowning with words everything in its path. This is the development of the second function auxiliary. This takes place from six to twelve years of age. The emotions that aid in its development are accident prone, emotional, idealistic and intelligence.

Feeling: Emotions

This is the use of your moral emotions.

Accident Prone- you are a social climber when it pertains to friends.

Emotional- you are miserly at expressing emotions.

Idealistic- having a sense of humor is a strength you possess.

Intelligence- when you are angry you are a nit-picker and you pick the least important thing to argue about.

Capricorn is the element of earth. Earth and the element of earth create a dusty, sandstorm of emotions, blinding everyone with words in its path. This is the development of the third function. This takes place from twelve to twenty-five years of age. The emotions that aid in its development are cunning, diplomatic, inventive and perfectionist.

Thinking: Intelligence

This is the use of your analytical thought.

Cunning-you are opportunistic when it pertains to money.

Diplomatic- you are prudent in the way you think.

Inventive- you are reliable when it pertains to family.

Capricorn is the element of earth. Earth and the element of fire create an eruption of emotions, burning and melting with words everyone in its path. This is the development of the fourth function. This takes place from twenty five to fifty years of age. The emotions that aid in its development are careless, indecisive, orderly and stubborn.

Judging: Judgment/ Intuition

This is the use of your moral thought.

Careless- when upset you are mean.

Indecisive- when you feel loved you are determined.

Orderly- your home life is organized.

Stubborn- when you face a difficult situation you are rigid.

Aquarius- The Element of Air

Aquarius is the element of air. Air and the element of air create a wurl wind of emotions, taking your breath away with words. This is the development of the dominant function. This takes place from birth to six years of age. The emotions that aid in its development are creativity, independence, intuition, and romantic.

Sensing: Vibes

This is the use of your analytical emotions.

Creativity- you are eccentric when it pertains to family and there is no one like you.

Independence- you are independent at your job.

Intuition- you are judgmental in the way you think.

Romantic-when you feel loved you are perverse.

Aquarius is the element of air. Air and the element of water create a hurricane of emotions, thrashing and drowning with words everyone in its path. This is the development of the second function auxiliary. This takes place from six to twelve years of age. The emotions that aid in its development are accident prone, emotional, idealistic and intelligence.

Feeling: Emotions

This is the use of your moral emotions.

Accident Prone- you are tactless when it pertains to friends.

Emotional- when expressing emotions you are friendly.

Idealistic-you are idealistic when it pertains to money.

Intelligence- when upset you are intelligent.

Aquarius is the element of air. Air and the element of earth create a tornado of emotions, thrashing and trashing with words everyone in its sight. . This is the development of the third function. This takes place from twelve to twenty-five years of age. The emotions that aid in its development are cunning, diplomatic, inventive and perfectionist.

Thinking: Intelligence

This is the use of your analytical thought.

Cunning- when angry you are unpredictable.

Diplomatic- you are human in your view of the world.

Inventive- being inventive is a strength you possess.

Perfectionist- when in love you are charismatic.

Aquarius is the element of air. Air and the element of fire create a bonfire of emotions, rising given the words and temperament. This is the development of the fourth function. This takes place from twenty five to fifty years of age. The emotions that aid in its development are careless, indecisive, orderly and stubborn.

Judging: Judgment/ Intuition

This is the use of your moral thought.

Careless- your home life is disorganized.

Indecisive- you are impulsive in your life.

Orderly- you are neat in appearance.

Stubborn- you are rebelllous when you face a difficult situation.

Pisces- The Element of Water

Pisces is the element of water. Water and the element of air create a hurricane of emotions, thrashing and drowning with words everyone in its path. This is the development of the dominant function. This takes place from birth to six years of age. The emotions that aid in its development are creativity, independence, intuition, and romantic.

Sensing: Vibes

This is the use of your analytical emotions.

Creativity- you are sensitive when it pertains to friends.

Independence- you are mysterious in your appearance.

Intuition- being judgmental is a strength possessed.

Romantic- when in love you are romantic.

Pisces is the element of water. Water and the element of water create a wave of emotions, crashing and drowning everyone in its path. This is the development of the second function auxiliary. This takes place from six to twelve years of age. The emotions that aid in its development are accident prone, emotional, idealistic and intelligence.

Feeling: Emotions

This is the use of your moral emotions.

Accident Prone- when you feel loved you are weak-willed.

Emotional-when upset you are emotional.

Idealistic- you are compassionate in your view of the world.

Intelligence- you are unworldly in the way you think.

Pisces is the element of water. Water and the element of earth create a flood of emotions, drowning with words everything in its path. This is the development of the third function. This takes place from twelve to twenty-five years of age. The emotions that aid in its development are cunning, diplomatic, inventive and perfectionist.

Thinking: Intelligence

This is the use of your analytical thought.

Cunning- when faced with a difficult situation you are secretive.

Diplomatic- you are compassionate in your view of the world.

Inventive-you are imaginative when it pertains to money.

Perfectionist- you are impressionable in your life.

Pisces is the element of water. Water and the element of fire create a steam of emotions; bursting with cloudy judgment toward everyone in its path. This is the development of the fourth function. This takes place from twenty five to fifty years of age. The emotions that aid in its development are careless, indecisive, orderly and stubborn.

Judging: Judgment/ Intuition

This is the use of your moral thought.

Careless- you are careless when it pertains to family.

Indecisive- when expressing emotions you are indecisive.

Orderly- you are receptive at your job.

Stubborn- when you are angry you are vague and don't reveal a lot of information as to why you feel the way you do.

Chapter 10: INFJ & ENFP
Judgment, Emotions, Intelligence, and Vibes

Masculine Sexuality Type

INFJ (Judge as an intuitive, feel as a feeler, think as an introvert, and sense as a sensor)

Judging (Masculine)

Indecisive- Have trouble keeping on track or following directions.

Careless- you are product oriented and less likely to deal with specifics because your emphasis is on completing the task and you prefer to focus on the big picture.

Orderly- you prefer to make plans and follow them accordingly. You are usually well organized. You set goals and work toward achieving them on time and are happiest after final decisions have been made and feel satisfaction from finishing the projects.

 Stubborn- you have a work ethic, work first play later, and prefer to know what you are getting into.

Behavior: Realistic

My natural temperament of fire uses the element of my judgment to created an attitude of being judgmental to activate the action of my intuition which effects my function of judging which leads to the behavior of being realistic. This behavioral person is a natural truth teller and their work has to tell things as they naturally are or they will not be content. They love representing the truth as described.

Feeling (Masculine)

Intelligence- you consider it important to be tactful as well as truthful. You step forward and consider the effects of your actions on others.

Idealistic- you show appreciation easily to others and believe any feeling is valid whether it makes sense or not. You naturally like to please others and may need to be encouraged to have own needs met.

Emotional- you value empathy and harmony but see the exception to the rule when it pertains to your own feelings. You make judgment based on your own feelings and values but you are people oriented and aware of others feelings. You are happiest in friendly, supportive, and cooperative environments.

Accident Prone- You may be seen as overemotional, illogical, and weak. You are an impatient person but are motivated by a desire to be appreciated.

Behavior: Patient

My natural temperament of water uses the element of my emotions to create an attitude of being emotional to activate the action of my introversion which effects my function of feeling which leads to the behavior of being patient. This behavioral person is very calm and capable of handling all. They have a high tolerance of bearing even the most difficult of challenges. They are very understanding and their for you as an individual.

Thinking (Masculine)

Cunning-you are private and are energized by spending time alone, you like to think things through inside your head and you share personal info with a select few people.

Inventive- you avoid being the center of attention and keep your enthusiasm to yourself.

Diplomatic- you think more than you react to any given situation and you prefer knowing more information than a little.

Perfectionist- you listen more than you talk and respond after taking the time to think things through inside your head.

Behavior: Impatient/ Rationalist

My natural temperament of earth uses the element of my intelligence to create an attitude of being intelligent to activate the action of my extroversion which effects my function of thinking which leads to the behavior of being a rationalist of impatient. This behavioral person is unable to wait patiently. They can't endure irritation for long periods of time. They have the ability to reason.

They are always on a quest for truth even when the truth is laid out honestly before them. They have a natural desire to constantly search things over for truth. They believe "reason" to be the main source of knowledge and spiritual truth meaning because you have asked the question of "why" this brings about intelligence.

Sensing (Feminine)

Intuition- you trust what is certain, can be proven and you present information in a step-by-step manner.

Independence- you are knowledgeable of your established skills and make a judgment by the facts you gather.

Creativity- you like new ideas only if they have practical applications and tend to be specific and literal about giving a detailed description.

Romantic- you value realism and common sense and are oriented towards the present.

Behavior: Illusionist

My natural temperament of air uses the element of my vibes that I pick up on from my sight, smelling, hearing, tasting, and touching to create an attitude of being sensitive to activate the action of my perception which effects my function sensing which leads to the behavior of being an illusionist. This behavioral person is a natural liar and their work has to have some form of illusions in it or they just won't be happy.

Feminine Sexuality Type
ENFP (Judge as an intuitive, feel as an extrovert, think as a thinker and sense as a perceiver)

Judging (Masculine)

Stubborn- you trust inspiration, spiritual guidance, and fiction and are oriented towards the future.

Careless- you like new ideas for your own sake, value imagination and innovation but tend to be general and figurative by using metaphors and analogies.

Indecisive- you enjoy learning new skills and get bored easily after mastering them. You present information through leaps and hurdles in a round about manner and are uncertain about your skills but make a judgment based on your own feelings.

Behavior: Realistic
My natural temperament of fire uses the element of my judgment to created an attitude of being judgmental to activate the action of my intuition which effects my function of judging which leads to the behavior of being realistic. This behavioral person is a natural truth teller and their work has to tell things as they naturally are or they

will not be content. They love representing the truth as described.

Feeling (Feminine)

Emotional- being with others energizes you. You react more than you think and you communicate to others with enthusiasm.

Accident Prone- You respond quickly without hearing the whole conversation. you enjoy being the center of attention, and enjoy a fast pace.

Idealistic- you think out loud and are easier to know and read. You were your emotions on your sleeve and talk with your body language. When your emotions have been hurt you feel the need to voice your opinion and you share personal information freely and sometimes without enough forethought.

Intelligence- you talk more than you listen and prefer to know a little information rather than it all.

Behavior: Patient

My natural temperament of water uses the element of my emotions to create an attitude of being emotional to activate the action of my introversion which effects my function of feeling which leads to the behavior of being patient. This behavioral person is very calm and capable of handling all. They have a high tolerance of bearing even the most difficult of challenges. They are very understanding and their for you as an individual.

Thinking (Feminine)

Diplomatic- You value logic, justice and fairness which to you is one standard for all. You step back and try to see the situation objectively before problem solving. You feel the need to be convinced that a specific event or activity makes sense before you will even believe.

Perfectionist- you naturally see flaws and tend to be critical of others and believe it is more important to be truthful than tactful. Believe others feelings are irrelevant to the situation at hand.

Inventive- Believe feelings are valid only if they are logical. You are motivated by a desire for achievement and accomplishment but have a hard time translating ideas into active steps.

Cunning- you may be seen as heartless, insensitive and uncaring but are impressed by competence and the end result.

Behavior: Impatient/ Rationalist

My natural temperament of earth uses the element of my intelligence to create an attitude of being intelligent to activate the action of my extroversion which effects my function of thinking which leads to the behavior of being a rationalist of impatient. This behavioral person is unable to wait patiently. They can't endure irritation for long periods of time. They have the ability to reason. They are always on a quest for truth even when the truth is laid out honestly before them. They have a natural desire to constantly search things over for truth. They believe "reason" to be the main source of knowledge and spiritual truth meaning because you have asked the question of "why" this brings about intelligence.

Sensing (Masculine)

Creativity- you are better at concentration exercises than fantasy or daydreaming. You have a play ethic, enjoy now and finish the job later, and enjoy exercises that allow you to learn new thing and have fun doing it. You are process oriented and your emphasis is on how the task is completed.

 Intuition- you are influenced by past experiences and this is your knowledge of doing things. You don't like to brainstorm for answers and are happiest leaving your options open. You change goals as new information becomes available and prefer to not decide but continue to collect information for later usage.

Romantic-you feel satisfaction from starting projects and see time as a renewable resource and set deadlines.

Independence- you are flexible, adaptable, and change gears quickly so that you may be available for many different approaches and techniques. You have a natural curiosity and like adapting to new situations.

Behavior: <u>Illusionist</u>

My natural temperament of air uses the element of my vibes that I pick up on from my sight, smelling, hearing, tasting, and touching to create an attitude of being sensitive to activate the action of my perception which effects my function sensing which leads to the behavior of being an illusionist. This behavioral person is a natural liar and their work has to have some form of illusions in it or they just won't be happy.

Aries- The Element of Fire

Aries is the element of fire. Fire and the element of Fire create heated emotions. This is the development of the dominant function and one of your strengths. This takes place from birth to six years of age. The emotions that aid in its development are careless, indecisive, orderly, and stubborn.

Judging: Judgment/ Intuition

This is the use of your moral thought.

> Careless- you're a procrastinator as it relates to your family.
> Indecisive- you are energetic about doing your job.
> Orderly- you are selfish when it comes to money.
> Stubborn- you are self-centered when expressing your emotions.

Aries is the element of fire. Fire and the element of water create a steam of emotions, bursting with cloudy judgment toward everyone in its path. This is the development of the auxiliary function. This takes place from six to twelve years of age. The emotions that aid in its development are accident prone, emotional, idealistic, and intelligence.

Feeling: Emotions

This is the use of your moral emotions.

Accident prone- your accident prone when your upset.

Emotional- you're quick tempered when you're angry.

Idealistic- being assertive is a strength you possess.

Intelligence- you're very tactless in the way you think.

Aries is the element of fire. Fire and element of earth create an eruption of emotions, burning everything and everyone, which crosses its path. This is the development of the third function. This takes place from twelve to twenty-five years of age. The four emotions, which aid in the growth of your intelligence are cunning, diplomatic, inventive and perfectionist.

Thinking: Intelligence

This is the use of your analytical thought.

Cunning- your adventuresome as it pertains to life shows cunning.

Diplomatic- your enthusiastic when experiencing love.

Inventive- your impulsive as it pertains to their appearance.

Perfectionist- you're innovative in your home life.

Aries is the element of fire. Fire and the element of Air create a bonfire of emotions, rising giving the temperaments. This is the development of the fourth function, which takes place from twenty five to fifty years of age. The emotions that aid in its development are creativity, independence, intuition, and romantic.

Sensing: Vibes

This is the use of your analytical emotions.

    Creativity-your optimistic as it pertains to your friends

    Independence- you're courageous when you face a difficult situation.

    Intuition- you're a free spirit in your view of the world.

    Romantic- your impatient when you feel loved.

Taurus- The Element of Earth

Taurus is the element of the earth. Earth and the element of fire create an eruption of emotions. This is the development of the dominant function, which takes place from birth to six years of age. The emotions that aid in its development are careless, indecisive, orderly and stubborn.

Judging: Judgment/ Intuition

This is the use of your moral thought.

        Careless- you're very practical in your views concerning home life.

Indecisive- when expressing emotions you are very lazy.

Orderly- you are very possessive about your
appearance.

Stubborn- you are very stubborn in your views of the
world.

Taurus is the element of the earth. Earth and the element of water create a flood of emotions; drowning everything in its path. This is the development of the auxiliary function. This takes place from six to twelve years of age. The emotions that aid in its development are accident prone, emotional, idealistic and intelligence.

Feeling: Emotions

This is the use of your moral emotions.

Accident Prone- you are violent when you are angry.

Emotional- you are greedy when in love.

Idealistic- you are warm hearted when it relates to your
family.

Intelligence- being strong- willed is a strength you
possess.

Taurus is the element of the earth. Earth and the element of earth produce a dusty sandstorm of emotions. Blinding everyone in sight. This is the development of the third function. This takes place from twelve to twenty-five years of age. The emotions that aid in its development are cunning, diplomatic, inventive and perfectionist.

Thinking: Intelligence

This is the use of your analytical thought.

> Cunning- when you face a difficult situation you're very resentful.
>
> Diplomatic- you are set in your ways when you think.
>
> Inventive- When upset you are very inflexible.
>
> Perfectionist- you are very reliable when it comes to your friends.

Taurus is the element of the earth. Earth and the element of air create a tornado of emotions, thrashing and trashing everything in its sight. This is the development of the fourth function. This takes place from twenty five to fifty years of age. The emotions that aid in its development are creativity, independence, intuition and romantic.

Sensing: Vibes

This is the use of your analytical emotions.

> Creativity-Your very solid in your view of life shows creativity.
>
> Independence- you're very persistent about doing your job.
>
> Intuition- when it comes to money you're very trustworthy.
>
> Romantic- you're very affectionate when you feel loved.

Gemini- The Element of Air

Gemini is the element of air. Air and the element of fire create a bonfire of emotions, rising given the temperament. This is the development of the dominant function. This takes place from birth to six years of age. The emotions that aid in its development are careless, indecisive, orderly and stubborn.

Judging: Judgment/ Intuition

This is the use of moral thought.

Careless-you are very secretive about your view of the world.

Indecisive- you can be superficial when it pertains to money.

Orderly-you are logical in your home life.

Stubborn- you are inconsistent when expressing your emotions.

Gemini is the element of air. Air and the element of water create a hurricane of emotions, thrashing and drowning with words everyone in its path. This is the development of the auxiliary function. This takes place from six to twelve years of age. The emotions that aid in its development are accident prone, emotional, idealistic and intelligence.

Feeling: Emotions

This is the use of moral emotions.

Accident Prone- you are very restless when it pertains to your family.

Emotional- you are nosey when you face a difficult situation.

369

Idealistic- you are very flighty in your appearance.

Intelligence- you are very spontaneous in your views of life.

Gemini is the element of air. Air and the element of earth create a tornado of emotions, thrashing and trashing everything in its sight. This is the development of the third function. This takes place from twelve to twenty-five years of age. The emotions that aid in its development are cunning, diplomatic, inventive and perfectionist.

Thinking: Intelligence

This is the use of analytical thought.

Cunning- you are very cunning when you are upset.

Diplomatic- when you are angry you are very devious.

Inventive- you are a communicator about the way you think.

Perfectionist- you can be very versatile when in love.

Gemini is the element of air. Air and the element of air create a world wind of emotions. This is the development of the fourth function. This takes place from twenty five to fifty years of age. The emotions that aid in its development are creativity, independence, intuition and romantic.

Sensing: Vibes

This is the use of analytical emotions.

Creativity- you are very energetic when it pertains to your friends.

Independence- you are adaptable as it relates to your job.

Intuition- being an intellectual is a strength possessed.

Romantic- you are very witty when in love.

Cancer- The Element of Water

Cancer is the element of water. Water and the element of fire create a steam of emotions. This is the development of the dominant function. This takes place from birth to six years of age. The emotions that aid in its development are careless, indecisive, orderly and stubborn.

Judging: Judgment/ Intuition

This is the use of moral thought.

Careless- you are very shrewd when you are angry.

Indecisive- your home life is very unstable.

Orderly- your appearance is changeable.

Stubborn- when upset you are unforgiving.

Cancer is the element of water. Water and the element of water create a wave of emotions, crashing and drowning everyone in its path. This is the development of the second function auxiliary. This takes place from six to twelve years of age. The emotions that aid in its development are accident prone, emotional, idealistic and intelligence.

Feeling: Emotions

This is the use of moral emotions.

Accident Prone-you are hyper sensitive when it pertains to
family.

Emotional- when you face a difficult situation you can be very
emotional.

Idealistic- you are thrifty when it pertains to money.

Intelligence- you are sensitive in your view of the world.

Cancer is the element of water. Water and the element of earth create a flood of emotions, drowning everything in its path. This is the development of the third function. This takes place from twelve to twenty-five years of age. The emotions that aid in its development are cunning, diplomatic, inventive and perfectionist.
Thinking: Intelligence
This is the use of analytical thought.

Cunning- being sympathetic is a strength possessed.

Diplomatic- when expressing emotions you can be over
indulgent in self-pity.

Inventive- you are very receptive when you think.

Perfectionist- when you feel loved you can be moody.

Cancer is the element of water. Water and the element of air create a hurricane of emotions. This is the development of the fourth function. This takes place from twenty five to fifty years of age. The emotions that aid in its development are creativity, independence, intuition, and romantic.

Sensing: Vibes

This is the use of analytical emotions.

Creativity- you're very kind to your friends.

Independence- your job is very messy.

Intuition- you're very judgmental in your views of life.

Romantic- when in love you can be overly emotional.

Leo- The Element of Fire

Leo is the element of fire. Fire and the element of fire create heated emotions. This is a very judgmental person. This is the development of the dominant function. This takes place from birth to six years of age. The emotions that aid in its development are careless, indecisive, orderly and stubborn.

Judging: Judgment/ Intuition

This is the use of your moral thought.

Careless- when you're angry you appear very snobbish.

Indecisive- at your job you are very egotistical.

Orderly- your home life is organized.

Stubborn- when upset you are intolerant.

Leo is the element of fire. Fire and water create a steam of emotions. This is the development of the second function auxiliary. This takes place from six to twelve years of age. The emotions that aid in its development are accident prone, emotional, idealistic and intelligence.

Feeling: Emotions

This is the use of your moral emotions.

Accident Prone- when expressing emotions you are attention-
seeking.

Emotional- when you feel loved you are generous.

Idealistic- being powerful is a strength possessed.

Intelligence- you are very broad-minded in the way you
think.

Leo is the element of fire. Fire and the element of earth create an eruption of emotions. This is the development of the third function. This takes place from twelve to twenty-five years of age. The emotions that aid in its development are cunning, diplomatic, inventive and perfectionist.

Thinking: Intelligence

This is the use of your analytical thought.

Cunning- you are patronizing when it relates to your family.

Diplomatic- when you face a difficult situation you are dogmatic.

Inventive- your view of the world is creative.

Perfectionist- when it comes to money you are extravagant.

Leo is the element of fire. Fire and the element of air create a bonfire of emotions, rising given the temperament. This is the development of the fourth function. This takes place from twenty five to fifty years of age. The emotions that aid in its development are creativity, independence, intuition, and romantic.

Sensing: Vibes

This is the use of your analytical emotions.

Creativity- you are very enthusiastic about life.

Independence- you are conceited about your appearance.

Intuition-you are very optimistic when it comes to your friends.

Romantic- when in love you are dramatic.

Virgo- The Element of Earth

Virgo is the element of earth. Earth and the element of fire create an eruption of emotions, burning and melting with words everyone in its path. This is the development of the dominant function. This takes place from birth to six years of age. The emotions that aid in its development are careless, indecisive, orderly and stubborn.

Judging: Judgment/ Intuition

This is the use of your moral thought.

Careless- you are neat in your appearance.

Indecisive- when angry you are grouchy.

Orderly- you are meticulous when it comes to money.

Stubborn- you are analytical in your view of family.

Virgo is the element of earth. Earth and the element of water create a flood of emotions, drowning with words everyone in its path. This is the development of the second function auxiliary. This takes place from six to twelve years of age. The emotions that aid in its development are accident prone, emotional, idealistic and intelligence.

Feeling: Emotions

This is the use of your moral emotions.

> Accident Prone- when you face a difficult situation you are fussy.
>
> Emotional- when expressing your emotions you are pessimistic.
>
> Idealistic- you are conscientious about your friends.
>
> Intelligence- you are hypercritical in your view of the world.

Virgo is the element of earth. Earth and the element of earth create a dusty sandstorm of emotions, blinding everyone in its path. This is the development of the third function. This takes place from twelve to twenty-five years of age. The emotions that aid in its development are cunning, diplomatic, inventive and perfectionist.

Thinking: Intelligence

This is the use of your analytical thought.

> Cunning- being prudish is a strength possessed.
>
> Diplomatic- when upset you are cranky.
>
> Inventive- you are a busy body in your home life.
>
> Perfectionist- you are a worrier when you feel loved.

Virgo is the element of earth. Earth and the element of air create a tornado of emotions, thrashing and trashing everyone in its path. This is the development of the fourth function. This takes place from birth to six years of age. The emotions that aid in its development are creativity, independence, intuition, and romantic.

Sensing: Vibes

This is the use of your analytical emotions.

Creativity- you are practical in the way you think.

Independence- at your job you are a workaholic.

Intuition- you are hypercritical in your view of life.

Romantic- when in love you are a perfectionist.

Libra- The Element of Air

Libra is the element of air. Air and the element of fire create a bonfire of emotions, rising given the words and temperament. This is the development of the dominant function. This takes place from birth to six years of age. The emotions that aid in its development are careless, indecisive, orderly and stubborn.

Judging: Judgment/ Intuition

This is the use of your moral thought.

Careless- you are extravagant when you have money.

Indecisive- when expressing emotions you are very indecisive and hard for you to make up your mind.

Orderly- your home life is orderly.

Stubborn- your view of life is easy going.

Perfectionist- you are a seeker in harmony when it relates to the world.

Libra is the element of air. Air and the element of water create a hurricane of emotions; thrashing and drowning with words everyone in its path. This is the development of the second function auxiliary. This takes place from six to twelve years of age. The emotions that aid in its development are accident prone, emotional, idealistic and intelligence.

Feeling: Emotions

This is the use of your moral emotions.

    Accident Prone- when angry you are resentful.

    Emotional- you are gullible when it comes to your family.

    Idealistic- your job is idealistic and you don't expect much.

    Intelligence- you are refined in the way you think.

Libra is the element of air. Air and the element of earth create a tornado of emotions, thrashing and drowning with words everyone in its path. This is the development of the third function. This takes place from twelve to twenty-five years of age. The emotions that aid in its development are cunning, diplomatic, inventive and perfectionist.

Thinking: Intelligence

This is the use of your analytical thought.

    Cunning- when you face a difficult situation you are charming.

    Diplomatic- when upset you are diplomatic.

    Inventive- you are changeable in your appearance.

Libra is the element of air. Air and the element of air create a world wind of emotions; taking your breath away with words. This is the development of the fourth function. This takes place from twenty five to fifty years of age. The emotions that aid in its development are creativity, independence, intuition, and romantic.

Sensing: Vibes

This is the use of your analytical emotions.

Creativity- when you feel loved you are flirtatious.

Independence- you are frivolous when it pertains to your friends.

Intuition- being two faced is a strength possessed.

Romantic- when in love you are romantic.

Scorpio- The Element of Water

Scorpio is the element of water. Water and the element of fire create a steam of emotions. This is the development of the dominant function. This takes place from birth to six years of age. The emotions that aid in its development are careless, indecisive, orderly and stubborn.

Judging: Judgment/ Intuition

This is the use of your moral thought.

Careless- when expressing emotions you are overly emotional.

Indecisive- you are energetic when it relates to your friends.

Orderly-being persistent is a strength possessed.

Stubborn-when upset you are stubborn.

Scorpio is the element of water. Water and the element of water create a wave of emotions, crashing and drowning everyone in its path. This is the development of the second function auxiliary. This takes place from six to twelve years of age. The emotions that aid in its development are accident prone, emotional, idealistic and intelligence.

Feeling: Emotions

This is the use of your moral emotions.

Accident Prone- you are violent when you are angry.

Emotional- when you feel loved you are emotional.

Idealistic- your appearance is practical.

Intelligence- you are very manipulative when it comes to money.

Scorpio is the element of water. Water and the element of earth create a flood of emotions, drowning with words everything in its path. This is the development of the third function. This takes place from twelve to twenty-five years of age. The emotions that aid in its development are cunning, diplomatic, inventive and perfectionist.

Thinking: Intelligence

This is the use of your analytical thought.

Cunning- you are vengeful in your views of the world.

Diplomatic- when you face a difficult situation you are jealous.

Inventive- you are determined when it relates to your family.

Perfectionist- your home life is secretive.

Scorpio is the element of water. Water and the element of air create a hurricane of emotions, thrashing and drowning with words everyone in its path. This is the development of the fourth function. This takes place from twenty five to fifty years of age. The emotions that aid in its development are creativity, independence, intuition, and romantic.

Sensing: Vibes

This is the use of your analytical emotions.

Creativity-you are creative in life.

Independence- you are independent in your job.

Intuition- you are very judgmental when you think.

Romantic- when in love you are passionate.

Sagittarius- The Element of Fire

Sagittarius is the element of fire. Fire and the element of fire create heated emotions, burning with words everything in its path. This is a very judgmental person. This is the development of the dominant function. This takes place from birth to six years of age. The emotions that aid in its development are careless, indecisive, orderly and stubborn.

Judging: Judgment/ Intuition

This is the use of your moral thought.

Careless- you are careless in the way you think.

Indecisive- when expressing emotions you are frank and give short answers.

Orderly- your home life is restless.

Stubborn- you are exaggerative when you have money.

Sagittarius is the element of fire. Fire and the element of water create a steam of emotions, bursting with cloudy judgment toward everyone in its path. This is the development of the second function auxiliary. This takes place from six to twelve years of age. The emotions that aid in its development are accident prone, emotional, idealistic and intelligence.

Feeling: Emotions

This is the use of your moral emotions.

Accident Prone- you are irresponsible when it pertains to family.

Emotional-when you feel loved you are ambitious.

Idealistic-you are very dependable when it pertains to friends.

Intelligence- you are energetic when it pertains to your job.

Sagittarius is the element of fire. Fire and the element of earth create an eruption of emotions, burning and melting with words everyone in its path. This is the development of the third function. This takes place from twelve to twenty-five years of age. The emotions that aid in its development are cunning, diplomatic, inventive and perfectionist.

Thinking: Intelligence

This is the use of your analytical thought.

Cunning- when faced with a difficult situation you remain sincere.

Diplomatic-you are frivolous when you are upset.

Inventive- you are tactless in your appearance.

Perfectionist-you are undisciplined in your life.

Sagittarius is the element of fire. Fire and the element of air create a bonfire of emotions, rising given the words and temperament. This is the development of the fourth function. This takes place from twenty five to fifty years of age. The emotions that aid in its development are creativity, independence, intuition, and romantic.

Sensing: Vibes

This is the use of your analytical emotions.

Creativity- you are erratic when upset.

Independence- you are free spirited in your view of the world.

Intuition- being optimistic is a strength you possess.

Romantic-when in love you are very passionate.

Capricorn- The Element of Earth

Capricorn is the element of earth. Earth and the element of fire create an eruption of emotions, burning and melting with words everyone in its path. This is the development of the dominant function. This takes place from birth to six years of age. The emotions that aid in its development are careless, indecisive, orderly and stubborn.

Judging: Judgment/ Intuition

This is the use of your moral thought.

Careless- when upset you are mean.

Indecisive- when you feel loved you are determined.

Orderly- your home life is organized.

Stubborn- when you face a difficult situation you are rigid.

Capricorn is the element of earth. Earth and the element of water create a flood of emotions, drowning with words everything in its path. This is the development of the second function auxiliary. This takes place from six to twelve years of age. The emotions that aid in its development are accident prone, emotional, idealistic and intelligence.

Feeling: Emotions

This is the use of your moral emotions.

Accident Prone- you are a social climber when it pertains to friends.

Emotional- you are miserly at expressing emotions.

Idealistic- having a sense of humor is a strength you possess.

Intelligence- when you are angry you are a nit-picker and you pick the least important thing to argue about.

Capricorn is the element of earth. Earth and the element of earth create a dusty, sandstorm of emotions, blinding everyone with words in its path. This is the development of the third function. This takes place from twelve to twenty-five years of age. The emotions that aid in its development are cunning, diplomatic, inventive and perfectionist.

Thinking: Intelligence

This is the use of your analytical thought.

Cunning-you are opportunistic when it pertains to money.

Diplomatic- you are prudent in the way you think.

Inventive- you are reliable when it pertains to family.

Perfectionist- you are overly ordinary in your life.

Capricorn is the element of earth. Earth and the element of air create a tornado of emotions, thrashing and trashing with words everyone in its sight. This is the development of the fourth function. This takes place from twenty five to fifty years of age. The emotions that aid in its development are creativity, independence, intuition, and romantic.

Sensing: Vibes

This is the use of your analytical emotions.

Creativity-you are ambitious about doing your job.

Independence- you are comfortable in your appearance.

Intuition- when in love you are generous.

Romantic-you are patient in your view of the world.

Aquarius- The Element of Air

Aquarius is the element of air. Air and the element of fire create a bonfire of emotions, rising given the words and temperament. This is the development of the dominant function. This takes place from birth to six years of age. The emotions that aid in its development are careless, indecisive, orderly and stubborn.

Judging: Judgment/ Intuition

This is the use of your moral thought.

Careless- your home life is disorganized.

Indecisive- you are impulsive in your life.

Orderly- you are neat in appearance.

Stubborn- you are rebellious when you face a difficult situation.

Aquarius is the element of air. Air and the element of water create a hurricane of emotions, thrashing and drowning with words everyone in its path. This is the development of the second function auxiliary. This takes place from six to twelve years of age. The emotions that aid in its development are accident prone, emotional, idealistic and intelligence.

Feeling: Emotions

This is the use of your moral emotions.

Accident Prone- you are tactless when it pertains to friends.

Emotional- when expressing emotions you are friendly.

Idealistic-you are idealistic when it pertains to money.

Intelligence- when upset you are intelligent.

Aquarius is the element of air. Air and the element of earth create a tornado of emotions, thrashing and trashing with words everyone in its sight. This is the development of the third function. This takes place from twelve to twenty-five years of age. The emotions that aid in its development are cunning, diplomatic, inventive and perfectionist.

Thinking: Intelligence

This is the use of your analytical thought.

Cunning- when angry you are unpredictable.

Diplomatic- you are human in your view of the world.

Inventive- being inventive is a strength you possess.

Perfectionist- when in love you are charismatic.

Aquarius is the element of air. Air and the element of air create a wurl wind of emotions, taking your breath away with words. This is the development of the fourth function. This takes place from twenty five to fifty years of age. The emotions that aid in its development are creativity, independence, intuition, and romantic.

Sensing: Vibes

This is the use of your analytical emotions.

Creativity- you are eccentric when it pertains to family and there is no one like you.

Independence- you are independent at your job.

Intuition- you are judgmental in the way you think.

Romantic-when you feel loved you are perverse.

Pisces- The Element of Water

Pisces is the element of water. Water and the element of fire create a steam of emotions; bursting with cloudy judgment toward everyone in its path. This is the development of the dominant function. This takes place from birth to six years of age. The emotions that aid in its development are careless, indecisive, orderly and stubborn.

Judging: Judgment/ Intuition

This is the use of your moral thought.

Careless- you are careless when it pertains to family.

Indecisive- when expressing emotions you are indecisive.

Orderly- you are receptive at your job.

Stubborn- when you are angry you are vague and don't reveal a lot of information as to why you feel the way you do.

Pisces is the element of water. Water and the element of water create a wave of emotions, crashing and drowning everyone in its path. This is the development of the second function auxiliary. This takes place from six to twelve years of age. The emotions that aid in its development are accident prone, emotional, idealistic and intelligence.

Feeling: Emotions

This is the use of your moral emotions.

    Accident Prone- when you feel loved you are weak-willed.

    Emotional-when upset you are emotional.

    Idealistic- you are compassionate in your view of the world.

    Intelligence- you are unworldly in the way you think.

Pisces is the element of water. Water and the element of earth create a flood of emotions, drowning with words everything in its path. This is the development of the third function. This takes place from twelve to twenty-five years of age. The emotions that aid in its development are cunning, diplomatic, inventive and perfectionist.

Thinking: Intelligence

This is the use of your analytical thought.

    Cunning- when faced with a difficult situation you are secretive.

    Diplomatic- you are compassionate in your view of the world.

    Inventive-you are imaginative when it pertains to money.

    Perfectionist- you are impressionable in your life.

Pisces is the element of water. Water and the element of air create a hurricane of emotions, thrashing and drowning with words everyone in its path. This is the development of the fourth function. This takes place from twenty five to fifty years of age. The emotions that aid in its development are creativity, independence, intuition, and romantic.

Sensing: Vibes

This is the use of your analytical emotions.

Creativity- you are sensitive when it pertains to friends.

Independence- you are mysterious in your appearance.

Intuition- being judgmental is a strength possessed.

Romantic- when in love you are romantic.

Chapter 11: ISFP & ESFJ
Emotions, Vibes, Judgment, and Intelligence

Masculine Sexuality Type

ISFP- Feel as a feeler, sense as a perceiver, judge as a judger, and think introverted

Feeling (Masculine)

Intelligence- you consider it important to be tactful as well as truthful. You step forward and consider the effects of your actions on others.

Idealistic- you show appreciation easily to others and believe any feeling is valid whether it makes sense or not. You naturally like to please others and may need to be encouraged to have own needs met.

 Emotional- you value empathy and harmony but see the exception to the rule when it pertains to your own feelings. You make judgment based on your own feelings and values but you are people oriented and aware of others feelings. You are happiest in friendly, supportive, and cooperative environments.

 Accident Prone- You may be seen as overemotional, illogical, and weak. You are an impatient person but are motivated by a desire to be appreciated.

Behavior: <u>Patient</u>

My natural temperament of water uses the element of my emotions to create an attitude of being emotional to activate the action of my introversion which effects my function of feeling which leads to the behavior of being patient. This behavioral person is very calm and capable of handling all. They have a high tolerance of bearing even the most difficult of challenges. They are very understanding and their for you as an individual.

Sensing (Masculine)

Creativity- you are better at concentration exercises than fantasy or daydreaming. You have a play ethic, enjoy now and finish the job later, and enjoy exercises that allow you to learn new thing and have fun doing it. You are process oriented and your emphasis is on how the task is completed.

Intuition- you are influenced by past experiences and this is your knowledge of doing things. You don't like to brainstorm for answers and are happiest leaving your options open. You change goals as new information becomes available and prefer to not decide but continue to collect information for later usage.

Romantic-you feel satisfaction from starting projects and see time as a renewable resource and set deadlines.

Independence- you are flexible, adaptable, and change gears quickly so that you may be available for many different approaches and techniques. You have a natural curiosity and like adapting to new situations.

Behavior: Illusionist

My natural temperament of air uses the element of my vibes that I pick up on from my sight, smelling, hearing, tasting, and touching to create an attitude of being sensitive to activate the action of my perception which effects my function sensing which leads to the behavior of being an illusionist. This behavioral person is a natural liar and their work has to have some form of illusions in it or they just won't be happy.

Judging (Feminine)

Indecisive- Have trouble keeping on track or following directions.
Careless- you are product oriented and less likely to deal with specifics because your emphasis is on completing the task and you prefer to focus on the big picture.
Orderly- you prefer to make plans and follow them accordingly. You are usually well organized. You set goals and work toward achieving them on time and are happiest after final decisions have been made and feel satisfaction from finishing the projects.

Stubborn- you have a work ethic, work first play later, and prefer to know what you are getting into.

Behavior: Realistic

My natural temperament of fire uses the element of my judgment to created an attitude of being judgmental to activate the action of my intuition which effects my function of judging which leads to the behavior of being realistic. This behavioral person is a natural truth teller and their work has to tell things as they naturally are or they will not be content. They love representing the truth as described.

Thinking (Masculine)

Cunning-you are private and are energized by spending time alone, you like to think things through inside your head and you share personal info with a select few people.

Inventive- you avoid being the center of attention and keep your enthusiasm to yourself.

Diplomatic- you think more than you react to any given situation and you prefer knowing more information than a little.

Perfectionist- you listen more than you talk and respond after taking the time to think things through inside your head.

Behavior: Impatient/ Rationalist

My natural temperament of earth uses the element of my intelligence to create an attitude of being intelligent to activate the action of my extroversion which effects my function of thinking which leads to the behavior of being a rationalist of impatient. This behavioral person is unable to wait patiently. They can't endure irritation for long periods of time. They have the ability to reason. They are always on a quest for truth even when the truth is laid out honestly before them. They have a natural desire to constantly search things over for truth. They believe "reason" to be the main source of knowledge and spiritual truth meaning because you have asked the question of "why" this brings about intelligence.

Feminine Sexuality Type
ESFJ- Feel as an Extrovert, sense as sensor, judge as a judger, and think as a thinker

Feeling (Feminine)

Emotional- being with others energizes you. You react more than you think and you communicate to others with enthusiasm.

Accident Prone- You respond quickly without hearing the whole conversation. you enjoy being the center of attention, and enjoy a fast pace.

Idealistic- you think out loud and are easier to know and read. You were your emotions on your sleeve and talk with your body language. When your emotions have been hurt you feel the need to voice your opinion and you share personal information freely and sometimes without enough forethought.

Intelligence- you talk more than you listen and prefer to know a little information rather than it all.

Behavior: Patient

My natural temperament of water uses the element of my emotions to create an attitude of being emotional to activate the action of my introversion which effects my function of feeling which leads to the behavior of being patient. This behavioral person is very calm and capable of handling all. They have a high tolerance of bearing even the most difficult of challenges. They are very understanding and their for you as an individual.

Sensing (Feminine)

Intuition- you trust what is certain, can be proven and you present information in a step-by-step manner.

Independence- you are knowledgeable of your established skills and make a judgment by the facts you gather.

Creativity- you like new ideas only if they have practical applications and tend to be specific and literal about giving a detailed description.

Romantic- you value realism and common sense and are oriented towards the present.

Behavior: <u>Illusionist</u>

My natural temperament of air uses the element of my vibes that I pick up on from my sight, smelling, hearing, tasting, and touching to create an attitude of being sensitive to activate the action of my perception which effects my function sensing which leads to the behavior of being an illusionist. This behavioral person is a natural liar and their work has to have some form of illusions in it or they just won't be happy.

<u>Judging</u> (Feminine)

Indecisive- Have trouble keeping on track or following directions.

Careless- you are product oriented and less likely to deal with specifics because your emphasis is on completing the task and you prefer to focus on the big picture.

Orderly- you prefer to make plans and follow them accordingly. You are usually well organized. You set goals and work toward achieving them on time and are happiest after final decisions have been made and feel satisfaction from finishing the projects.

 Stubborn- you have a work ethic, work first play later, and prefer to know what you are getting into.

Behavior: <u>Realistic</u>

My natural temperament of fire uses the element of my judgment to created an attitude of being judgmental to activate the action of my intuition which effects my function of judging which leads to the behavior of being realistic. This behavioral person is a natural truth teller and their work has to tell things as they naturally are or they will not be content. They love representing the truth as described.

Thinking (Feminine)

Diplomatic- You value logic, justice and fairness which to you is one standard for all. You step back and try to see the situation objectively before problem solving. You feel the need to be convinced that a specific event or activity makes sense before you will even believe.

Perfectionist- you naturally see flaws and tend to be critical of others and believe it is more important to be truthful than tactful. Believe others feelings are irrelevant to the situation at hand.

Inventive- Believe feelings are valid only if they are logical. You are motivated by a desire for achievement and accomplishment but have a hard time translating ideas into active steps.

Cunning- you may be seen as heartless, insensitive and uncaring but are impressed by competence and the end result.

Behavior: <u>Impatient/ Rationalist</u>

My natural temperament of earth uses the element of my intelligence to create an attitude of being intelligent to activate the action of my extroversion which effects my function of thinking which leads to the behavior of being a rationalist of impatient. This behavioral person is unable to wait patiently. They can't endure irritation for long periods of time. They have the ability to reason. They are always on a quest for truth even when the truth is laid out honestly before them. They have a natural desire to constantly search things over for truth. They believe "reason" to be the main source of knowledge and spiritual truth meaning because you have asked the question of "why" this brings about intelligence.

Aries- The Element of Fire

Aries is the element of fire. Fire and the element of water create a steam of emotions, bursting with cloudy judgment toward everyone in its path. This is the development of the dominant function and one of your strengths. This takes place from birth to six years of age. The emotions that aid in its development are accident prone, emotional, idealistic, and intelligence.

Feeling: Emotions

This is the use of your moral emotions.

    Accident prone- your accident prone when your upset.

    Emotional- you're quick tempered when you're angry.

Idealistic- being assertive is a strength you possess.

Intelligence- you're very tactless in the way you think.

Aries is the element of fire. Fire and the element of Air create a bonfire of emotions, rising giving the temperaments. This is the development of the second function auxiliary. This takes place from six to twelve years of age. The emotions that aid in its development are creativity, independence, intuition, and romantic.

Sensing: Vibes

This is the use of your analytical emotions.

Creativity-your optimistic as it pertains to your friends

Independence- you're courageous when you face a difficult situation.

Intuition- you're a free spirit in your view of the world.

Romantic- your impatient when you feel loved.

Aries is the element of fire. Fire and the element of Fire create heated emotions. This is the development of the third function. This takes place from twelve to twenty-five years of age. This function will never be as strong as the dominant and auxiliary functions. The emotions that aid in its development are careless, indecisive, orderly, and stubborn.

Judging: Judgment/ Intuition

This is the use of your moral thought.

Careless- you're a procrastinator as it relates to your family.

Indecisive- you are energetic about doing your job.

Orderly- you are selfish when it comes to money.

Stubborn- you are self-centered when expressing your
emotions.

Aries is the element of fire. Fire and element of Earth create an eruption of emotions, burning everything and everyone, which crosses its path. This is the development of the fourth function, which takes place from twenty five to fifty years of age. The four emotions, which aid in the growth of your intelligence are cunning, diplomatic, inventive and perfectionist.

Thinking: Intelligence

This is the use of your analytical thought.

Cunning- your adventuresome as it pertains to life shows
cunning.

Diplomatic- your enthusiastic when experiencing love.

Inventive- your impulsive as it pertains to their appearance.

Perfectionist- you're innovative in your home life.

Taurus- The Element of Earth

Taurus is the element of the earth. Earth and the element of water create a flood of emotions, drowning everything in its path. This is the development of the dominant function, which takes place from birth to six years of age. The emotions that aid in its development are accident prone, emotional, idealistic and intelligence.

Feeling: Emotions

This is the use of your moral emotions.

> Accident Prone- you are violent when you are angry.
>
> Emotional- you are greedy when in love.
>
> Idealistic- you are warm hearted when it relates to your family.
>
> Intelligence- being strong- willed is a strength you possess.

Taurus is the element of the earth. Earth and the element of air create a tornado of emotions, thrashing and trashing everything in its sight. This is the development of the auxiliary function. This takes place from six to twelve years of age. The emotions that aid in its development are creativity, independence, intuition and romantic.

Sensing: Vibes

This is the use of your analytical emotions.

> Creativity-Your very solid in your view of life shows creativity.

Independence- you're very persistent about doing your
   job.
Intuition- when it comes to money you're very
   trustworthy.
Romantic- you're very affectionate when you feel loved.

Taurus is the element of the earth. Earth and the element of fire
create an eruption of emotions. This is the development of the
third function. This takes place from twelve to twenty-five years of
age. The emotions that aid in its development are careless,
indecisive, orderly and stubborn.
Judging: Judgment/ Intuition
This is the use of your moral thought.

   Careless- you're very practical in your views concerning
      home life.
   Indecisive- when expressing emotions you are very lazy.
   Orderly- you are very possessive about your
      appearance.
   Stubborn- you are very stubborn in your views of the
      world.

Taurus is the element of the earth. Earth and the element of earth
produce a dusty sandstorm of emotions. Blinding everyone in sight.
This is the development of the fourth function. This takes place
from twenty five to fifty years of age. The emotions that aid in its

development are cunning, diplomatic, inventive and perfectionist.

Thinking: Intelligence

This is the use of your analytical thought.

>Cunning- when you face a difficult situation you're very
>resentful.
>
>Diplomatic- you are set in your ways when you think.
>
>Inventive- When upset you are very inflexible.
>
>Perfectionist- you are very reliable when it comes to
>your friends.

Gemini- The Element of Air

Gemini is the element of air. Air and the element of water create a
hurricane of emotions. This is the development of the dominant
function. This takes place from birth to six years of age. The
emotions that aid in its development are accident prone, emotional,
idealistic and intelligence.

Feeling: Emotions

This is the use of moral emotions.

>Accident Prone- you are very restless when it pertains to
>your family.
>
>Emotional- you are nosey when you face a difficult
>situation.
>
>Idealistic- you are very flighty in your appearance.
>
>Intelligence- you are very spontaneous in your views of
>life.

Gemini is the element of air. Air and the element of air create a world wind of emotions. This is the development of the auxiliary function. This takes place from six to twelve years of age. The emotions that aid in its development are creativity, independence, intuition and romantic.

Sensing: Vibes

This is the use of analytical emotions.

Creativity- you are very energetic when it pertains to your friends.

Independence- you are adaptable as it relates to your job.

Intuition- being an intellectual is a strength possessed.

Romantic- you are very witty when in love.

Gemini is the element of air. Air and the element of fire create a bonfire of emotions, rising given the temperament. This is the development of the third function. This takes place from twelve to twenty-five years of age. The emotions that aid in its development are careless, indecisive, orderly and stubborn.

Judging: Judgment/ Intuition

This is the use of moral thought.

Careless-you are very secretive about your view of the world.

Indecisive- you can be superficial when it pertains to money.

Orderly-you are logical in your home life.

Stubborn- you are inconsistent when expressing your emotions.

Gemini is the element of air. Air and the element of earth create a tornado of emotions, thrashing and trashing everything in its sight. This is the development of the fourth function. This takes place from twenty five to fifty years of age. The emotions that aid in its development are cunning, diplomatic, inventive and perfectionist.

Thinking: Intelligence

This is the use of analytical thought.

Cunning- you are very cunning when you are upset.

Diplomatic- when you are angry you are very devious.

Inventive- you are a communicator about the way you think.

Perfectionist- you can be very versatile when in love.

Cancer- The Element of Water

Cancer is the element of water. Water and the element of water create a wave of emotions. This is the development of the dominant function. This takes place from birth to six years of age. The emotions that aid in its development are accident prone, emotional, idealistic and intelligence.

Feeling: Emotions

This is the use of moral emotions.

Accident Prone-you are hyper sensitive when it pertains to family.

Emotional- when you face a difficult situation you can be very emotional.

Idealistic- you are thrifty when it pertains to money.

Intelligence- you are sensitive in your view of the world.

Cancer is the element of water. Water and the element of air create a hurricane of emotions. This is the development of the second function auxiliary. This takes place from six to twelve years of age. The emotions that aid in its development are creativity, independence, intuition, and romantic.

Sensing: Vibes

This is the use of analytical emotions.

Creativity- you're very kind to your friends.

Independence- your job is very messy.

Intuition- you're very judgmental in your views of life.

Romantic- when in love you can be overly emotional.

Cancer is the element of water. Water and the element of fire create a steam of emotions. This is the development of the third function. This takes place from twelve to twenty-five years of age. The emotions that aid in its development are careless, indecisive, orderly and stubborn.

Judging: Judgment/ Intuition

This is the use of moral thought.

Careless- you are very shrewd when you are angry.

Indecisive- your home life is very unstable.

Orderly- your appearance is changeable.

Stubborn- when upset you are unforgiving.

Cancer is the element of water. Water and the element of earth create a flood of emotions, drowning everything in its path. This is the development of the fourth function. This takes place from twenty five to fifty years of age. The emotions that aid in its development are cunning, diplomatic, inventive and perfectionist.
Thinking: Intelligence
This is the use of analytical thought.

Cunning- being sympathetic is a strength possessed.

Diplomatic- when expressing emotions you can be over indulgent in self-pity.

Inventive- you are very receptive when you think.

Perfectionist- when you feel loved you can be moody.

Leo- The Element of Fire

Leo is the element of fire. Fire and water create a steam of emotions. This is the development of the dominant function. This takes place from birth to six years of age. The emotions that aid in its development are accident prone, emotional, idealistic and intelligence.
Feeling: Emotions
This is the use of your moral emotions.

Accident Prone- when expressing emotions you are attention-seeking.

Emotional- when you feel loved you are generous.

Idealistic- being powerful is a strength possessed.

Intelligence- you are very broad-minded in the way you think.

Leo is the element of fire. Fire and the element of air create a bonfire of emotions, rising given the temperament. This is the development of the second function auxiliary. This takes place from six to twelve years of age. The emotions that aid in its development are creativity, independence, intuition, and romantic.

Sensing: Vibes

This is the use of your analytical emotions.

Creativity- you are very enthusiastic about life.

Independence- you are conceited about your appearance.

Intuition-you are very optimistic when it comes to your friends.

Romantic- when in love you are dramatic.

Leo is the element of fire. Fire and the element of fire create heated emotions. This is a very judgmental person. This is the development of the third function. This takes place from twelve to twenty-five years of age. The emotions that aid in its development are careless, indecisive, orderly and stubborn.

Judging: Judgment/ Intuition

This is the use of your moral thought.

Careless- when you're angry you appear very snobbish.

Indecisive- at your job you are very egotistical.

Orderly- your home life is organized.

Stubborn- when upset you are intolerant.

Leo is the element of fire. Fire and the element of earth create an eruption of emotions. This is the development of the fourth function. This takes place from twenty five to fifty years of age. The emotions that aid in its development are cunning, diplomatic, inventive and perfectionist.

Thinking: Intelligence

This is the use of your analytical thought.

Cunning- you are patronizing when it relates to your family.

Diplomatic- when you face a difficult situation you are dogmatic.

Inventive- your view of the world is creative.

Perfectionist- when it comes to money you are extravagant.

Virgo- The Element of Earth

Virgo is the element of earth. Earth and the element of water create a flood of emotions, drowning with words everyone in its path. This is the development of the dominant function. This takes place from birth to six years of age. The emotions that aid in its development are accident prone, emotional, idealistic and intelligence.

Feeling: Emotions

This is the use of your moral emotions.

Accident Prone- when you face a difficult situation you are
   fussy.
Emotional- when expressing your emotions you are pessimistic.
Idealistic- you are conscientious about your friends.
Intelligence- you are hypercritical in your view of the world.

Virgo is the element of earth. Earth and the element of air create a tornado of emotions, thrashing and trashing everyone in its path. This is the development of the second function auxiliary. This takes place from six to twelve years of age. The emotions that aid in its development are creativity, independence, intuition, and romantic.
Sensing: Vibes
This is the use of your analytical emotions.
   Creativity- you are practical in the way you think.
   Independence- at your job you are a workaholic.
   Intuition- you are hypercritical in your view of life.
   Romantic- when in love you are a perfectionist.

Virgo is the element of earth. Earth and the element of fire create an eruption of emotions, burning and melting with words everyone in its path. This is the development of the third function. This takes place from twelve to twenty-five years of age. The emotions that aid in its development are careless, indecisive, orderly and stubborn.
Judging: Judgment/ Intuition

This is the use of your moral thought.

Careless- you are neat in your appearance.

Indecisive- when angry you are grouchy.

Orderly- you are meticulous when it comes to money.

Stubborn- you are analytical in your view of family.

Virgo is the element of earth. Earth and the element of earth create a dusty sandstorm of emotions, blinding everyone in its path. This is the development of the fourth function. This takes place from birth to six years of age. The emotions that aid in its development are cunning, diplomatic, inventive and perfectionist.

Thinking: Intelligence

This is the use of your analytical thought.

Cunning- being prudish is a strength possessed.

Diplomatic- when upset you are cranky.

Inventive- you are a busy body in your home life.

Perfectionist- you are a worrier when you feel loved.

Libra- The Element of Air

Libra is the element of air. Air and the element of water create a hurricane of emotions; thrashing and drowning with words everyone in its path. This is the development of the dominant function. This takes place from birth to six years of age. The emotions that aid in its development are accident prone, emotional, idealistic and intelligence.

Feeling: Emotions

This is the use of your moral emotions.

Accident Prone- when angry you are resentful.

Emotional- you are gullible when it comes to your family.

Idealistic- your job is idealistic and you don't expect much.

Intelligence- you are refined in the way you think.

Libra is the element of air. Air and the element of air create a world wind of emotions; taking your breath away with words. This is the development of the second function auxiliary. This takes place from six to twelve years of age. The emotions that aid in its development are creativity, independence, intuition, and romantic.

Sensing: Vibes

This is the use of your analytical emotions.

Creativity- when you feel loved you are flirtatious.

Independence- you are frivolous when it pertains to your friends.

Intuition- being two faced is a strength possessed.

Romantic- when in love you are romantic.

Libra is the element of air. Air and the element of fire create a bonfire of emotions, rising given the words and temperament. This is the development of the third function. This takes place from twelve to twenty-five years of age. The emotions that aid in its development are careless, indecisive, orderly and stubborn.

Judging: Judgment/ Intuition

This is the use of your moral thought.

 Careless- you are extravagant when you have money.

 Indecisive- when expressing emotions you are very indecisive
   and hard for you to make up your mind.

 Orderly- your home life is orderly.

 Stubborn- your view of life is easy going.

Libra is the element of air. Air and the element of earth create a tornado of emotions, thrashing and drowning with words everyone in its path. This is the development of the fourth function. This takes place from twenty five to fifty years of age. The emotions that aid in its development are cunning, diplomatic, inventive and perfectionist.

Thinking: Intelligence

This is the use of your analytical thought.

 Cunning- when you face a difficult situation you are charming.

 Diplomatic- when upset you are diplomatic.

 Inventive- you are changeable in your appearance.

 Perfectionist- you are a seeker in harmony when it relates to
the world.

Scorpio- The Element of Water

Scorpio is the element of water. Water and the element of water create a wave of emotions, crashing and drowning everyone in its path. This is the development of the dominant function. This takes place from birth to slx years of age. The emotions that aid in its development are accident prone, emotional, idealistic and intelligence.

Feeling: Emotions

This is the use of your moral emotions.

Accident Prone- you are violent when you are angry.

Emotional- when you feel loved you are emotional.

Idealistic- your appearance is practical.

Intelligence- you are very manipulative when it comes to money.

Scorpio is the element of water. Water and the element of air create a hurricane of emotions, thrashing and drowning with words everyone in its path. This is the development of the second function auxiliary. This takes place from six to twelve years of age. The emotions that aid in its development are creativity, independence, intuition, and romantic.

Sensing: Vibes

This is the use of your analytical emotions.

Creativity-you are creative in life.

Independence- you are independent in your job.

Intuition- you are very judgmental when you think.

Romantic- when in love you are passionate.

Scorpio is the element of water. Water and the element of fire create a steam of emotions. This is the development of the third function. This takes place from twelve to twenty-five years of age. The emotions that aid in its development are careless, indecisive, orderly and stubborn.

Judging: Judgment/ Intuition

This is the use of your moral thought.

Careless- when expressing emotions you are overly emotional.

Indecisive- you are energetic when it relates to your friends.

Orderly-being persistent is a strength possessed.

Stubborn-when upset you are stubborn.

Scorpio is the element of water. Water and the element of earth create a flood of emotions, drowning with words everything in its path. This is the development of the fourth function. This takes place from twenty five to fifty years of age. The emotions that aid in its development are cunning, diplomatic, inventive and perfectionist.

Thinking: Intelligence

This is the use of your analytical thought.

Cunning- you are vengeful in your views of the world.

Diplomatic- when you face a difficult situation you are jealous.

Inventive- you are determined when it relates to your family.

Perfectionist- your home life is secretive.

Sagittarius- The Element of Fire

Sagittarius is the element of fire. Fire and the element of water create a steam of emotions, bursting with cloudy judgment toward everyone in its path. This is the development of the dominant function. This takes place from birth to six years of age. The emotions that aid in its development are accident prone, emotional, idealistic and intelligence.

Feeling: Emotions

This is the use of your moral emotions.

Accident Prone- you are irresponsible when it pertains to family.

Emotional-when you feel loved you are ambitious.

Idealistic-you are very dependable when it pertains to friends.

Intelligence- you are energetic when it pertains to your job.

Sagittarius is the element of fire. Fire and the element of air create a bonfire of emotions, rising given the words and temperament. This is the development of the second function auxiliary. This takes place from six to twelve years of age. The emotions that aid in its development are creativity, independence, intuition, and romantic.

Sensing: Vibes

This is the use of your analytical emotions.

Creativity- you are erratic when upset.

Independence- you are free spirited in your view of the world.

Intuition- being optimistic is a strength you possess.

Romantic-when in love you are very passionate.

Sagittarius is the element of fire. Fire and the element of fire create heated emotions, burning with words everything in its path. This is a very judgmental person. This is the development of the third function. This takes place from twelve to twenty-five years of age. The emotions that aid in its development are careless, indecisive, orderly and stubborn.

Judging: Judgment/ Intuition

This is the use of your moral thought.

Careless- you are careless in the way you think.

Indecisive- when expressing emotions you are frank and give short answers.

Orderly- your home life is restless.

Stubborn- you are exaggerative when you have money.

Sagittarius is the element of fire. Fire and the element of earth create an eruption of emotions, burning and melting with words everyone in its path. This is the development of the fourth function. This takes place from twenty five to fifty years of age. The emotions that aid in its development are cunning, diplomatic, inventive and perfectionist.

Thinking: Intelligence

This is the use of your analytical thought.

Cunning- when faced with a difficult situation you remain

sincere.

Diplomatic-you are frivolous when you are upset.

Inventive- you are tactless in your appearance.

Perfectionist-you are undisciplined in your life.

Capricorn- The Element of Earth

Capricorn is the element of earth. Earth and the element of water create a flood of emotions, drowning with words everything in its path. This is the development of the dominant function. This takes place from birth to six years of age. The emotions that aid in its development are accident prone, emotional, idealistic and intelligence.

Feeling: Emotions

This is the use of your moral emotions.

Accident Prone- you are a social climber when it pertains to friends.

Emotional- you are miserly at expressing emotions.

Idealistic- having a sense of humor is a strength you possess.

Intelligence- when you are angry you are a nit-picker and you pick the least important thing to argue about.

Capricorn is the element of earth. Earth and the element of air create a tornado of emotions, thrashing and trashing with words everyone in its sight. This is the development of the second function auxiliary. This takes place from six to twelve years of age.

The emotions that aid in its development are creativity, independence, intuition, and romantic.

Sensing: Vibes

This is the use of your analytical emotions.

Creativity-you are ambitious about doing your job.

Independence- you are comfortable in your appearance.

Intuition- when in love you are generous.

Romantic-you are patient in your view of the world.

Capricorn is the element of earth. Earth and the element of fire create an eruption of emotions, burning and melting with words everyone in its path. This is the development of the third function. This takes place from twelve to twenty-five years of age. The emotions that aid in its development are careless, indecisive, orderly and stubborn.

Judging: Judgment/ Intuition

This is the use of your moral thought.

Careless- when upset you are mean.

Indecisive- when you feel loved you are determined.

Orderly- your home life is organized.

Stubborn- when you face a difficult situation you are rigid.

Capricorn is the element of earth. Earth and the element of earth create a dusty, sandstorm of emotions, blinding everyone with words in its path. This is the development of the fourth function.

This takes place from twenty five to fifty years of age. The emotions that aid in its development are cunning, diplomatic, inventive and perfectionist.

Thinking: Intelligence

This is the use of your analytical thought.

Cunning-you are opportunistic when it pertains to money.

Diplomatic- you are prudent in the way you think.

Inventive- you are reliable when it pertains to family.

Perfectionist- you are overly ordinary in your life.

Aquarius- The Element of Air

Aquarius is the element of air. Air and the element of water create a hurricane of emotions, thrashing and drowning with words everyone in its path. This is the development of the dominant function. This takes place from birth to six years of age. The emotions that aid in its development are accident prone, emotional, idealistic and intelligence.

Feeling: Emotions

This is the use of your moral emotions.

Accident Prone- you are tactless when it pertains to friends.

Emotional- when expressing emotions you are friendly.

Idealistic-you are idealistic when it pertains to money.

Intelligence- when upset you are intelligent.

Aquarius is the element of air. Air and the element of air create a world wind of emotions, taking your breath away with words. This is the development of the second function auxiliary. This takes place from six to twelve years of age. The emotions that aid in its development are creativity, independence, intuition, and romantic.

Sensing: Vibes

This is the use of your analytical emotions.

Creativity- you are eccentric when it pertains to family and there is no one like you.

Independence- you are independent at your job.

Intuition- you are judgmental in the way you think.

Romantic-when you feel loved you are perverse.

Aquarius is the element of air. Air and the element of fire create a bonfire of emotions, rising given the words and temperament. This is the development of the third function. This takes place from twelve to twenty-five years of age. The emotions that aid in its development are careless, indecisive, orderly and stubborn.

Judging: Judgment/ Intuition

This is the use of your moral thought.

Careless- your home life is disorganized.

Indecisive- you are impulsive in your life.

Orderly- you are neat in appearance.

Stubborn- you are rebellious when you face a difficult situation.

Aquarius is the element of air. Air and the element of earth create a tornado of emotions, thrashing and trashing with words everyone in its sight. This is the development of the fourth function. This takes place from twenty five to fifty years of age. The emotions that aid in its development are cunning, diplomatic, inventive and perfectionist.

Thinking: Intelligence

This is the use of your analytical thought.

Cunning- when angry you are unpredictable.

Diplomatic- you are human in your view of the world.

Inventive- being inventive is a strength you possess.

Perfectionist- when in love you are charismatic.

Pisces- The Element of Water

Pisces is the element of water. Water and the element of water create a wave of emotions, crashing and drowning everyone in its path. This is the development of the dominant function. This takes place from birth to six years of age. The emotions that aid in its development are accident prone, emotional, idealistic and intelligence.

Feeling: Emotions

This is the use of your moral emotions.

Accident Prone- when you feel loved you are weak-willed.

Emotional-when upset you are emotional.

Idealistic- you are compassionate in your view of the world.

Intelligence- you are unworldly in the way you think.

Pisces is the element of water. Water and the element of air create a hurricane of emotions, thrashing and drowning with words everyone in its path. This is the development of the second function auxiliary. This takes place from six to twelve years of age. The emotions that aid in its development are creativity, independence, intuition, and romantic.

Sensing: Vibes

This is the use of your analytical emotions.

Creativity- you are sensitive when it pertains to friends.

Independence- you are mysterious in your appearance.

Intuition- being judgmental is a strength possessed.

Romantic- when in love you are romantic.

Pisces is the element of water. Water and the element of fire create a steam of emotions; bursting with cloudy judgment toward everyone in its path. This is the development of the third function. This takes place from twelve to twenty-five years of age. The emotions that aid in its development are careless, indecisive, orderly and stubborn.

Judging: Judgment/ Intuition

This is the use of your moral thought.

Careless- you are careless when it pertains to family.

Indecisive- when expressing emotions you are indecisive.

Orderly- you are receptive at your job.

Stubborn- when you are angry you are vague and don't reveal a lot of information as to why you feel the way you do.

Pisces is the element of water. Water and the element of earth create a flood of emotions, drowning with words everything in its path. This is the development of the fourth function. This takes place from twenty five to fifty years of age. The emotions that aid in its development are cunning, diplomatic, inventive and perfectionist.

Thinking: Intelligence

This is the use of your analytical thought.

    Cunning- when faced with a difficult situation you are secretive.

    Diplomatic- you are compassionate in your view of the world.

    Inventive-you are imaginative when it pertains to money.

    Perfectionist- you are impressionable in your life.

Chapter 12: INFP & ENFJ
Emotions, Judgment, Vibes, and Intelligence

The INFP and ENFJ are similar in a lot of the ways except for the way how they use there functions is quite different. The INFP's are introverted and masculine and ENFJ's are extroverted and feminine. Extrovert's likes crowds and Introvert's likes to be left alone.

INFP- Feel as a feeler, judge as an intuitive, sense as a perceiver and think as an introvert

Feeling
Intelligence- you consider it important to be tactful as well as truthful.

You step forward and consider the effects of your actions on others.

Idealistic- you show appreciation easily to others and believe any feeling is valid whether it makes sense or not.
You naturally like to please others and may need to be encouraged to have own needs met.

 Emotional- you value empathy and harmony but see the

exception to the rule when it pertains to your own feelings.
You make judgment based on your own feelings and values but
you are people oriented and aware of others feelings.
You are happiest in friendly, supportive, and cooperative
environments.

Accident Prone- You may be seen as overemotional, illogical,
and weak.
You are an impatient person but are motivated by a desire to be
appreciated.

Behavior: <u>Patient</u>
My natural temperament of water uses the element of my emotions
to create an attitude of being emotional to activate the action of
my introversion which effects my function of feeling which leads to
the behavior of being patient. This behavioral person is very calm
and capable of handling all. They have a high tolerance of bearing
even the most difficult of challenges. They are very understanding
and their for you as an individual.

Judging

Stubborn- you trust inspiration, spiritual guidance, and fiction and
are oriented towards the future.

Careless- you like new ideas for your own sake, value imagination and innovation but tend to be general and figurative by using metaphors and analogies.

Indecisive- you enjoy learning new skills and get bored easily after mastering them.

 You present information through leaps and hurdles in a round about manner.

 You are uncertain about the skills you posses but make a judgment based on your own gut feelings anyway.

Behavior: Realistic

My natural temperament of fire uses the element of my judgment to created an attitude of being judgmental to activate the action of my intuition which effects my function of judging which leads to the behavior of being realistic. This behavioral person is a natural truth teller and their work has to tell things as they naturally are or they will not be content. They love representing the truth as described.

Sensing

Creativity- you are better at concentration exercises than fantasy or daydreaming. You have a play ethic, enjoy now and finish the job later, and enjoy exercises that allow you to learn new thing and have fun doing it. You are process oriented and your emphasis is on how the task is completed.

 Intuition- you are influenced by past experiences and this is your knowledge of doing things. You don't like to brainstorm for answers and are happiest leaving your options open. You change goals as new information becomes available and prefer to not decide but continue to collect information for later usage.

Romantic-you feel satisfaction from starting projects and see time as a renewable resource and set deadlines.

Independence- you are flexible, adaptable, and change gears quickly so that you may be available for many different approaches and techniques.

You have a natural curiosity and like adapting to new situations.

Behavior: Illusionist

My natural temperament of air uses the element of my vibes that I pick up on from my sight, smelling, hearing, tasting, and touching to create an attitude of being sensitive to activate the action of my perception which effects my function sensing which leads to the behavior of being an illusionist. This behavioral person is a natural liar and their work has to have some form of illusions in it or they just won't be happy.

Thinking-

Cunning-you are private and are energized by spending time alone, you like to think things through inside your head and you share personal info with a select few people.

Inventive- you avoid being the center of attention and keep your enthusiasm to yourself.

Diplomatic- you think more than you react to any given situation and you prefer knowing more information than a little.

Perfectionist- you listen more than you talk and respond after taking the time to think things through inside your head.

Behavior: Impatient/ Rationalist

My natural temperament of earth uses the element of my intelligence to create an attitude of being intelligent to activate the action of my extroversion which effects my function of thinking which leads to the behavior of being a rationalist of impatient. This behavioral person is unable to wait patiently. They can't endure irritation for long periods of time. They have the ability to reason. They are always on a quest for truth even when the truth is laid out honestly before them. They have a natural desire to constantly search things over for truth. They believe "reason" to be the main source of knowledge and spiritual truth meaning because you have asked the question of "why" this brings about intelligence.

ENFJ- Feel as an extrovert, judge as an intuitive, sense as a sensor, think as a thinker

Feeling

Emotional- being with others energizes you. You react more than you think and you communicate to others with enthusiasm.

Accident Prone- You respond quickly without hearing the whole conversation. you enjoy being the center of attention, and enjoy a fast pace.

Idealistic- you think out loud and are easier to know and read. You were your emotions on your sleeve and talk with your body language. When your emotions have been hurt you feel the need to voice your opinion and you share personal information freely and sometimes without enough forethought.

Intelligence- you talk more than you listen and prefer to know a little information rather than it all.

Behavior: Patient

My natural temperament of water uses the element of my emotions to create an attitude of being emotional to activate the action of my introversion which effects my function of feeling which leads to the behavior of being patient. This behavioral person is very calm and capable of handling all. They have a high tolerance of bearing even the most difficult of challenges. They are very understanding and their for you as an individual.

431

Judging

Stubborn- you trust inspiration, spiritual guidance, and fiction and are oriented towards the future.

Careless- you like new ideas for your own sake, value imagination and innovation but tend to be general and figurative by using metaphors and analogies.

Indecisive- you enjoy learning new skills and get bored easily after mastering them. You present information through leaps and hurdles in a round about manner and are uncertain about your skills but make a judgment based on your own feelings.

Behavior: <u>Realistic</u>

My natural temperament of fire uses the element of my judgment to created an attitude of being judgmental to activate the action of my intuition which effects my function of judging which leads to the behavior of being realistic. This behavioral person is a natural truth teller and their work has to tell things as they naturally are or they will not be content. They love representing the truth as described.

Sensing

Intuition- you trust what is certain, can be proven and you present information in a step-by-step manner.

Independence- you are knowledgeable of your established skills and make a judgment by the facts you gather.

Creativity- you like new ideas only if they have practical applications and tend to be specific and literal about giving a detailed description.

Romantic- you value realism and common sense and are oriented towards the present.

Behavior: Illusionist

My natural temperament of air uses the element of my vibes that I pick up on from my sight, smelling, hearing, tasting, and touching to create an attitude of being sensitive to activate the action of my perception which effects my function sensing which leads to the behavior of being an illusionist. This behavioral person is a natural liar and their work has to have some form of illusions in it or they just won't be happy.

Thinking

Diplomatic- You value logic, justice and fairness which to you is one standard for all. You step back and try to see the situation objectively before problem solving. You feel the need to be convinced that a specific event or activity makes sense before you will even believe.

Perfectionist- you naturally see flaws and tend to be critical of others and believe it is more important to be truthful than tactful. Believe others feelings are irrelevant to the situation at hand.

Inventive- Believe feelings are valid only if they are logical. You are motivated by a desire for achievement and accomplishment but have a hard time translating ideas into active steps.

Cunning- you may be seen as heartless, insensitive and uncaring but are impressed by competence and the end result.

Behavior: Impatient/ Rationalist

My natural temperament of earth uses the element of my intelligence to create an attitude of being intelligent to activate the action of my extroversion which effects my function of thinking which leads to the behavior of being a rationalist of impatient. This behavioral person is unable to wait patiently. They can't endure irritation for long periods of time. They have the ability to reason. They are always on a quest for truth even when the truth is laid out honestly before them. They have a natural desire to constantly search things over for truth. They believe "reason" to be the main source of knowledge and spiritual truth meaning because you have asked the question of "why" this brings about intelligence.

Aries INFP or ENFJ- The Element of Fire

Aries is the element of fire. Fire and the element of water create a steam of emotions, bursting with cloudy judgment toward everyone in its path. This is the development of the dominant function and one of your strengths. This takes place from birth to six years of age. The emotions that aid in its development are accident prone, emotional, idealistic, and intelligence.

Feeling: Emotions

This is the use of your moral emotions.

Accident prone- your accident prone when your upset.

Emotional- you're quick tempered when you're angry.

Idealistic- being assertive is a strength you possess.

Intelligence- you're very tactless in the way you think.

Aries is the element of fire. Fire and the element of Fire create heated emotions. This is the development of the second function auxiliary. This takes place from six to twelve years of age. The emotions that aid in its development are careless, indecisive, orderly, and stubborn.

Judging: Judgment/ Intuition

This is the use of your moral thought.

Careless- you're a procrastinator as it relates to your family.

Indecisive- you are energetic about doing your job.

Orderly- you are selfish when it comes to money.

Stubborn- you are self-centered when expressing your

emotions.

Aries is the element of fire. Fire and the element of Air create a bonfire of emotions, rising giving the temperaments. This is the development of the third function. This takes place from twelve to twenty-five years of age. This function will never be as strong as the dominant and auxiliary functions. The emotions that aid in its development are creativity, independence, intuition, and romantic.
Sensing: Vibes
This is the use of your analytical emotions.

Creativity-your optimistic as it pertains to your friends

Independence- you're courageous when you face a difficult situation.

Intuition- you're a free spirit in your view of the world.

Romantic- your impatient when you feel loved.

Aries is the element of fire. Fire and element of Earth create an eruption of emotions, burning everything and everyone, which crosses its path. This is the development of the fourth function, which takes place from twenty five to fifty years of age. The four emotions, which aid in the growth of your intelligence which are cunning, diplomatic, inventive and perfectionist.
Thinking: Intelligence
This is the use of your analytical thought.

Cunning- your adventuresome as it pertains to life shows

cunning.

Diplomatic- your enthuslastic when experiencing love.

Inventive- your impulsive as it pertains to their appearance.

Perfectionist- you're innovative in your home life.

Taurus INFP or ENFJ- The Element of Earth

Taurus is the element of the earth. Earth and the element of water create a flood of emotions, drowning everything in its path. This is the development of the dominant function, which takes place from birth to six years of age. The emotions that aid in its development are accident prone, emotional, idealistic and intelligence.

Feeling: Emotions

This is the use of your moral emotions.

> Accident Prone- you are violent when you are angry.
>
> Emotional- you are greedy when in love.
>
> Idealistic- you are warm hearted when it relates to your family.
>
> Intelligence- being strong- willed is a strength you possess.

Taurus is the element of the earth. Earth and the element of fire create an eruption of emotions. This is the development of the auxiliary function. This takes place from six to twelve years of age. The emotions that aid in its development are careless, indecisive, orderly and stubborn.

Judging: Judgment/ Intuition

This is the use of your moral thought.

> Careless- you're very practical in your views concerning home life.
>
> Indecisive- when expressing emotions you are very lazy.
>
> Orderly- you are very possessive about your appearance.
>
> Stubborn- you are very stubborn in your views of the world.

Taurus is the element of the earth. Earth and the element of air create a tornado of emotions, thrashing and trashing everything in its sight. This is the development of the third function. This takes place from twelve to twenty-five years of age. The emotions that aid in its development are creativity, independence, intuition and romantic.

Sensing: Vibes

This is the use of your analytical emotions.

> Creativity-Your very solid in your view of life shows creativity.
>
> Independence- you're very persistent about doing your job.
>
> Intuition- when it comes to money you're very trustworthy.
>
> Romantic- you're very affectionate when you feel loved.

Taurus is the element of the earth. Earth and the element of earth produce a dusty sandstorm of emotions. Blinding everyone in sight. This is the development of the fourth function. This takes place from twenty five to fifty years of age. The emotions that aid in its development are cunning, diplomatic, inventive and perfectionist.

Thinking: Intelligence

This is the use of your analytical thought.

>Cunning- when you face a difficult situation you're very resentful.

>Diplomatic- you are set in your ways when you think.

>Inventive- When upset you are very inflexible.

>Perfectionist- you are very reliable when it comes to your friends.

Gemini INFP or ENFJ- The Element of Air

Gemini is the element of air. Air and the element of water create a hurricane of emotions. This is the development of the dominant function. This takes place from birth to six years of age. The emotions that aid in its development are accident prone, emotional, idealistic and intelligence.

Feeling: Emotions

This is the use of moral emotions.

>Accident Prone- you are very restless when it pertains to your family.

Emotional- you are nosey when you face a difficult
situation.

Idealistic- you are very flighty in your appearance.

Intelligence- you are very spontaneous in your views of
life.

Gemini is the element of air. Air and the element of fire create a bonfire of emotions, rising given the temperament. This is the development of the third function. This takes place from twelve to twenty-five years of age. The emotions that aid in its development are careless, indecisive, orderly and stubborn.

Judging: Judgment/ Intuition

This is the use of moral thought.

Careless-you are very secretive about your view of the world.

Indecisive- you can be superficial when it pertains to money.

Orderly-you are logical in your home life.

Stubborn- you are inconsistent when expressing your emotions.

Gemini is the element of air. Air and the element of air create a world wind of emotions. This is the development of the auxiliary function. This takes place from six to twelve years of age. The emotions that aid in its development are creativity, independence, intuition and romantic.

Sensing: Vibes

This is the use of analytical emotions.

Creativity- you are very energetic when it pertains to your
friends.

Independence- you are adaptable as it relates to your job.

Intuition- being an intellectual is a strength possessed.

Romantic- you are very witty when in love.

Gemini is the element of air. Air and the element of earth create a tornado of emotions, thrashing and trashing everything in its sight. This is the development of the fourth function. This takes place from twenty five to fifty years of age. The emotions that aid in its development are cunning, diplomatic, inventive and perfectionist.

Thinking: Intelligence

This is the use of analytical thought.

Cunning- you are very cunning when you are upset.

Diplomatic- when you are angry you are very devious.

Inventive- you are a communicator about the way you think.

Perfectionist- you can be very versatile when in love.

Cancer INFP or ENFJ- The Element of Water

Cancer is the element of water. Water and the element of water create a wave of emotions. This is the development of the dominant function. This takes place from birth to six years of age. The emotions that aid in its development are accident prone, emotional, idealistic and intelligence.

Feeling: Emotions

This is the use of moral emotions.

Accident Prone-you are hyper sensitive when it pertains to family.

Emotional- when you face a difficult situation you can be very emotional.

Idealistic- you are thrifty when it pertains to money.

Intelligence- you are sensitive in your view of the world.

Cancer is the element of water. Water and the element of fire create a steam of emotions. This is the development of the second function auxiliary. This takes place from six to twelve years of age. The emotions that aid in its development are careless, indecisive, orderly and stubborn.

Judging: Judgment/ Intuition

This is the use of moral thought.

Careless- you are very shrewd when you are angry.

Indecisive- your home life is very unstable.

Orderly- your appearance is changeable.

Stubborn- when upset you are unforgiving.

Cancer is the element of water. Water and the element of air create a hurricane of emotions. This is the development of the third function. This takes place from twelve to twenty-five years of age. The emotions that aid in its development are creativity, independence, intuition, and romantic.

Sensing: Vibes

This is the use of analytical emotions.

Creativity- you're very kind to your friends.

Independence- your job is very messy.

Intuition- you're very judgmental in your views of life.

Romantic- when in love you can be overly emotional.

Cancer is the element of water. Water and the element of earth create a flood of emotions, drowning everything in its path. This is the development of the fourth function. This takes place from twenty five to fifty years of age. The emotions that aid in its development are cunning, diplomatic, inventive and perfectionist.

Thinking: Intelligence

This is the use of analytical thought.

Cunning- being sympathetic is a strength possessed.

Diplomatic- when expressing emotions you can be over indulgent in self-pity.

Inventive- you are very receptive when you think.

Perfectionist- when you feel loved you can be moody.

Leo INFP or ENFJ- The Element of Fire

Leo is the element of fire. Fire and water create a steam of emotions. This is the development of the dominant function. This takes place from birth to six years of age. The emotions that aid in its development are accident prone, emotional, idealistic and intelligence.

Feeling: Emotions

This is the use of your moral emotions.

Accident Prone- when expressing emotions you are attention-seeking.

Emotional- when you feel loved you are generous.

Idealistic- being powerful is a strength possessed.

Intelligence- you are very broad-minded in the way you think.

Leo is the element of fire. Fire and the element of fire create heated emotions. This is a very judgmental person. This is the development of the third function. This takes place from twelve to twenty-five years of age. The emotions that aid in its development are careless, indecisive, orderly and stubborn.

Judging: Judgment/ Intuition

This is the use of your moral thought.

Careless- when you're angry you appear very snobbish.

Indecisive- at your job you are very egotistical.

Orderly- your home life is organized.

Stubborn- when upset you are intolerant.

Leo is the element of fire. Fire and the element of air create a bonfire of emotions, rising given the temperament. This is the development of the second function auxiliary. This takes place from six to twelve years of age. The emotions that aid in its development are creativity, independence, intuition, and romantic..

Sensing: Vibes

This is the use of your analytical emotions.

Creativity- you are very enthusiastic about life.

Independence- you are conceited about your appearance.

Intuition-you are very optimistic when it comes to your friends.

Romantic- when in love you are dramatic.

Leo is the element of fire. Fire and the element of earth create an eruption of emotions. This is the development of the fourth function. This takes place from twenty five to fifty years of age. The emotions that aid in its development are cunning, diplomatic, inventive and perfectionist.

Thinking: Intelligence

This is the use of your analytical thought.

Cunning- you are patronizing when it relates to your family.

Diplomatic- when you face a difficult situation you are dogmatic.

Inventive- your view of the world is creative.

Perfectionist- when it comes to money you are extravagant.

Virgo INFP or ENFJ- The Element of Earth

Virgo is the element of earth. Earth and the element of water create a flood of emotions, drowning with words everyone in its path. This is the development of the dominant function. This takes place from birth to six years of age. The emotions that aid in its development are accident prone, emotional, idealistic and intelligence.

Feeling: Emotions

This is the use of your moral emotions.

Accident Prone- when you face a difficult situation you are fussy.

Emotional- when expressing your emotions you are pessimistic.

Idealistic- you are conscientious about your friends.

Intelligence- you are hypercritical in your view of the world.

Virgo is the element of earth. Earth and the element of fire create an eruption of emotions, burning and melting with words everyone in its path. This is the development of the second function auxiliary. This takes place from six to twelve years of age. The emotions that aid in its development are careless, indecisive, orderly and stubborn.

Judging: Judgment/ Intuition

This is the use of your moral thought.

Careless- you are neat in your appearance.

Indecisive- when angry you are grouchy.

Orderly- you are meticulous when it comes to money.

Stubborn- you are analytical in your view of family.

Virgo is the element of earth. Earth and the element of air create a tornado of emotions, thrashing and trashing everyone in its path. This is the development of the third function. This takes place from twelve to twenty-five years of age. The emotions that aid in its development are creativity, independence, intuition, and romantic.

Sensing: Vibes

This is the use of your analytical emotions.

Creativity- you are practical in the way you think.

Independence- at your job you are a workaholic.

Intuition- you are hypercritical in your view of life.

Romantic- when in love you are a perfectionist.

Virgo is the element of earth. Earth and the element of earth create a dusty sandstorm of emotions, blinding everyone in its path. This is the development of the fourth function. This takes place from birth to six years of age. The emotions that aid in its development are cunning, diplomatic, inventive and perfectionist.

Thinking: Intelligence

This is the use of your analytical thought.

Cunning- being prudish is a strength possessed.

Diplomatic- when upset you are cranky.

Inventive- you are a busy body in your home life.

Perfectionist- you are a worrier when you feel loved.

Libra INFP or ENFJ- The Element of Air

Libra is the element of air. Air and the element of water create a hurricane of emotions; thrashing and drowning with words everyone in its path. This is the development of the dominant function. This takes place from birth to six years of age. The emotions that aid in its development are accident prone, emotional, idealistic and intelligence.

Feeling: Emotions

This is the use of your moral emotions.

Accident Prone- when angry you are resentful.

Emotional- you are gullible when it comes to your family.

Idealistic- your job is idealistic and you don't expect much.

Intelligence- you are refined in the way you think.

Libra is the element of air. Air and the element of fire create a bonfire of emotions, rising given the words and temperament. This is the development of the second function auxiliary. This takes place from six to twelve years of age. The emotions that aid in its development are careless, indecisive, orderly and stubborn.

Judging: Judgment/ Intuition

This is the use of your moral thought.

Careless- you are extravagant when you have money.

Indecisive- when expressing emotions you are very indecisive and hard for you to make up your mind.

Orderly- your home life is orderly.

Stubborn- your view of life is easy going.

Libra is the element of air. Air and the element of air create a world wind of emotions; taking your breath away with words. This is the development of the third function. This takes place from twelve to twenty-five years of age. The emotions that aid in its development are creativity, independence, intuition, and romantic.

Sensing: Vibes

This is the use of your analytical emotions.

Creativity- when you feel loved you are flirtatious.

Independence- you are frivolous when it pertains to your friends.

Intuition- being two faced is a strength possessed.

Romantic- when in love you are romantic.

Libra is the element of air. Air and the element of earth create a tornado of emotions, thrashing and drowning with words everyone in its path. This is the development of the fourth function. This takes place from twenty five to fifty years of age. The emotions that aid in its development are cunning, diplomatic, inventive and perfectionist.

Thinking: Intelligence

This is the use of your analytical thought.

Cunning- when you face a difficult situation you are charming.

Diplomatic- when upset you are diplomatic.

Inventive- you are changeable in your appearance.

Perfectionist- you are a seeker in harmony when it relates to the world.

Scorpio INFP or ENFJ- The Element of Water

Scorpio is the element of water. Water and the element of water create a wave of emotions, crashing and drowning everyone in its path. This is the development of the dominant function. This takes place from birth to six years of age. The emotions that aid in its development are accident prone, emotional, idealistic and intelligence.

Feeling: Emotions

This is the use of your moral emotions.

Accident Prone- you are violent when you are angry.

Emotional- when you feel loved you are emotional.

Idealistic- your appearance is practical.

Intelligence- you are very manipulative when it comes to money.

Scorpio is the element of water. Water and the element of fire create a steam of emotions. This is the development of the second function auxiliary. This takes place from six to twelve years of age. The emotions that aid in its development are careless, indecisive, orderly and stubborn.

Judging: Judgment/ Intuition

This is the use of your moral thought.

Careless- when expressing emotions you are overly emotional.

Indecisive- you are energetic when it relates to your friends.

Orderly-being persistent is a strength possessed.

Stubborn-when upset you are stubborn.

Scorpio is the element of water. Water and the element of air create a hurricane of emotions, thrashing and drowning with words everyone in its path. This is the development of the third function. This takes place from twelve to twenty-five years of age. The emotions that aid in its development are creativity, independence, intuition, and romantic.

Sensing: Vibes

This is the use of your analytical emotions.

Creativity-you are creative in life.

Independence- you are independent in your job.

Intuition- you are very judgmental when you think.

Romantic- when in love you are passionate.

Scorpio is the element of water. Water and the element of earth create a flood of emotions, drowning with words everything in its path. This is the development of the fourth function. This takes place from twenty five to fifty years of age. The emotions that aid in its development are cunning, diplomatic, inventive and perfectionist.

Thinking: Intelligence

This is the use of your analytical thought.

Cunning- you are vengeful in your views of the world.

Diplomatic- when you face a difficult situation you are jealous.

Inventive- you are determined when it relates to your family.

Perfectionist- your home life is secretive.

Sagittarius INFP or ENFJ- The Element of Fire

Sagittarius is the element of fire. Fire and the element of water create a steam of emotions, bursting with cloudy judgment toward everyone in its path. This is the development of the dominant function. This takes place from birth to six years of age. The emotions that aid in its development are accident prone, emotional, idealistic and intelligence.

Feeling: Emotions

This is the use of your moral emotions.

Accident Prone- you are irresponsible when it pertains to family.

Emotional-when you feel loved you are ambitious.

Idealistic-you are very dependable when it pertains to friends.

Intelligence- you are energetic when it pertains to your job.

Sagittarius is the element of fire. Fire and the element of fire create heated emotions, burning with words everything in its path. This is a very judgmental person. This is the development of the second function auxiliary. This takes place from six to twelve years of age. The emotions that aid in its development are careless, indecisive, orderly and stubborn.

Judging: Judgment/ Intuition

This is the use of your moral thought.

Careless- you are careless in the way you think.

Indecisive- when expressing emotions you are frank and give short answers.

Orderly- your home life is restless.

Stubborn- you are exaggerative when you have money.

Sagittarius is the element of fire. Fire and the element of air create a bonfire of emotions, rising given the words and temperament. This is the development of the third function. This takes place from twelve to twenty-five years of age. The emotions that aid in its development are creativity, independence, intuition, and romantic.

Sensing: Vibes

This is the use of your analytical emotions.

Creativity- you are erratic when upset.

Independence- you are free spirited in your view of the world.

Intuition- being optimistic is a strength you possess.

Romantic-when in love you are very passionate.

Sagittarius is the element of fire. Fire and the element of earth create an eruption of emotions, burning and melting with words everyone in its path. This is the development of the fourth function. This takes place from twenty five to fifty years of age. The emotions that aid in its development are cunning, diplomatic, inventive and perfectionist.

Thinking: Intelligence

This is the use of your analytical thought.

Cunning- when faced with a difficult situation you remain
sincere.

Diplomatic-you are frivolous when you are upset.

Inventive- you are tactless in your appearance.

Perfectionist-you are undisciplined in your life.

Capricorn INFP or ENFJ- The Element of Earth

Capricorn is the element of earth. Earth and the element of water
create a flood of emotions, drowning with words everything in its
path. This is the development of the dominant function. This takes
place from birth to six years of age. The emotions that aid in its
development are accident prone, emotional, idealistic and
intelligence.

Feeling: Emotions

This is the use of your moral emotions.

Accident Prone- you are a social climber when it pertains to
friends.

Emotional- you are miserly at expressing emotions.

Idealistic- having a sense of humor is a strength you possess.

Intelligence- when you are angry you are a nit-picker and you
pick the least important thing to argue about.

Capricorn is the element of earth. Earth and the element of fire create an eruption of emotions, burning and melting with words everyone in its path. This is the development of the second function auxiliary. This takes place from six to twelve years of age. The emotions that aid in its development are careless, indecisive, orderly and stubborn.

Judging: Judgment/ Intuition

This is the use of your moral thought.

Careless- when upset you are mean.

Indecisive- when you feel loved you are determined.

Orderly- your home life is organized.

Stubborn- when you face a difficult situation you are rigid.

Capricorn is the element of earth. Earth and the element of air create a tornado of emotions, thrashing and trashing with words everyone in its sight. This is the development of the third function. This takes place from twelve to twenty-five years of age. The emotions that aid in its development are creativity, independence, intuition, and romantic.

Sensing: Vibes

This is the use of your analytical emotions.

Creativity-you are ambitious about doing your job.

Independence- you are comfortable in your appearance.

Intuition- when in love you are generous.

Romantic-you are patient in your view of the world.

Capricorn is the element of earth. Earth and the element of earth create a dusty, sandstorm of emotions, blinding everyone with words in its path. This is the development of the fourth function. This takes place from twenty five to fifty years of age. The emotions that aid in its development are cunning, diplomatic, inventive and perfectionist.

    Thinking: Intelligence

This is the use of your analytical thought.

    Cunning-you are opportunistic when it pertains to money.

    Diplomatic- you are prudent in the way you think.

    Inventive- you are reliable when it pertains to family.

    Perfectionist- you are overly ordinary in your life.

Aquarius INFP or ENFJ- The Element of Air

Aquarius is the element of air. Air and the element of water create a hurricane of emotions, thrashing and drowning with words everyone in its path. This is the development of the dominant function. This takes place from birth to six years of age. The emotions that aid in its development are accident prone, emotional, idealistic and intelligence.

Feeling: Emotions

This is the use of your moral emotions.

    Accident Prone- you are tactless when it pertains to friends.

Emotional- when expressing emotions you are friendly.

Idealistic-you are idealistic when it pertains to money.

Intelligence- when upset you are intelligent.

Aquarius is the element of air. Air and the element of fire create a bonfire of emotions, rising given the words and temperament. This is the development of the second function auxiliary. This takes place from six to twelve years of age. The emotions that aid in its development are careless, indecisive, orderly and stubborn.

Judging: Judgment/ Intuition

This is the use of your moral thought.

Careless- your home life is disorganized.

Indecisive- you are impulsive in your life.

Orderly- you are neat in appearance.

Stubborn- you are rebellious when you face a difficult situation.

Aquarius is the element of air. Air and the element of air create a world wind of emotions, taking your breath away with words. This is the development of the third function. This takes place from twelve to twenty-five years of age. The emotions that aid in its development are creativity, independence, intuition, and romantic.

Sensing: Vibes

This is the use of your analytical emotions.

Creativity- you are eccentric when it pertains to family and there is no one like you.

Independence- you are independent at your job.

Intuition- you are judgmental in the way you think.

Romantic-when you feel loved you are perverse.

Aquarius is the element of air. Air and the element of earth create a tornado of emotions, thrashing and trashing with words everyone in its sight. This is the development of the fourth function. This takes place from twenty five to fifty years of age. The emotions that aid in its development are cunning, diplomatic, inventive and perfectionist.

Thinking: Intelligence

This is the use of your analytical thought.

Cunning- when angry you are unpredictable.

Diplomatic- you are human in your view of the world.

Inventive- being inventive is a strength you possess.

Perfectionist- when in love you are charismatic.

Pisces INFP or ENFJ- The Element of Water

Pisces is the element of water. Water and the element of water create a wave of emotions, crashing and drowning everyone in its path. This is the development of the dominant function. This takes place from birth to six years of age. The emotions that aid in its development are accident prone, emotional, idealistic and intelligence.

Feeling: Emotions

This is the use of your moral emotions.

   Accident Prone- when you feel loved you are weak-willed.

   Emotional-when upset you are emotional.

   Idealistic- you are compassionate in your view of the world.

   Intelligence- you are unworldly in the way you think.

Pisces is the element of water. Water and the element of fire create a steam of emotions; bursting with cloudy judgment toward everyone in its path. This is the development of the second function auxiliary. This takes place from six to twelve years of age. The emotions that aid in its development are careless, indecisive, orderly and stubborn.

Judging: Judgment/ Intuition

This is the use of your moral thought.

   Careless- you are careless when it pertains to family.

   Indecisive- when expressing emotions you are indecisive.

   Orderly- you are receptive at your job.

   Stubborn- when you are angry you are vague and don't reveal a
      lot of information as to why you feel the way you do.

Pisces is the element of water. Water and the element of air create a hurricane of emotions, thrashing and drowning with words everyone in its path. This is the development of the third function. This takes place from twelve to twenty-five years of age. The emotions that aid in its development are creativity, independence, intuition, and romantic.

Sensing: Vibes

This is the use of your analytical emotions.

Creativity- you are sensitive when it pertains to friends.

Independence- you are mysterious in your appearance.

Intuition- being judgmental is a strength possessed.

Romantic- when in love you are romantic.

Pisces is the element of water. Water and the element of earth create a flood of emotions, drowning with words everything in its path. This is the development of the fourth function. This takes place from twenty five to fifty years of age. The emotions that aid in its development are cunning, diplomatic, inventive and perfectionist.

Thinking: Intelligence

This is the use of your analytical thought.

Cunning- when faced with a difficult situation you are secretive.

Diplomatic- you are compassionate in your view of the world.

Inventive-you are imaginative when it pertains to money.

Perfectionist- you are impressionable in your life.

"BUILDING YOUR PERSONALITY TYPE PROFILE"

-Chapter 13-

Building Your Personality Type Profile

This chapter of the book is a self-survey designed to help the reader to understand their individual personality type. Please feel in the answers to the best of your ability.

1. What is your astrological sign? _____

2. What is the natural temperament of your astrological sign?

_____

3. How does the temperament function?

_____

_____

_____

4. List the four major emotions affected by your astrological sign?

_____

5. Define the duties of the four emotions of your astrological sign?

_____

_____.

_____

_____.

_____

_____

_____.

6. How do you use your gift of free will?

_____

_____

_____

_____

_____

7. How do you use your gift of morals?

_____

_____

_____

_____.

8. Are your morals a strength or a weakness for your given personality type?

_____

9. What is your dominant personality type?

_____

10. List the four functions in order of your personality type:

1. _____

2. _____

3. _____

4. _____

11. List the four temperaments in order of your personality type:

1. _____

2. _____

3. _____

4. _____

12. Define how your dominant function and temperament work together?

_____

_____

_____

_____.

13. Define your dominant behavior?

_____

_____

_____

_____.

14. List the four emotions that aid in the dominant functions development:

1. _____

2. _____

3. _____

4. _____

15. Define the duties of the four emotions of your dominant function?

1.

_____

_____

_____

_____.

2.

_____

_____

_____

_____

3.

_____

_____

_____

_____

4.

_____

_____

_____

_____

16. Define how your auxiliary function and temperament work together?

_____

_____

_____.

17. Define your auxiliary behavior?

_____

_____

_____.

18. List the four emotions that aid in the auxiliary functions development:

1. _____

2. _____

3. _____

4. _____

19. Define the duties of the four emotions of your auxiliary function?

1.

_____

_____

2.

_____

_____

3.

_____

_____.

4.

_____

_____.

20. Define how your third function and temperament work together?

_____

_____

_____

21. Define the third behavior of your personality type?

_____

_____

_____.

22. List the four emotions that aid in the third functions development:

1. _____

2. _____

3. _____

4. _____

23. Define the duties of the four emotions of your third function?

1._____

_____

_____

2.

_____

_____

_____.

3.

_____

_____

_____.

4.

_____

_____

_____.

24. Define how your fourth function and temperament work together?

_____

_____

_____.

25. Define the fourth behavior of your personality type?

_____

_____

_____.

26. List the four emotions that aid in the fourth functions development:

1. _____

2. _____

3. _____

4. _____

27. Define the duties of the four emotions of your fourth function?

1.

_____

_____

_____

_____

2.

_____

_____

_____

3.

_____

_____

_____

4.

_____

_____

_____

28. What are your two strengths?

_____

29. What are your two weaknesses?

_____

30. List the 6 Emotional Healing Steps that will aid in keeping your emotions in order?

1. _____

2. _____

3. _____

4. _____

5. _____

6. _____

Know you can successfully say you know yourself. Congratulations and I mean that from the bottom of my heart.

-Chapter 14-
Bodily Healing: Preparing Physically

"Jesus said to him, I am the way, the truth, and the life. No one comes to the Father except through Me". - **John 14:6**

Everyone is not ready to leave his or her comfort zone. They would rather spend a lifetime not dealing with the issues at hand than facing them. They get caught up in all the negative habits of the world like Drugs, sex, women, and food.

My aunt once told me that my family loves to over indulge. If it were a drink you wanted to have they'll drink you under the table, if you were dating and having sex with one person, no they'll just have to have a couple partners. Everything must be to the limit allowed and that goes for drugs, sex, women and food.

Any problem that has every existed I most likely have a relative or friend whose experienced it first hand which helps me to translate it to paper to be studied as a referenced to help others. It makes a lot of sense her theory but I have a more detailed approach. What if I said even with all the negative experiences a person has went through in there entire lifetime those where just the steps they had to take place to develop there personality traits. Would you believe me? Speaking from a religious standpoint, what if this were the best way God could give you lesson to be learned. I believe in this answer to be true because I've spent the majority of my life watching and helping others to find a better solution to the problems they face everyday. I'm no psychiatrist but you can say I play one everyday in my neighborhood and family surroundings. I believe the answer lies within our DNA, the blueprint to our design.

There is only one person responsible for our design and not a team of aliens, but then that's my opinion. I once read in a magazine about the discovery of our DNA.

It read, " Another early surprise: Many of the newly discovered disease- promoting variations don't lie inside the active genes. Instead, they lurk deep inside "junk" or "dark" DNA, the mysterious and seemingly inactive regions that compose 98.5 % of the genome and whose functions are unknown. These findings hint at a powerful and previously unknown command and control apparatus inside our DNA." (Forbes Life April 2007 p.62)

They believe the dark and mysterious regions of the genome and not the active genes are forming diseases in the body. They believe our genes are being controlled and told when to release the devastating diseases. What part of the genes could have that much control over our entire body? No one knows the name for this portion but I believe I have an idea. I believe this mysterious portion's of the genes is related to our emotions and personality. They are the powerful and unknown command and control apparatus inside of our DNA. History and hormones can prove this theory.

In the bible, *The woman said to the serpent, "We may eat fruit from the trees on the garden but God did say, 'You must not eat fruit from the tree that is in the middle of the garden and you must not touch it, or you will die". -**Genesis 3:2-7***

"You will not surely die," the serpent sad to the woman. "For God knows that when you eat of it your eyes will be opened and you will be like God, knowing good and evil."

When the woman saw that the fruit of the tree was good for food and pleasing to the eye, and also desirable for gaining wisdom, she took some and ate it. She also gave some to her husband, who was with her, and he ate it. Then the eyes of both of them were opened, and they realized they were naked; so they sewed fig leaves together and made coverings for themselves. Why would it even shame them to know that they were naked?

Could this be the both of them in the Garden of Eden are recognizing emotions. I believe the Lord was making us aware of our emotions killing us. If God were talking from an emotional standpoint than every time our emotions become over whelmed isn't the feeling as If we have died. Eventually we do die when we don't get our emotions in control. Take for instance the first time you fell in love and then the relationship ended, wasn't the feeling as if you had died? So he could have meant that when they ate of the fruit that they would become emotional and then it would kill them. Eventually we do die when we don't get our emotions in control. Science can prove this theory. Science has done nothing but prove in the lords existence.

The reason I wrote both of these quotes one from the bible which is more than 8,000- 10,000 years old and the quote of a scientist whom researches DNA is to help you to understand that science and religion go hand and hand, even for those who do not believe. They are conveying the same story and the same theory. The bible just told us without the research. If more people took the time to understand what they were reading they would not have the need to do the research. Just as the lord said because you see this beautiful world that I have created with your eyes you should believe in me. That is so true. We as people witness the lord everyday in his teaching's still. For me writing this book is taking the lord out of the mental or imagination and putting him in the physical form because we are all children of the lord whether we choose to acknowledge it or not and when we have him spiritually we have direct lessons being learnt everyday without the stress and dangers of the world.

I read in this book once that if I would learn to loose my blind spot than I would be a better person. I asked myself what could my blind spot be? Could it be the illusions I continued to feed myself for years? Well, if so, I no longer have any blind spots because the illusions have been removed. I no longer feed myself illusions. I'm dealing with reality. Reality is much better anyway and I'm going to teach you the steps I took to help me loose my illusion as well. Don't get me wrong illusions are wonderful for your development from birth to becoming an adult but once you have reached the levels of higher mental state the illusions we continue to carry can cripple us. Everyone mental perception is not supposed to be open completely because the way everyone thinks is differently. Drugs feed our illusions. Everything in the world is taken in excessive amounts and because we take them in excessive amounts for prolonged periods of time they cause harm to our bodies. Look at the description of the purpose for drugs below.

Stimulants are drugs that speed up activity in the central nervous system.	**Depressants** are drugs that slow down activity in the central nervous system.	**Opiates** relieves pain and commonly produces euphoria.	**Psychedelic drugs** produce hallucinations, change thought processes or disrupt the normal perception of time and space.

Below is a list of drug and the lasting results. I put this here to help you to think of your life in the long run.

Drug Habits

Type of Drug	Type	Natural Response to Drug	Lasting Results
Cigarettes (nicotine and tobacco)	Stimulant	Varies from alertness to calmness, depending on mental set, and prior arousal; decreases appetite for carbohydrates	Heart disease, high blood pressure, impaired circulation, erectile problems in men, cancer and other health risks.
Beer & Alcohol	Depressant	Slow reaction time, tension, depression, reduced ability to store new memories or to retrieve old ones, poor	Blackouts, cirrhosis of the liver, other organ damage, mental and neurological impairment, psychosis,
Marijuana (Weed)	Mild Psychedelic	Relaxation, Euphoria, increased appetite, reduced ability to store new memories other effects depending on mental set and settings	Throat and lung irritation, lung damage, impaired immunity, long term effects not well listed
PCP/ Dipped Squares	Psychedelic	Euphoria, Hallucinations, Numbness	
Crack/Cocaine	Stimulant	Euphoria, excitation, burst of energy, suppressed appetite	Excitability, sleeplessness, sweating, paranoia, anxiety, panic, depression, heart damage, heart failure, injury to nose if snorted
Opium, Heroin, Morphine	Opiate	Euphoria, relief of pain	Loss of appetite, nausea, constipation, withdrawal symptoms, convulsions, coma, possibly death

The drug Cocaine blocks the brains reabsorption of the neurotransmitters dopamine and norepinephrine. When this happens, levels of dopamine and norepinephrine rise in the body. The result is overstimulation of certain brain circuits and a brief euphoric high. This is the reason why you aren't going to beat up a crack head as the saying goes, because they have so many endorphins working to protect them from pain that they don't feel a thing. When the drugs wear off, a depletion of dopamine may cause the user to crash and become sleepy and depressed. This is the reason why they may rest for a week and then return to the habit.

The majority of drugs cloud up your judgment. It impairs your ability to think responsibly and often you just go with the flow, unlike other times when you weren't impaired you'd just say no.

If you can't do it for your health, then try to stop for your wallets sake, because "A free high is the worst high". I heard this saying my entire life and I believe it. Why is it that a free high is the worst high? I believe It is the worst high because you can obtain it so easily everyday since your not the one whose spending money. Look back at the list of drugs, and find which ones you believe are easily obtained.

What I have observed is what is easiest to attain is the drugs that are legal. Let's stop being fools for a minute, no one is growing drugs in their own backyards and even if they were you need to understand that the creator of the universe made each and every type of plant as well as human beings. Do to the fact, we've become civilized, we accept the rules made by our governments. The government tells us that this or that drug is bad or good for us. They must manufacture it, test it and make sure that it is safe for man, because of this process; you as a person no longer own the rights to process or manufacture the same product. The government found it first and now owns the rights to it. We play the patent game on the creator's inventions. Think for a minute, a piece of crack and an apple do the same thing. They are not responsible on their own, but have to join with something or someone else to make a difference. An apple does not eat a person, but a person has to eat an apple for an apple to be of use. Just like crack, until a person smokes a piece of crack it isn't of use. Crack doesn't smoke man, man smokes crack. Cigarettes don't just jump in your mouth, man puts it there. It is an extension. Man has basically given man permission to enslave them. People need to stop lying and twisting the laws for there benefit. The rules are not set in place because they want to help us as a people, but to control us as a people. The people stand around like mindless fools waiting for others to save them. They don't want to do the footwork themselves giving other entities permission to enslave your mind.

Back to the subject at hand, take for instance cigarettes they are very cheap, well at least when I use to buy them, the average pack cost about $4.50. Everyone can't afford to buy a Carton for the week, so we'll just multiply the average cost of a pack times the seven days giving a total of $31.50 for your week's expense and that's only if you smoke a pack per day. Imagine if everyone in the United States smoked. How much money would that be? If people didn't smoke they wouldn't have to spend the large amounts needed for healthcare, or are these just the illusions I like to feed myself. My truth can be proven. These drugs do nothing for our bodies but play off our emotions and feed our illusions. Don't get me wrong, for those that are very ill the effects of certain drugs can be quite useful and alleviating of pain but for those who haven't troubling conditions and aren't suffering mentally or physically why even indulge. It took me eleven years, of being a victim to my emotions, to want to quit smoking cigarettes. Hopefully it won't take anyone else as long.

A friend of mine, who was haunted by the demons of his past, sat down with me and told me his story. He is a good example of my theory. Firstly you need to understand that he is a Leo with a personality trait of INTP. Which means his emotions flow in this format thinking, judging, sensing and feeling. If you add these functions with the elements of his personality you have a ready to explode, eruption, bonfire, hurricane of a person on your hands. So be careful when dealing with this fire sign and personality.

Example Profile 1: Thomas

In the year 1967, he was about the age of six and was a very happy and healthy boy, as long as he got his way. His parents made sure that he was well provide for. As a side hustle to make ends meet, his father ran an after hour spot from their home. There were always bottles of liquor laying around and people constantly came by to get serviced. He remembers on his birthday receiving a new bike every year for a total of six years. His home life was very organized which taught him to be an orderly person. Everything had its place and he had been trained to keep his things together. Any task his parents gave him to complete he'd finish in a timely manner but the majority of the time he became confrontational as most little kids are. By the time he was eight his parents started allowing him to make errands for them by running to the store to purchase cigarettes. Sad to say, back in those days no one really paid attention to what was appropriate for children. Five years past and he got older and taller. He noticed his mom and dad were having difficult times in there marriage. They argued constantly and his father began to stray. By the time he was eleven, his father and mother divorced. This angered and hurt him deeply. He thought he had the perfect family. He blamed himself and soon started experimenting with alcohol as a method of rebellion.

The first time was at home when he opened the cabinet and grabbed a bottle. He said to me, it was on from there. I asked him if he remembered why he had done it? He said part of it was to punish his parents for splitting up and the other reason was he was chasing that happy moment he remembered when he was younger, a time when his parents sold liquor together, and made money and were happy just from the profit. He had wanted to relive those moments where he was happiest. He soon started going to the bars at about twelve years of age ordering his shots. In those days no one bothered anyone or instilled the value of what was appropriate and wrong behavior, for children or adults. People were proud to just be free and living by their rules. Most business owners didn't have a clue of the effects it would have on children and were just out to get paid. He didn't have the support of others to tell him at that age that what he was doing was inappropriate. He started dating by the time he was fourteen, and dropped out of school by the age of sixteen. His life started spiraling out of control.

In the year 1979, he remembers having both of his girlfriends pregnant at the same time. He continued to date one of the girls and later found out that he had not fathered the child with her that he had grown to love. The woman eventually gave him a son but the process had already been set in motion. He started drinking more and trying different drugs. He told himself he was not going to fall in love again because he had invested so much of his feelings into his girlfriend. His father had helped him to furnish there home together with a lot of second hand furniture. By this time he was a tried and true alcoholic who didn't trust women too much. In the relationship they didn't deal with their issues. One day his girlfriend went out dancing with a girl friend and returned home. He was drunk of course, he thought they were going to have a wonderful night and to his surprise he saw passion kisses going down her back, or at least that is what he thought. So much time has passed and he was so drunk that he can barely remember the realness of the story. They got into an argument, and then went there own separate ways because his heart couldn't take it. He's a very sweet simple man who still hasn't really addressed his issues. He used a lot of drugs after there separation like speed, weed and crack. He's even been to jail on three separate occasions for drug use where he served six months in prison twice and eight months in prison for his last crime. None of the experiences (jail time included) have taught him anything, but has given him more of an appreciation for his freedom. This man would rather take the easy way out rather than facing his emotions. That is the hurdle that mankind need's to learn to jump over.

The purpose of writing the story about Thomas was to show the relationship between emotions and drugs. When your emotions are not in order, it throws the body's hormonal balance off and your body then becomes depressed. Your body then starts its search for solutions to alleviate the mood. It starts to release these hormones with the hope of repairing the damaged tissues but the mind is so impatient that it finds another answer, a quick solution to the problem. This is when we indulge in different drugs and often become addicted. Our bodies are naturally trying to repair its damage when we add to the problem.

So many people put so much energy into escaping than facing. The truth is not always hard. I, myself have spent eleven years escaping while under the effects of cigarette smoke. I didn't make it to the harder drugs because my body wasn't even tolerant of the small drugs, and I also didn't have a desire to do them.

When I became committed to quitting cigarettes I made a schedule. I had heard that the majority of successful people have a schedule, and this is why I made one. The best place I found to start was to make a 24-hour schedule and then start of simple. There are 24-hours in a day, 8 of those hours are spent sleeping, another 8 hours spent working, and the other 8 hours juggling the rest of your day. A person barely gets to spend that time with loved ones. There is a time and place for everything. If you miss a day of recording, it's okay and don't worry, just continue on in the same pace.

Making a schedule is giving yourself something to be judge; it is putting your problems into the physical form. How can you fight a ghost if you can't see it? You have to make it visible to the naked eye. This is not a hard technique to follow. Im tired of others creating systems for personal gain, others need to learn the same method. Only you know what is best for you, I can only make suggestions and inform you of the steps that I took that helped me. Everyone has a bit of expert in him or her when it pertains to certain situations. I have been smoke free for 3 years and counting. I feel great. Negativity can't have me back anymore because I've learned my individual behavior.

To take my mind off of smoking, I did things that were opposite and "**different**" of what my mind were use to, I ate Eclipse cinnamon flavored mints every time the urge hit me. The urge lasted for only 15 minutes and I faced it head on. It wasn't as bad afterwards as I had built it up to be in my mind. I broke the pattern of the cycle in which my body had become accustomed too. My brother once told me it only takes 21 days to get the nicotine out of your system. So therefore the first 21 days for me were the hardest, but after you've broken the cycle of the pattern, your body won't be chemically dependent on it anymore. It's upon you to realize that you no longer need it. Fill the time slot of your day with other positive techniques. Get away from what you are use to because it hurts your body in the end. Just as with chicken and most African-American's, we love fried chicken, but if we'd learn to incorporate other foods in our diet, rather than just what taste good, and stop lying about our fiber intake, we wood be healthier physically. Now, this format can be used for drugs, sex, women and food. For those that use hard drugs you may also need to go to Detox Classes and other programs to assist you but this book can be used as a guideline to stay focused. You will also need a strong supportive team to help you. Look at the schedule below.

Time	Mood	Activity
5:30 a.m.		
6:00 a.m.		Had quick breakfast; smoked a cigarette
6:30 a.m.	neutral	
7:00 a.m.	mad	Have to go to work; smoked a cigarette
7:30 a.m.		
8:00 a.m.		
8:30 a.m.		
9:00 a.m.		
9:30 a.m.		
10:00 a.m.		
10:30 a.m.	bored	Don't have money for lunch; smoked a cigarette
11:00 a.m.		
11:30 a.m.		
12:00 p.m.		
12:30 p.m.	angry	Co-worker got on my nerves; smoked a cigarette
1:00 p.m.		
1:30 p.m.		
2:00 p.m.		
2:30 p.m.		
3:00 p.m.		
3:30 p.m.	happy	Just got off work; smoked a cigarette
4:00 p.m.		
4:30 p.m.		
5:00 p.m.		
5:30 p.m.	upset	Children acted up today; smoked a cigarette
6:00 p.m.		
6:30 p.m.		
7:00 p.m.	Happy & full	Ate Diner; smoked a cigarette
7:30 p.m.		
8:00 p.m.		
8:30 p.m.	moody	Watched a good movie; smoked a cigarette
9:00 p.m.		
9:30 p.m.	bored	Getting ready for bed; smoked a cigarette
10:00 p.m.		Sleep
12:00 a.m.		
12:30 a.m.		
1:00 a.m.		
1:30 p.m.		
2:00 a.m.		
2:30 a.m.		
3:00 a.m.		
3:30 a.m.		
4:00 a.m.		
4:30 a.m.		
5:00 a.m.		

There is no set time to stop smoking cigarettes. Everyone is different. I advice that if your trying to get over the hurdles in your life that you make an attempt to quite smoking for your physical

486

health and the damage that it does to your soul. I use this example to show a pattern in smoking behavior because I believe that if you knew your pattern and the moods affecting your behavior at a particular given time then you would be able to take control and cut down on the amount of times you smoke in any given day. You must seriously consider the effects cigarette smoking has on your life.

-Chapter 15-

Emotional Healing: Bearing your Cross

*"For the message of the cross is foolishness to those who are perishing, but to us who are being saved it is the power of God. For it is written: I will destroy the wisdom of the wise, and bring to nothing the understanding of the prudent". –**1Corinthians 1:18-19***

The Six Steps to Emotional Healing

Until others start admitting the truth about harmful and drastic situations that have taken place within their lives, such as abuse, the cycle of violence and harm to one another will continue. You have to understand that the situations you experience are mere stages of development. Every given situation aids in the development of a function. It's never personal. Do you think the creator does not see the father who rapes and molests his daughter, or the uncle who takes advantage of his nephew? He does, he's just waiting to see if you're going to be foolish enough to keep it a secret and not commit to helping others with the information.

"Where is the wise? Where is the scribe? Where is the disputer of this age? Has not God made foolish the wisdom of the world? For

since, in the wisdom of God, the world through wisdom did not know God, it pleased God through the foolishness of the message preached to save those who believe". -1Corinthians 1:20-21

In order for Physical, Emotional and Mental Healing to take place within your life, there must be an understanding that certain genes are responsible for negative storage of memories. Remember, each event helps to build up an emotion, and each emotion gives you diversity in the way in which you think and operate.

Genes	Duty	Masculine	Emotions	Feminine	Emotions
G	Sensing	I- Introvert	Cunning Inventive Diplomatic Perfectionist	E- Extrovert	Emotional Accident Prone Idealistic Intelligence
T	Thinking	P- Perceiver	Creativity Intuition Romantic Independence	J- Judger	Indecisive Careless Orderly Stubborn

Sensing- is the use of the analytical emotions from stored emotional memories of the individual or others. It gathers information from the five senses tasting, touching, smelling, hearing, and seeing. Storage is formed by dating, cheating, fashion, dramatically experienced situations, illusions of love, and anything else that requires illusions.

Thinking- is the use of the analytical thought from the stored intellectual memories of the individual or others. Storage is formed by puzzles, debates, mathematical problems, arguments, fighting, problem solving and any event with a negative action that has little to do with the act of being emotional.

The memory section of the individuals mind stores analytical emotions and analytical thought. **Memory** is the rational and emotional faculty of retaining and recalling past experiences.

Within this chapter you will find all of the necessary steps to cleansing the emotions and getting rid of the effects of the storage of the negative memories. To cleanse the emotion there must be an understanding that you are receiving the son, and the son is Jesus. It is the password that makes it possible for the father to hear you. Think of it this way as being a parent with your children, we don't pay attention to the pains or ills of others until our children or loves are hurt because it is not important but the minute our children are impacted it effects are very being. The concept is the same with the Lord. It's not personal but the way for him to hear you. The body (father) takes care of the soul (son), and the soul (son) takes care of the body (father), but the mind (holy ghost) governs all. Every aspect of the individual must be lined up for complete healing of all 3 Layers of the self.

Step One- Making the list

"Because the foolishness of God is wiser than men and the weakness of God is stronger than men. For you see your calling, brethren, that not many wise according to the flesh, not many mighty, not many noble are called". - **1Corinthians 1:25-26**

Sit down and make a list of all the events that have ever happened in your life that you can remember from birth to current. Write down the experiences you've had and the people that you've met as well. You actually have to write down the year of birth and the following year, so on and so on. Even if you don't believe the event relates to anything write it down anyway. It could have shaped someone else's life and you'll be able to show them the same method and help them out as well. As I stated earlier some personality types learn from the thoughts of others therefore negative events and positive events, as well as the people we meet impact our lives. We are humans and we have emotions; our hearts react to the feelings they give off. If you can't remember some of the events or people, but have heard stories about you participating in certain event or being around at certain place write them down. The more the merrier. Below I have written an example of how to format your list. You can skip over the years you don't remember, but once you recollect go backward and write it down.

Example 1:

Year	Event	The Effect it had on me
1976	Born March 12, with a scare on my face because of surgical removal	I live with an impression mark that draws attention to my face
1977		
1978	For Christmas I received a powered truck from my dad	I loved it because I received it from my dad even though I rarely got to ride it
1979	My father was arrested and sent to	I missed him very much
1980		
1981		
1982		
1983		
1984		
1985	I was able to visit with my father	I hadn't seen him in such a long time
1986		
1987		
1988		
1989		

Now attempt to recreate your life story in the same manner. On this page you'll be able to begin as a rough draft, but you know as well as I do, you'll need a bigger notebook. Use the next page as a starter page.

_____

_____

_____

_____

_____

_____

_____

_____

_____

_____

_____

_____

_____

_____

_____

_____

_____

_____

Step Two- Preparing Mentally

"This includes you who were once so far away from God. You were his enemies, separated from him by your evil thoughts and actions, yet now he has brought you back as his friends. He has done this through his death on the cross in his own human body. As a result, he has brought you into the very presence of God, and you are holy and blameless as you stand before him without a single fault. But you must continue to believe this truth and stand in it firmly. Don't drift away from the assurance you received when you heard the Good News. The Good News has been preached all over

*the world, and I, Paul, have been appointed by God to proclaim it. **-Colossians 1:21-23***

No one likes to go backwards into their past. In the past is a buildup of a bunch of events that pertain to hurtful memories. We have been taught to keep pushing forward and to leave the past in the past as a method of resolving old issues; but how can you go forwards when the past continues to haunt your everyday? I don't need to research this area of my book. Life has been a good teacher and I've been an even better student. Just the observation of others has helped me to come to this conclusion. I have a knack when it comes to people and they love to confess their problems to me all the time. From listening to others and their problems I've learned that you must go backwards and address all your past problems or they will continue to return one by one. For some people it takes years, because the memories of what happened to them remains very unpleasant and frightening.

It's like reliving a nightmare over and over. This is the use of your analytical emotions defeating you by playing events over and over in your mind. The reality of the events isn't what's affecting you but the illusions your holding on too and many people wonder why others turn to drugs as therapy. When you find the courage to face the problem, life becomes so rewarding and stress free. You have just learned to put yourself in control of what happens to you and the way you choose to react to a given situation. To master this step you must reflect on the list you previously made and think about how it may have affected your life. Ask questions, like what part of your personality do you believe the event was stimulating? Why did I take it so personally? When events happen in our lives that we can't make since of in our minds because of the pain realize this, the pain that you feel is just strengthening an emotion. The event, which happened, had to cause some type of growth to your character profile. When you are able to do this you will see which one of your emotions were actively stimulated or were over stimulated and know the reason why it is so hard for you to deal with the problems and get beyond them. We are full of different emotions, 16 major emotions recognized for sure. That's our gift, it's our Pandora's box or the fruit Eve gave to Adam, which was passed on down to us generation to generation, whether you believe it or not.

In the scripture, Mark 7:15-23, it reads, There is nothing that enters a man from outside which can defile him; but the things which come out of him, those are the things that defile a man. "If anyone has ears to hear, let him hear!" When He had entered a house away from the crowd, His disciples asked Him concerning the parable. So He said to them, "Are you thus without understanding also? Do you not perceive that whatever enters a man from outside cannot defile him, "Because it does not enter his heart but his stomach, and is eliminated, thus purifying all foods? And He said, "What comes out of a man, that defiles a man". "For from within, out of the heart of men, proceed evil thoughts, adulteries, fornications, murders, thefts, covetousness, wickedness, deceit, lewdness, an evil eye, blasphemy, pride, foolishness". "All these evil things come from within and defile a man."

This scripture conveys the same message in which I speak. The emotional baggage in which you hold on to can defile and hurt you. It can even turn a good person into a negative one. That is why you must let go.

Step Three- Facing Your Fears

"You were dead because of your sins and because your sinful nature was not yet cut away. Then God made you alive with Christ. He forgave all our sins. He cancelled the record that contained the charges against us. He took it and destroyed it by nailing it to Christ cross. In this way, God disarmed the evil rulers and authorities. He shamed them publicly by his victory over them on the cross of Christ. **-Colossians 2:13-15**

You need to grieve as a method of getting rid of all the negative energy. It's okay to allow your emotions to become expressed either privately or with the aid of someone. Remember we are all human and it is a natural process to become emotional, that's what you have tear ducts for.

Part of the problem is over the years we've accumulated so many illusions. We enjoy feeding them to ourselves just like that song goes, "don't worry be happy". Why would anyone want to worry? Worrying is very stressful. When you worry your body releases these hormones to lesson the effects of stress and sometimes your body doesn't shut down the production of these hormones until your body feels better. So what do you think happens if you never get better? Correct, your body continues to release the hormones till eventually you receive a fatal dosage. Pay attention to the reality of it all, your fine one day, and then you have a bad day, your mind tries to assist your body, the your body continues to break down, then you develop some terminal disease which no one can explain because you were just fine or appeared to be a minute ago, and lastly you die.

Don't get me wrong there is nothing wrong with death because it is a natural process, but why die when it's something you can correct. No one has to look at the internal plumbing anymore just to know when something is wrong. It's the greatest lie ever told. I'd rather die happy because it was my time to go. So get your emotions in order.

It makes a lot of sense to me that when we don't face our issues over time we develop a lot of seriously negative habits that eventually lead to our death. If you need an example all you have to do is turn on your TV and watch those who are successful. We forget they are people with feelings because they put on a great show by entertaining us, they have more money than us and we enjoy watching them and feeding our illusions. They have become the focal point of our grief. They've become pride and we've become envy, the two deadly sins. It's not there fault, they were just telling another persons story. It never happened to them. They just made us love the character they brought to life but truth is they do not really exist. It's there job to feed us the illusions; you are the audience whom they entertain and do a great job at it. There are healthy illusions and negative illusions. Do you see what I mean by illusions now? Reality is much better. Now that you've learned a little about illusions here are some of the questions you need to ask yourself about each and every event you remember. This will help you to loose your illusions. What is the fear you hold on to? Who gave you the fear? Why do you have this fear? What did it do to your trust? Was it because of a loved one that you took it so personally? When did it take place? How old was I? Where did it take place? Was I in a comfort zone? Why did it take place (My version of story)? How did I let it become so personal?

Face the fears. Admit the wrong in the fear and unassociated yourself from it. Let the emotions come out of hiding and experience the pain from it and own it. Don't give it any more power over you. You have to take each event one by one and address it. I am a living testament you can get past it. Example 1, for those who were molested like myself, ask yourself these questions then remove the personal out of it so you can heal. I had to tell myself, "It could have been anyone at that time I just so happen to be there". It would have happened anyway, it just would have been someone else's daughter. Forgive it, because it was not personal. It was wrong and should not have happened to you, but it wasn't personal.

Example 2, For those acts that you feel were personal I'd say to myself, I just so happen to be related to this man and if I were not his daughter the other person who committed this crime against me would have done it anyway but it would have been my sister. He was going to get either one of us. So because of my knowledge of this I'm not going to take it personal as an attack on my character, and forgive it for me. Take the power back. Say, "It has done nothing but strengthened me".

You can't expect to run through the list of past events in one complete day and believe that you have completely healed because you haven't. This is a process and it has taken years for all the emotions to build you into the person that you are today, be it negative or positive it has affected your life, so it's going to take just as much time to undo all the damage. You need to compare note and see why it hurts you so much before. You have to be your own private investigator over your mind. I want you to see why this event personally attacked your character. Why did you take it so personal? When you can see why it relates to you so well, you'll learn how to deal with it more effectively the next time it strikes. In other words see why you took it so personal so you can let it go. You'll know when you've correctly healed from the event because when you discuss it openly with family and friends you no longer hurt from hearing about it.

Step Four- Acceptance: Owning it

"If you forgive the sins of any they are forgiven them; if you retain the sins of any, they are retained". –John 20:23

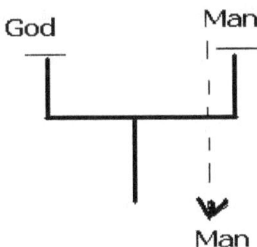

Man must learn to except the fact that man is not God and quit trying to stack them up next to God because they don't measure up. We put people on these pedestals that they don't belong on. When our emotions are hurt by others it creates the illusion of the one whom hurt our hearts becoming hero's. When man puts everything on that pedestal they must give it to God and watch it fall to Earth. I mean you must actually allow yourself to see it happen in your mind because then you'll be free.

Let me give you an example, my whole life my uncle had been telling all of his nieces and nephews that he was the total package, which is saying a lot for a person's character. This allowed us to place him so high in our mind that we actually believed there was nothing that he couldn't do until he started to let all of us down. We could have held on to the memories and kept building him up. Our heart and minds were so confused by this because our love for our uncle was so deep even more than he loved us at times. I had to give it to God as well as my brother, sisters and cousins. I said Lord I know my uncle is just a man and that when I receive his love I'm just receiving a mere sample of you because you are love completely and he was just the vessel that you used. Than I watched him fall from the total package into a man who makes mistakes, because it was my relatives and I who had placed his love high with God and it was a lie. Because the one thing about love it never changes and is unconditional, God never lets you down even when you let yourself down.

This is how you except what has happened to you when the effects of it seem so lasting. Any given circumstance, if there was love it was bound to hurt you. I can look back at a lot of events from my past and hurt behind them but that doesn't change the fact that while it was happening to me, at times I loved every minute of it. It has truly shaped my life and I love the beautiful yet complex woman that I've grown to become today. People are scared to death of facing reality. They don't think their current situation will get any better than the illusions they like to feed themselves, but it does. You just have to dig deep down within your heart to understand one clear truth and that is, "Everything that has happened in your life was not personal". It was just the building blocks that helped to craft you into the person you were made to be and have become. You should be happy and able to look in the mirror and love yourself everyday without being tormented by pain.

Jerry Springer is someone I use to love to watch and not just for the excitement of his crazy shows. Jerry! Jerry! I loved him so much for exposing the world to what people attempt to keep a secret everyday. He's no psychiatrist but he makes an attempt at least to help others deal with there negative issues. It's hard for a lot of people to relate to his shows because they've never experienced the stories most of his guest talk about. What do you think some of the people who are guest on his shows where thinking when they decided to come and expose there inner most secret? I don't think they went there because they get a kick out of airing their dirty laundry. Why is it easier for most people to express their feelings to millions rather than to the one they love? A lot of his guest claim to be too afraid to tell their significant other at home for fear of what they might do to them or others. I think going on the Jerry Springer Show has made them the bravest people on the planet because Jerry Shows are very judgmental. By facing the music on his show the worst part is over. The story has been told and everything is then laid on the table to be judged. As the saying goes, Let he who is without sin cast the first stone and I don't think there would be anyone to stand on Jerry's show. Just from being there they've sinned as well. I take the lords laws and hold them dear to my heart. I'm attempting to give the world its wake up call.

God does not judge by man-made laws, he has his own laws. God promises to make right what went wrong in everyone's life if you can just believe in him. The Lord I believe in knows that the same man that grew up to be a child molester was molested as a boy himself, as well as the man who abuses was abused himself. I'm not saying the world should release the criminals of the world, I'm just saying take a minute to understand that your neighbor was once just like you on the right path till that one episode knocked his emotions off balance. No ones life is more valuable to the Lord than that of your neighbors; meaning you are both equally important to the lord's purpose. One of The Lords commandment is that you love your neighbor as you love yourself and this is how you show him that you love him.

504

Although negativity has plagued your life this far you do have the opportunity to get it right and get your emotions back In order; as well as that of your neighbor's. Just follow the steps I've written.

Acceptance is about bearing your own cross. Own the negativity and positivity that has happened to you. It helped to get you to were you are today, still able to breath and repent of your sins. After you've addressed each event personally I want you to accept and own what has happened to you. I want you to understand it was just the building blocks that helped you to get to the person you are today, and every time you look in a mirror you should be very proud of what you see.

Yes, I had a very strong, short, 4'9, but wise grandmother in Ms. Lula Mae Guyon. She called us all her tribe. She had seventeen children and three died at birth. My father is her youngest child. I wasn't raised around her but she put up the effort to be included in my life and my brother's. She even accepted my two sisters as if they were her grandchildren as well. At the age of 14 she became more active in my life. The majority of my cousins were grown so when I'd visit she'd also have over to the house my younger, great-cousins. Grandma was the best; she'd have a baby in each arm and still have time for you. I had gotten pregnant by the time I was 15 and delivered my baby by the time I was 16. When my daughter was a couple of months old my grandmother came into the lounge room where I was sitting and asked everyone to leave so she could talk to me. I was in shock thinking what I could have done wrong. Grandma just said "baby, don't forget to let your baby's father be a part of that girls life". I said, "I am letting him grandma". She said no baby, that's not the daddy. You find that girls real father and let him be a part of that girl's life. Wow! You know those real grandma's from back in the day just tell you like it is. I didn't want to accept her truth because I was in love with the person I thought was my baby's father.

When I had gotten pregnant a big secret came out. I had been involved with my adopted cousin. He ran away from home just to be with me. I hid him in my room and left for school the next day as if nothing had happened. We were hanging out downtown waiting on the stores to open so we could get something to eat and play hooky the rest of the day. When the stores finally opened we went to a restaurant that had the sit down booths. A friend of his from summer school came in to use the john. He spoke and I didn't think much of it. When he returned he came over to the table were we where sitting and asked my adopted cousin who I was. I just looked at him because I wanted to hear his answer too. Now mind you this person had never seen me before until that day so it was okay for my adopted cousin to be honest. He told him I was his cousin. My mouth dropped. I thought to myself "okay, now I'm your cousin, a cousin with benefits". The friend, we'll just call him lavadez, said, "how are you doing", "Do you have a boyfriend"? I looked right at my adopted cousin and said "No I don't". He then said, "Good, good can we talk". I said "I don't' mind". One thing led to another, and we eventually made it to Lavadez house off 116th Corlette. We had needed a place to hand out till school hours had past. My cousin went to sleep then Lavadez and me had unprotected sex.

I didn't see Lavadez again until 3 months later to show him that I was pregnant. We kept in contact over the phone for a brief moment than we lost touch. Over the phone when I revealed my truth to him, he kept insisting that I was pregnant by him. We exchanged information but when I moved to another address the information was lost to me.

Love is blind. My own baby's father told me the truth and I didn't want to believe because I allowed my emotions to lead me. I had a DNA test done on my adopted cousin, which confirmed he wasn't the father. In the process I hurt so many people for my sin. My aunt because she was a grand-daughter short, my cousin who invested the time into what he perceived was his daughter, my daughter who never got to know her biological father and Lavadez who has yet to know his daughter. It has been sixteen years since the day I first was pregnant. Had I taken the time to just heath my grandmother's words I would not be in the situation today? The problem would have been fixed sooner, but I accept my situation for what it is. This is the way the Lord wanted it to work out.

Just as I said earlier, I understand now that it was the building blocks that made me into the person I am today. I love what I see every time I look in the mirror. I made a lot of wrong choices in my youth, and adult life almost everyone does. I am just acceptable today of what has happened. I own every event from my past. I couldn't picture the person I am today without the event there to help shape my life. I own it.

Step Five- Can't fix it, so let it go

This is the fairy-tale section of the book. We've all been looking for prince charming, and the perfect getaway since the moment we learned to read. Right, Ladies? We were told to read more because reading helped to nurture our imagination. Lord knows reality is tough enough with our work, home life, family and friends. We just don't need the added aggravations, and stress to our daily lives, but we all need some form of comfort.

Everyone needs something positive to hold onto for strength just to see our way threw to the next day. So sometimes we get lost in our imagination. Some of us take a short trip, which ends up being an extended vacation, or a permanent residence. We didn't mean for it to happen but the dream world is so beautiful and stress free. The illusions captivate us.

We have to learn to enjoy the fantasy for what it is, everyone loves Disney Land, but when it's time to return to reality make every effort to loose all your illusions.

We must train our mind to see beyond our blind spot. I was

told a long time ago, if I could learn to look beyond the rose colored glasses I would be a better person. When I had also read it that was when I decided to find a better solution to aid in making me a better person. I've been searching for a way I could do this. I finally came up with the answer that I've been sharing in my book the whole time.

How do we open our minds to forgiveness? What does it take? First, you must learn to accept the situations, or events that have fashioned your life for what they are. It's all about developing your emotions and functions. How else will you receive the information? Id like to think, had I not had a boyfriend who loved to indulge in other women, I wouldn't know what cheating meant, nor would I have learned why or what it was that I loved about him. Love fed me hate, if you can understand that. Everything has a cause and effect. I don't like to get caught up in simple emotions. I like to see the whole picture from every angle possible. I remove my emotions from the equation. That is the only way you will receive the best picture. My sister in-law would tell me; there are three sides to a story my story, his story, and what God knows. I believe it. All three stories are the truth; it's just each person has there own perspective of the events that have happened but given different interpretations because of their personality type and astrological sign. Actually, they couldn't help the way they perceived the conversation. It was destined to happen that way. What do we gain from being able to notice beyond our blind spot?

You gain a clearer outlook on the emotions, and yourself as an individual.

What I've trained my mind to do when I'm ready to let go is to take the fairy tale side of the story out of it. We have to learn to accept what is going on right now for what it is.

Let me give you an example, all my life I've corresponded with my father from jail. When I became an adult my mom had gotten rid of her horrible boyfriend and started dating another guy by the name of David. I felt like the Lord sent her what she needed at that particular time because her heart had been broken so bad. My mom and David dated for 10 years before they had even considered marriage. I was grown and on my own, but I accepted David as my stepfather and father figure, because in all the time that I had gotten to know him, he never caused me harm or my child. I saw him for the man that he was and gave praise to him for making my mother so happy.

My biological father, Melvin, couldn't accept me calling another man dad. It hurt him deeply. I didn't call him dad to hurt him, or because he had taken my father's place, but out of respect. From my point of view, he was the first stepfather whom respected my body, space, and mind. I grew to love and respect him for it. It was the years of this man tolerating my hate towards him that made me appreciate him. He was a wonderful person to my daughter, which he considered his to also be his granddaughter.

My mother had adopted a little girl at 6 months old and he

was a wonderful father to my little sister. He wasn't perverted and this made me look at men differently, I saw that they can be trusted.

My biological father even wrote a letter through the mail to further show his disgust in the matter. I in return didn't understand what was happening because I wasn't looking at the story from all angles. The only side I could see was mines and my stepfather. My stepfather was proud and excepting of me relating to him as my parent. He felt bonded to me an appreciative. He even knew my father when he was a child and they were considered friends. He gave me stories of my father when others couldn't. He had great respect for my father and I loved him for it. I took time to reflect and to see the story from my father's side. He was a parent whom felt like he was striped from his child's life. She was the daughter that he prayed for. He got to correspond and raise her giving his soul and mind. In ways he felt that his love for his daughter is what imprisoned him to begin with. He lives with the thought, had he not come to save his baby girl, he would not be in prison today. He adored and loved his baby girl. He wanted very much to be apart of her life and felt threatened by another man even attempting to be or mean what he should mean, to his daughter and to dismiss his feeling as if they were nothing was heart wrenching.

I later apologized to my father for not feeling his emotions because I understood now where he was coming from. No man could ever replace my father in my life, he is my Hero. I tried to make him aware of my feelings and why I had done it but he didn't want to hear my story, he was venting and I accepted it. He had to deal with his issues about it. It didn't change the fact that I had a stepfather and a father who love me dearly. I love my dad and I love David, but they're not in the same boat competing for my heart and love. No one can even stack up to meaning as much to me as my father. He raised my soul and mind from prison. God gave me the best parts of him. He has educated me to so many situations and is constantly giving me the gift of his time, which I am so thankful for.

My relationship to David was not going to change because of my father's feelings because he was now a part of my mother, little sister and my world. I did how ever do some adjusting because I didn't want to hurt anyone's feelings. So sometimes you can't always fix situations. You have to allow yourself the chance to try and get your point across, then let it go. I'm not going to beat myself up and give myself some unwanted emotions that harm my body. The hormonal effects can be devastating. You must allow that part of your illusions to die because no one is perfect. Don't hold hate, resentment or fear on your heart. Allow your self to hurt and heal. You've got to learn to move past your feelings and the events that shape your lives. This is what Jesus would do. It's all about training our mind to forgive. As I said earlier reality is much better. You need to un attach yourself from the negativity. You must learn to look at events objectively. See the event if it were happening to someone else. Then you'll be better able to judge the event. What would be your opinion then? Let it go because life Is too short to worry.

Step Six- Recognize but Never forget

It is okay to remember what has happened to you. It's a part of your makeup and the reason you are the person you are today. Had the events never happened, you would not be fashioned in the way you are. You should love what you see and not be hurt when ever the issues are discussed because it's a part of your makeup and it's not your current situation. You now have the control. Everyone has a story to tell and a servitude to complete. The positive energy must always be recycled and passed on because it is always better to give than receive. When you remember events from your past it prevents you from mentally and physically making the same mistakes over and falling into the same pattern. Patterns are nasty little traps.

Reflection is great because it alleviates the mind of past stresses and worries. You should spend at least 30 minutes per day meditating on past events. This restores your health and emotions. Remembering past event could be of benefit to others as well because it gives you a subject to relate to as servitude to relieve others of the same burdens or problems. Maybe hearing a story from you would convince a person to get away from the same negativity. The majority of people learn from example. The more you talk about past situations the easier the subjects become. Recognize the truth in the story for what it is. Don't allow yourself to get caught up in the trap of self-pity. Like the saying goes about trouble it's easy to get in and hard to get out so never forget your past troubles or you will repeat them.

Chapter 16-

Mental Healing: Coming Back to the Same Circle

"But of Him you are in Christ Jesus, who became for us wisdom from God- and righteousness and sanctification and redemption- That as it is written, He who glories let him glory in the Lord." - **1Corinthians 1:30-31**

When something tragic happens to us in our life and we grieve because of it, our minds are just reminding us of the prior events which happened deep within our past, this is what we relate the current event to, and that is the reason for it hurting us so much.

Let's look at the situation logically; events and environments' are nourishment for the emotions. In order for an emotion to do its job it has to be stimulated. The relating of the emotion, such as feeding it prior events helps the emotion grow big and strong. It is never personal and just a natural part of your design. It is what helps you to exist as an individual, mind body and soul.

As I stated earlier the part that no one pays attention too is we all have a central nervous system (kingdom of God) and a peripheral nervous system (kingdom of Satan). The peripheral nervous system (Kingdom of Satan) handles the central nervous system's (Kingdom of God) input and output. It is what connects the mind to the body, just as the emotions connect the mind and body to the soul. What ever information you gather from your feeling and judging, your sensing and thinking interprets the information and adds a hint of spice by throwing in an old memory or two at you that relates to the same topic just to intensify the emotional response which is also known as your mood. Therefore, whatever is going on in the central nervous system (Kingdom of God) the peripheral nervous system (Kingdom of Satan) is always looking for a way to use it against you.

For example, my little brother use to get jumped on so much because he was a church boy. He would stay at the church all day with his bible in hand. When he left the church to come home the neighborhood boys would be waiting in the bushes for him and would attack him every time throwing rocks at him and chasing him home. This scenario happened everyday, the same time because he was unsuspecting, naive and giving others the benefit of doubt.

One day my mother got upset and made my brother stand and fight. She politely told him to kick their behind or she was going to kick his behind. Well that put the fear in him that he needed because my mother had never raised a hand to hit her only son and he didn't want to take a chance on experiencing it. So he took off one of his dress shoes and got to swinging. He was not an experienced fighter but just like the rocks that were thrown at him, he knew that the heel of his shoe would hurt as well. My brother won the battle that day and the experience from the guys jumping out the bushes on him taught him to be more alert of his surroundings. The emotion did it's job well.

Later in life, when my brother got a bit more weight and height on him he started jumping out the bushes on the guys as they did him. He disliked bullies so much that the event from his past became a part of his mission in life. He had not forgiven the kids for disrupting his life as a church boy.

This is what I mean by the past experiences coming back to haunt you now. It may give the illusion that the event bothering you is a current situation, but in truth, if it were current then it wouldn't even hurt or trouble your minds as much as it does. Your mind has not had built up enough data or had enough exposure to the event to become grievous. We have to learn to let go of the past events, at least within our minds. This is what I consider coming back to the same circle.

How are we, as a people, going to move past the current events now, which take place within our life if we can't get rid of the old junk. We must learn that it's not personal and move past the pain, even as hard as it may seem, you can do it.

Remember I stated earlier, the events were the building blocks that helped to formulate you into the person the creator already picked for you to be.

Learn from those events that happened in your life and then let it go. If you continue to hold onto those events the emotions will first cripple your soul, body and then eventually your mind.

A good example is cigarettes and tobacco. A billion dollar a year industry with a product that's so easy to attain. For starters cigarettes have no life form, they do not actually walk and jump into the mouths of it's victims who desire to smoke. What they do as a job is stimulate an emotion, and if you make a habit of smoking them than you over stimulate an emotion that does not need to be constantly stimulated. Everything on this planet stimulates an emotion, down to the food we eat. We as a people are addictive and have addictive behaviors. Change must start with us not the product. People wouldn't be richer than others if they didn't' allow themselves to be slaves. Keyword **allow.** People indulge in this bad habit because of a traumatic life event in there life. They are drawn to the fact that they can escape their mind's problems for a minute. It is a product of the world and is but a distraction in itself because it solves no problems, yet destroys physical man and woman. The devil always knows when to come calling.

A part of my life story is a good example of this. I'm not innocent, I was sucked in too, I smoked cigarettes for 11 years because of depression. I had lost at the same time two key figures that were very important in my life. My grandmother died on her 77th birthday and my first love went to jail.

I was grief stricken and didn't want to face the emotion so I turned to cigarettes for comfort. Remember, when you're at your lowest point the devil always knows when to strike. Something so simple that could have been treated within a couple of months from just visiting a psychiatrist office. At the least the psychiatrist would have probably given me better choices that I had available to for myself.

Smokers take a chance everyday on developing some form of cancer or early death sentence because of it. I am not the creator and I don't know the day expected for a person death, but I do know from common-sense smoking cigarettes shorten your chance of living a full life. It doesn't take a rocket scientist to figure out how our emotions relate to our behavior, Does it? Everyone's life story has a cause and an effect. What is your story? Have you shared it?

Once we are relieved of the physical and spiritual negativity it always finds a way to reintroduce itself back into our lives through the mental negativity. As that age old saying goes, Misery loves company. It is so true because Misery use to be my best company. Think of what I said earlier peripheral nervous system against central nervous system. My simple emotions of loving and missing the two key figures within my life, the peripheral nervous system (Kingdom of Satan) decided to throw the memories that I have stored in my emotional memory and my intellectual memory right back at me, in order to make it harder on my emotions to deal with the event. Can you hear the violin (Tear jerk, tear jerk). This as I said stimulates the growth of an emotion. I recognize this now about my emotions but I didn't when I was younger and going through the episode.

When I sit back and think about how good God is, I can't help but say, He is Raw"! He is my championship fighter who always comes out on top. He knows me completely. He knew that loosing the both of them when I did would prompt me to look for deeper answers within him.

A lot of the problems with the world is due largely to the fact that they have forgotten their first love. God is love and the first expression of receiving his love is when we first date and mate. This mate tells our body, mind and soul what qualities to appreciate in another person and what not to. You are set basically the way that you are meant to be and you have the answers to the questions already encoded within you by the time you are 14-16 years of age. As a matter of fact, the first person that broke your heart and you appreciated is encoded within your genes and there is no escaping it. This is the first person you looked at as "love", behavior that they did you didn't like or behavior they did that you approved of was all encoded within your genes. This is your marriage and union the creator has joined together. Every person that you meet after your first love will possess the same characteristics and qualities that remind you of that first love. That is the reason why you indulge and entertain the relationship. So many people get a kick out of being thieves and stilling a person's virginity. You just don't know the damage you do. Everyone needs to stop focusing on what the sex feels like because it is a mere illusion. It doesn't last and regardless the thrill is never as good as the first time.

People get into this habit believing they can just switch up and things will be all right. As a matter of fact they think they are upgrading when they are actually downgrading to a less expensive model. The damage has already been done to your heart and now, you have to start the process all over of recording the codes.

Your brain goes into overdrive when you constantly change the codes and tell your mind, body and soul no I've changed my mind I like this now too. All from jumping person to person. Think about the Ten Commandment "Thou shalt not commit adultery" for a minute, back in the day's people were getting married when they found a suitable companion. They didn't change up mates and they stayed together because their mate was there first expression of love. Forever beautiful.

Regardless, to how crappy he looked as he aged or how fat she got from having children they loved each other endlessly. Every time she looked at him she saw her first love and he saw his first love that is beautiful. Marriage meant so much more back in the days. Because of the encoding, this is the very reason people get mad at their current spouses. People are so jealous about hearing stories of others. No one wants to learn why you behave the way you do. It hurts people to hear about prior loved ones, they think everything is just about sex. I heard once from an ex, "I don't wanna hear about how another man made you happy, I wanna make you happy". To make one happy one must learn them or the person of interest. You have to do your research about the one you claim to love most.

A couple of months ago though for me that wasn't the case. Let me tell you my story... My family and I had moved to this new neighborhood because we had needed time to heal emotionally and spiritually because of my daughter being physically assaulted by previous neighbors. I'm not going to sugarcoat anything, my daughter is no chump but instead of playing tick for tack and hurting another mother's child I relocated. We had been at the new location for a period of three months when I started noticing changes in my husband's behavior.

To break it down for you I am a dominant sensor of negative emotions and an auxiliary thinker of negative thoughts. Therefore I'm always analyzing, breaking down and building events over for truth. My strengths are to stack analytical emotions and analytical thoughts within my mind. I deal with the logics of things, so I am aware that I don't have all of my husband's time.

This is a key element that most people need to pay attention to within there own lives, there are only 24 hours in a day, 8 hours of work, 8 hours of play and 8 hours of sleep. It is a constant juggle to include everyone you love in daily life activities. It's amazing that one actually spend enough time with another.

For my husband at 4:00 a.m. he wakes up to prepare

himself for the day ahead. He takes a shower for 30 minutes, brushes his teeth for 5-10 minutes, and Irons his clothes for about 10 minutes, and then he may have a sensible breakfast. By the time 5:30 a.m. comes around he's out the door so he can catch his bus so he wont be late for work. I myself, don't see him again normally until about 4:30 p.m.- 5:30 p.m. because of the commute it takes him to make it home. I don't get to see my husband until twelve hours later, and that's if he decides to come straight home. He makes stops along the way visiting relative's, friend and throwing back a couple of beers. I would get so upset at the hours my husband would return home because me or his children would get no time to spend with him. As quoted from the bible when a man marries he is joined to his wife and they are one, but why do I feel like a half? I already know I married the wrong man; I'm just trying to get my point across.

I'm talking about three o'clock a.m. to six o'clock a.m. and him strolling through the door. This isn't the way I believe a marriage is supposed to be.

The few hours before it's time for him to go back to work. I don't want to hear anything about bar hours or such a things because this type of behavior was unlike my husband. I've been with him a total of eight years so I should know his behavior by now. Sometimes he's a no call no show. Just to think that I might have to call the cops, hospital or morgue looking for my husband is not fair to my emotions. I shouldn't have to worry. I'd sit and think to myself, "Why would he want to put me through this type of grief?" I felt like he was personally attacking my character.

Usually when he'd come home, he'd assist me with the girls by entertaining them while I cooked and cleaned the house, then he'd play a little video game and would normally be asleep in the bed by the time twelve midnight came rolling around, but that changed for him. It seemed I never got a break from the girls. I was always busy. I never even had the time to tend to my own health and my cholesterol was up. I would say to myself out of anger "Oh, he must not know who I am". "He must not know I will hurt him". I would get so enraged.

I had reached my limit and I didn't allow that type of behavior to continue anymore. I waited to confront him, I first kept a journal of the hours and his behavior for about a good two weeks before I brought it to his attention. One afternoon he came home and I was so upset. I felt very disrespected because we were to be as one, this kept ringing in my head and he was just doing what he wanted without consulting me.

A voice inside my head said if he doesn't respect you than what chances do you have with the rest of the world. I felt he was cheating on me with the streets because I wasn't getting his time. I immediately lashed out at him. We had a screaming match. Hurtful words were exchanged and I slugged him out of anger. Being the man he is, he attempted to restrain me, but I'm a tough cookie to handle, what happened next was I just cried and cried. He asked me to calm down. He said he didn't mean to upset me so much. I eventually walked away from him and ran to the bathroom to be alone. I was disgusted. He followed me there and wanted to talk. When I opened the door I immediately looked up to catch his eyes when I noticed the bruise I had done. I burst into more tears. I said, "I can't believe this. This relationship is bringing someone out of me that I do not want to exist. I can't be with you anymore".

This was a fear of mine that came rolling back around. The devil knew the right words to play off in my mind to make the action happen.

It was a fear of mine because I spent the majority of my youth watching my mother and her boyfriend of thirteen years battle each other everyday and his drug habit didn't help it either. One day, I walked in on the both of them wrestling, in the bed, over a twenty-two-caliber handgun. The emotions were racing in my mind. I immediately became enraged because I had just heard a story from a friend that her mom died in this same way and it was the reason for her living with her grandmother. So I intervened and took the handgun from the both of them. It could have misfired or anything. My father was already not very much a part of my life because of gunplay. Anyone could have been shot that day. He stood up and began to walk in my direction so I slugged him with everything that I had than cursed him out, I already had mad hate for him, what I felt at that moment was that it was very immature for him to bring a gun in the home in the first place and second, for the both of them let alone to be wrestling over it.

I left and went to my aunt's house to cool off and I returned when they started acting their age and not there shoe size. I also returned cause I had to watch my brother and sisters.

I had returned to the same circle in my adult life that I had experienced as a child, as far as both adults acting immature. This had happened because I had not fully forgiven my mom or her boyfriend at the time for what happened. I had not even forgiven myself for witnessing it.

So now I was reliving my past in my own life story. My husband said I apologize and I said no, "we are both at fault". All of the emotions came out of me then. I said, "it's not fair that I should have to do everything for these babies all by myself". Where suppose to be married! I mean, I did it the right way this time; I got married before having the babies. Why did you marry me? What would happen if the shoes were on the other foot and I decided to not come home?

See everyone assumes because you're a woman you have a natural instinct to mother your children. That's not always the case. In the bible, in genesis god said he was going to make man a helper so he sent woman. Therefore she was meant to assist man and it was not meant to be her full time job. It's fifty, fifty.

He said, I know baby I just wanted to spend time with my father and Thee; I just lost track of time, but I love you and need you in my life. I said, you can't just say those words and think everything is fine with us. The job is not done by your words alone and actions speak louder than words. Show me. Do your part. I said, you know what, I'm going to do me and you do you. He said, what does that mean bay. I said, saying that doesn't mean I want a divorce. He was frightened. He said, Oh because you were scaring me with that one. You know I can't live without you or the kids.

I'm just saying I can no longer stress myself out worrying about you and your ware bouts. One of us has to be sane and healthy mentally in this relationship. So I'm going to be the first to make an attempt to get it together. He said oh, okay baby. You do you first, and then you can help me because I don't want to loose you.

So that's what I did. I turned to the bible for comfort but it wasn't my first step. Firstly, I use to pray to the lord to keep me safe and then that He would just walk with me. My husband from time to time still made the same mistakes but I didn't allow it to upset me as much. I got a handle on my emotions. Everything I've wrote in this book I've practiced. I even put a little distance on our relationship because I realize all of us have a journey and servitude that we must take.

I got back acquainted with myself. I started reading this book called Reading People by Jo-Ellan Dimitrius, Ph.D., and Mark Mazzarella because I was inspired because of my husband's actions. I had now become a detective about behavior in people.

Part of me was still struggling for answers and I had wanted to know the real reason why he had suddenly changed, instead of just listening to what he wanted to tell me.

The book was very insightful; it hit on a bunch of good points. I remember saying to myself "oh, this book is really great, only if they had a book to read emotions". Emotions, emotions rang in my head. I remembered reading this book years ago in my early twenties that went into great details describing the emotions we were born with in the astrological signs. The only problem with the book that I saw was each of the emotions were different but I knew there had to be some common ground about them. So I re-read the book and still with a lot of good points I found, I got to thinking about emotions and another book I had also read and said to myself what if these character traits influenced our emotions. When I looked a little closer at the book I noticed the character traits had emotions they were just not defined. Wouldn't that be something? The more I read the more I saw the lord working in my life. He was giving me the answers that I needed within these two books. It was with this theory that I had pulled God from out the heavens and into the physical form to be witnessed by each and every man because I then realized he and his kingdom exist in each and every one of us whether we want him there or not. I had finally grasped the understanding of the verse in Genesis 3:16, "your desire shall be for your husband, and he shall rule over you."

That was exactly what I was experiencing now, my desire

was for my husband and he wasn't putting my feeling into consideration at all, he just did what he'd felt like doing. It was already stated in the bible, and I had accepted that it was already predestined for my husband to think this way, regardless to my feelings he was never going to live up to my standard or expectation of what I felt was appropriate behavior. The lord was not punishing Eve or the feminine gene by what The Creator had said, The Creator was making her aware of the actions she had put into play.

I had to learn to forgive him big-time, because I had witnessed it was a natural flaw or reaction that he would always make. He wasn't trying purposely to hurt my emotions and to experience the true essence of love; you have to go through the negativity. How do you think the genes within learn to appreciate a person?

This is what sets him apart as being his own man. If his boys called him for pool and drinks he'd tell me anything just to get the opportunity to go, if he wanted to play his Xbox rather than curling up in bed with me and a movie than he would play his game because that is the way he'd feel. Men, they are naturally rebellious and it didn't just start with him. Men need to learn how to do things for themselves just like women need to learn how do things for themselves. It's never personal.

Now because the lessons in the bible are written doesn't mean they have to become lessons that you have to experience personally. You can learn from others pitfalls and triumphs. Everything doesn't have to always be experienced for you to learn from it. You can learn from events without actually having to go threw the same events yourself just by opening your mind.

They are all The Creator's lessons for us to learn from. Just because it's predestined to happen in the bible does not mean you can't learn to lessen the effects it has on your life by not taking it personal. Example, just because it's predestined for my husband to rule over me doesn't have to mean I suffer from wanting to be around him. We both need to practice bending in our views 50% of the time. Divorcing your spouse or running away from the situation all together, what does it show the demon that resides in them? That they have won and you have given up on them and your just like everyone else who has let them down in there life. You have to continue the flow of love regardless to the cost. People must learn to quit being so selfish with there time.

Sometimes you can learn from other peoples mistake without having lived it. That's the whole point. I'm not going to sugar coat anything because I am a person who naturally feels emotions, but I am not as angry a person as I use to be, because I took the time to understand what was happening to me and will continue to take place in my life. So I too am destined to get upset from time to time but because of the knowledge I acquired the effects of it wont be as lasting, nor will it be a fear attempting to come back into my life. Doing so will prevent you as well from having to come back to the same circle. After you firmly deal with the problem and your wounds have healed, your mind and body can no longer hurt behind your past pains. For some people, depending on the circumstances, you actually have to remove yourself from what is troubling you and this is not giving up. This is taking a vacation. This is helping to calm down those emotions that have taken over.

Conclusion:

The moral of my story is to face each event as if it were fresh and new within your mind. Learn not be as judgmental concerning others actions because there is a higher power running the show, and he does not allow the events which have happened to take place because he wants to hurt you but because he wishes to help you. You must learn to look at events objectively and witness that all these processes happen because a specific function is in development. You are a vessel for God to distribute his love. He lives within you. Try not to let your analytical thoughts run away with you. Let it go and remove the personal from the event. It's a small request to ask.

-Deciphering the Bible-

The bible is the best book ever read and sold more copies across
the globe. It contains all of the creator's laws and commandments.
The bible is the basis information before leaving earth because it
contains the keys to receiving heaven within thy self. It tells a lot of
emotional stories for the creation or mankind to understand it's
design and the mistakes made by the creation throughout life.
Regardless to what many may question as I once stated, they get
lost with all the distractions and analyzing the nothing, be it you're
a non believe or true to Christ, the bible and Christ have still done
there job. You're the one that needs to catch up.

The key element that has been over looked by many is the fact
that the stories are emotional stories and the thoughts of God
translated through the word of mankind. Why do you think God
decided to relay his words in such a manner? He could have told
the stories without the emotions if he wanted and it would have
produce some positive results.

Let me tell you what I see, remember I'm a sensor; part of
sensing is storing the analytical emotion in the memories section of
the brain of the self or others. God has beaten the Devil at his own
game. God is good, and he has already played checkmate with the
Devil. My belief is that the Lord chose to tell his stories in such an
emotional manner because that is the way in which the sensing

function of the brain decides to store the analytical emotional stories told by the individual or others in the memory section of the emotional mind. Remember I told you that sensing was the use of the analytical emotions from the stored emotional memories of self and others. The sensing section of the brain of the individual has to house the emotional stories here. Think what this result must do to the devil? It binds him and locks him away in his dungeon unable to destroy another mind for centuries. Praise Jesus! All you have to do is read the words of the lord for true help and salvation, and believe it and it shall be.

I am not mad at those for questioning the bibles truth because it shows that they are not lazy and at least their doing their research and homework for the truth. But as I said earlier the bible proves in the existence of God and Christ because it contains mankind's design and only the creator has that type of information.

Now that you've had a little insight into my mind, pick up your bible and read with your newly acquired eyes.

Resources

The creator is the one whom sets your feet onto the path of knowledge that is obtained. I could not have found these answers had the creator not already prepared them for me.

Below is a list of books that aided the development of my discovering the duties of the gene. I thank all of these individual's that gave me their personal stories within their books.

The Holy Bible

The American Heritage Dictionary
ISBN: 0-395-32944-2

Black Sun Signs   1996
Thelma Balfour   ISBN: 0-684-81209-6

Do What You Are 1992, 1995
Tieger, Paul D. and Barron-Tieger, Barbara
ISBN: 978-0-316-84522-9

Molecule of Emotion 1997

Pert Ph.D., Candace B. ISBN: 0-684-83187-2

Reading People 1998, 1999

Dimitrius Ph.D., Jo-Ellan and Mazzarella Mark

ISBN: 0-345-42587-1

The Gospel and the Zodiac

ISBN: 978-1-590-20037-7

And any Psychology Book

ABOUT THE AUTHOR

Katrina Stradford is a wife, mother of 3 beautiful daughters and a grandmother of one. She dedicates her time to giving others a better understanding of their design with the hope that mankind will stop taking events so personally and attempt to love and help one another. She is currently working on her other book projects and companies. For more information on the author you can view her web pages listed below:

www.mskstradford.com
www.katrinastradford.info
www.autoentology.info
www.mskstradfordpublishing.info
www.karetrinamentoringfoundation.info
www.knowledgeofself.info